Worldwide Mobilizations

DISLOCATIONS

General Editors: August Carbonella, *Memorial University of Newfoundland*; Don Kalb, *University of Bergen & Utrecht University*; Linda Green, *University of Arizona*

The immense dislocations and suffering caused by neoliberal globalization, the retreat of the welfare state in the last decades of the twentieth century, and the heightened military imperialism at the turn of the twenty-first century have raised urgent questions about the temporal and spatial dimensions of power. Through stimulating critical perspectives and new and cross-disciplinary frameworks that reflect recent innovations in the social and human sciences, this series provides a forum for politically engaged and theoretically imaginative responses to these important issues of late modernity.

For a full volume listing, please see back matter.

Worldwide Mobilizations

Class Struggles and Urban Commoning

Edited by Don Kalb and Massimiliano Mollona

First published in 2018 by
Berghahn Books
www.berghahnbooks.com

© 2018, 2026 Don Kalb and Massimiliano Mollona
First paperback edition published in 2026

All rights reserved. Except for the quotation of short passages
for the purposes of criticism and review, no part of this book
may be reproduced in any form or by any means, electronic or
mechanical, including photocopying, recording, or any information
storage and retrieval system now known or to be invented,
without written permission of the publisher.

Library of Congress Cataloging-in-Publication Data
Names: Kalb, Don, 1959- editor. | Mollona, Massimiliano, 1969- editor.
Title: Worldwide mobilizations : class struggles and urban commoning / edited by Don Kalb and Massimiliano Mollona.
Description: New York, NY : Berghahn Books, 2018. | Series: Dislocations ; Volume 24 | Includes bibliographical references and index.
Identifiers: LCCN 2017055530 (print) | LCCN 2018008972 (ebook) | ISBN 9781785339073 (ebook) | ISBN 9781785339066 (hardback : alk. paper)
Subjects: LCSH: Social movements--Case studies. | Sociology, Urban--Case studies. | Social stratification--Case studies. | Social structure--Case studies. | Economic anthropology--Case studies.
Classification: LCC HM881 (ebook) | LCC HM881 .W68 2018 (print) | DDC 307.76--dc23
LC record available at https://lccn.loc.gov/2017055530

British Library Cataloguing in Publication Data
A catalogue record for this book is available from the British Library

EU GPSR Authorized Representative
LOGOS EUROPE, 9 rue Nicolas Poussin, 17000, LA ROCHELLE, France
Email: Contact@logoseurope.eu

ISBN 978-1-78533-906-6 hardback
ISBN 978-1-83695-689-1 paperback
ISBN 978-1-80758-196-1 epub
ISBN 978-1-78533-907-3 web pdf

https://doi.org/10.3167/9781785339066

Contents

Preface   vii

Acknowledgements   xi

Introduction   Introductory Thoughts on Anthropology and Urban Insurrection   1
Don Kalb and Massimiliano Mollona

Chapter 1   Confronting 'Aggressive Urbanism': Frictional Heterogeneity in the 'Gezi Protests' of Turkey   31
Mehmet Barış Kuymulu

Chapter 2   Reconfiguring 'the People'? Notes on the 2014 Winter Revolt in Bosnia and Herzegovina   52
Stef Jansen

Chapter 3   'Sofia 2014, Feels Like 1989': Abstention from the Protests and Declining Market Teleology in Bulgaria   73
Dimitra Kofti

Chapter 4   Spontaneity, Antagonism and the Moral Politics of Outrage: Urban Protest in Argentina since 2001   92
Sian Lazar

Chapter 5   'Neither Left nor Right': Crisis, Wane of Politics and Struggles for Sovereignty   118
Giacomo Loperfido

Chapter 6   Rebels and Revolutionaries: Urban Mobilizations of the Kamaiya Movement in Post-conflict Western Nepal   142
Michael Peter Hoffmann

Chapter 7 The Brazilian 'June' Revolution: Urban Struggles,
Composite Articulations and New Class Analysis   163
Massimiliano Mollona

Chapter 8 Contradictions of the 'Common Man':
A Realist Approach to India's Aam Aadmi Party   187
Luisa Steur

Chapter 9 Re-envisioning Social Movements in the Global City:
From Fordism to the Neoliberal Era   208
Ida Susser

Afterword Notes for a Contemporary Urban Class Analysis   223
Massimiliano Mollona and Don Kalb

Index   235

PREFACE

This book was first published as a hardback in 2018. The subsequent Covid pandemic was not the right moment for the launching of a paperback edition. But 2026 is.

The world is witnessing another round of 'spontaneous' social uprisings once again, as in the 2010s. Under the rubric of 'generation Z' protests, a label derived from marketing, young and less young people in Latin America, Nepal, Indonesia, Bangkok, Morocco, Kenya, Mozambique, Bangladesh and other countries are rebelling once more against incumbent 'authoritarian neoliberal' regimes. 'Spontaneous' in this context means: little visible organization beyond the internet and the social media, let alone party and labor union involvement. Also, with little intellectual preparation. Predictably, they are smoothly adopting again, in their anger and rejectionism, the global liberal vocabulary of (anti) corruption and 'democracy'. As in the 2010s, this register of protest points to changing the personnel but not the system. Urban rebellions in the last decades, while continuing to proliferate, in particular in 'spontaneous' format, seem to have become ever less efficacious, as widely noted.

In the Global North (and various places in the Global South), meanwhile, radical Right-wing regimes, some of them bordering on and inspired by an uncannily neoliberal form of fascism, have succeeded the Left-wing mobilizations of the early 2010s. The latter's last eruptions were around the Black Lives Matter protests in 2020 and the environmental mobilizations of 2021-23. A classical historical pattern has repeated itself: failed revolutions of the Left lead to crack downs by a radical revanchist Right and consequent reactionary domination. The recent Left, of course, though full of radical ideas and values, did generally not even seek that revolution but just 'reform' and 'regulation'. And of course, there was 'identity' all around, enjoying prefigurative action over the hard work of building new versions of Gramsci's 'historical bloc.'

This book, coming out of a session held in 2014, reflected that massive and memorable cycle of Left-democratic anti-neoliberal protests in the early 2010's, a 'new 1848'. In 2014 subsequent years as we getting this book ready, we were keenly aware of the turn of the political tide and the reactionary descents that many countries were making. With Brexit and Trump, the global system as a whole was moving towards Right-wing nationalism. We were also aware of reactionary potentials in the mobilizations in India, Brazil, Chile, Italy, Bosnia and Bulgaria described in our chapters.

We also had a message for social anthropological theory and method. Against this background of Left-wing exhaustion and Right-wing ascendance we wrote against the reigning habits in anthropological research on Left-wing politics: ethnographic presentism, idealism, and culturalism, often amounting to a celebration of Left identity politics. Ethnographies often focused on small groups of utopian and prefigurative actors, creating 'new cultural worlds'. They were big on autonomous, egalitarian and ecological desire as expressed in their subjects' actions and words recorded during fieldwork. Keen to share the activists' excitement, often written by field researchers who easily identified with these groups and were part of the action, they produced a sense that all of this was profoundly new and original, and surely leading to an increasingly egalitarian and sustainable future. However, such studies were often very thin on historical and global context, weak in their understanding of capitalism, and reluctant to link ethnographic subjects and sites to mass processes. Our book advocated social realism versus cultural idealism, sought to connect small scale ethnography with theory, history and comparison, and deployed classical but updated concepts of labor, class, capital and the commons, reshaping classical traditions into active agendas for research and discovery.

Anthropologists have recently caught up with history and have started studying the ascendant reactionary networks. With its fetishism of small scale cultural ethnographies, however, it remains prone to making the old errors, now concerning the opposite camp. Ethnographic excitement around spoken words, titbits from social media, actions without much context, actors with little history, small fleeting groups and passing encounters, little sense of place, can blind one for the fact that, like the Left-wing wave of the early 2000s and 2010s, these are largescale global developments, embedded in profound and uneven transformations of capitalism, also, and very much so, on an intimate scale. Webs of meaning must be studied within the webs of life as it is lived.

Antwerp/Bergen/London/Bologna January 2026

Acknowledgements

The editors want to acknowledge the inspiration received from friends, students and collaborators over the years, several of whom have been associated with Berghahn's *Dislocations Series* and with *Focaal – Journal of Global and Historical Anthropology*. This volume reflects a mere moment in an ongoing conversation with all of them. Of course we also would like to thank once more the contributors, including those who presented their work at the original EASA session in 2014 but could not appear in this volume. Finally, we are grateful for the editorial support of Oana Mateescu in Bucharest, whose efficiency and perfectionism carried us through the last stages as both of us got absorbed by other tasks.

Don Kalb, Bergen, Budapest and Antwerpen
Massimiliano Mollona, London

INTRODUCTION

Introductory Thoughts on Anthropology and
Urban Insurrection

Don Kalb and Massimiliano Mollona

The year 2011 was a classical annus mirabilis. Larger numbers of citizens went onto the streets to demonstrate, to occupy, and to strike – simultaneously, in a tight sequence, inspired by each other – in more locations than perhaps at any earlier moment in human history. As such it counts among a very small collection of exceptionally rebellious years: 1848 and 1968 are the examples. The years preceding and following 2011 were also extraordinarily turbulent and politically flamboyant, forming one rolling cycle of worldwide protest, or perhaps more precisely one worldwide wave of regionally embedded cycles.

Remarkably, for the first time since a generation (since '1968'), capitalism was once again denounced, sometimes literally so without metaphorical digressions. True, calls for 'democracy', 'transparency' and 'fairness' against corruption, and increasingly 'for the people and against the elites', did dominate the banners, the social and public media and the wider public discourses. These were symbols, slogans and narratives shaped in earlier conjunctures, such as the protest wave against local oligarchies, governmental cliques and selfish bureaucracies in the 1990s and early 2000s. Such symbols originated partly from the 1989 'refolutions' in Central and Eastern Europe, the subsequent colour revolutions in Serbia, Georgia, Kyrgyzstan and Ukraine, the pro-democracy NGO-world, and to some extent from the alter-globalist movement; but they also came from Latin America. Protesters sought to use and adapt this liberal heritage in 2011 in order to make a new context intelligible. But in particular in the Global North, with (neo-) liberalism dominant for a whole generation, neoliberal capitalism itself, as well as its local instantiations, was now clearly under popular critical scrutiny, more directly so than ever before. The financial crisis, the credit crunch, the subsequent imposition of draconian austerity on nations that had just paid up to save the bankers and speculators, the recognition of long running social stagnation amid gentrification, the loss of popular sovereignty, and ever deepening inequalities both within cities, nations, and worldwide, particularly also within the Global North, indicated that the engine that had unified the world into a neoliberal 'free market' under US leadership since 1989 was stuttering towards the end of its shelf life.

The crisis also had profound consequences for food and energy prices, in particular in the Global South and the Middle East. The decades preceding the crisis, in addition, had witnessed a steady and sometimes explosive rise in costs associated with education and urban housing, almost everywhere, despite and because of the cheap credit boom that had sparked the crunch on Wall Street.

The worldwide mobilizations of 2011 were set off by an act of a modest person in an out of the way place: the self-immolation of market vendor Mohammed Bouazizi before the municipal building in Sidi Bouzid, Tunisia, in December 2010: it was a dramatic and desperate gesture against corruption and humiliation by local police officers in a context of sharply rising costs of living that Mohammed could not meet for his family. As his kin and friends mobilized, supported by the street vendors trade union of which Bouazizi was a member, the news of what seemed like a local uprising in the Tunisian provinces went viral via the new social media and Al-Jazeera. Within a few weeks, the Arab street was in revolt against their rulers: in Cairo, Damascus, Tripoli, and in many smaller places (see for good chronologies of the 2011 Arab Spring and subsequent 'world insurgency' Khosrokhavar 2012; Mason 2012; Castells 2015; Werbner, Webb and Spellman-Poots 2014).

As the Arab Spring intensified, tumultuously and increasingly bloodily, just across the water Spanish Indignados and Greek protesters followed up in the spring and summer of 2011 with massive and sustained mobilizations that continued the 'Movement of the Squares'. They were decrying imposed austerity, elite corruption, popular indebtedness and aggravating inequality; also, the handling of these syndromes of capitalist rule within an EU that was unashamedly shifting towards internal financial imperialism of the North over the South, and thus silently cancelling the ideals of 'democracy', 'social cohesion', 'ever closer union' and 'convergence of living standards' that had ostensibly driven the European project until then.

In the early fall, the Occupy Movement in the United States, inspired by all this, succeeded in mobilizing millions of citizens in dozens of cities. They occupied parks and squares – iconically so in Zuccotti Park – around the corner from Wall Street, denouncing the state socialism for the bankers who had gone bust in 2008 and who were being resurrected, along with the capitalist economy they had wrecked, by the Obama government at stupefying public costs in a social context where the '99 per cent' had been stagnating for decades and financialized capitalism had demonstrably only served the '1 per cent' – a powerful slogan against inequality that was popularized by Occupy, sticking 'forever'.

Demonstrations and square occupations further proliferated as the year went by. In Israel, massive demonstrations denounced urban inequality, gentrification and rising costs of living. Moscow and other big Russian cities rose up in an almost Mediterranean mode against the usurpation of state power by Vladimir Putin in late 2011 and early 2012. North-western Europe was restive throughout, though significantly less rebellious than the circum-Mediterranean or the United States. A twin protest with Zuccotti Park emerged in London in front of the London Stock Exchange – this, after London had already witnessed its 'feral summer' of violent youth rioting and student protest in the spring of 2010; the German left scene followed suit with blockades of the ECB. Many places in postsocialist Europe, in particular Bosnia (see Jansen's chapter), Bulgaria (Kofti, this volume), Romania and the Baltic countries saw sustained waves of bigger and smaller movements rocking incumbent governments in 2012–14. Ukraine had its momentous, spectacular and, in retrospect, politically disastrous Maidan moment in November 2012–February 2013. Hungary had witnessed big protests against austerity for years in a row, and was now, perhaps paradoxically, in the midst of a full scale right-wing transformation towards an 'illiberal' dual state (Szombati, forthcoming); Poland would follow in its wake in 2015. The French left was re-energized, as it split from President Hollande's neoliberal accommodations with Germany, aligning itself intellectually with the new-New Lefts in the European South. Outside Euro-America, Maoist guerrillas in the central forest band of India and massive mobilizations against corruption and violence in New Delhi (see the chapter by Steur) signalled the immense stresses of capitalist liberalization cum dispossession in the second most populous state on earth, and the biggest formally democratic one. China, meanwhile, was counting 60,000 official acts of popular rebellion per year as mobile workers protested against exploitative factory regimes on the coast and peasants and citizens mobilized against large-scale dispossession of land by industrializing local states and real-estate mafias. Hong Kong saw its 'umbrella revolution' in the early fall of 2014 against the encroachments of Main Land bureaucratic power-holders. In Thailand and Nepal (see the chapter by Hoffmann), radical popular movements were contesting the hierarchical constitutions of these states. South African workers and students, meanwhile, were mobilizing ever more vocally and systematically against durable inequalities and corruption, and increasingly running amok against the neoliberal stagnation of the ANC. Latin America (Lazar, Mollona, this volume) saw the last intense rounds of popular struggle for equality, redistribution and recognition by workers, with inhabitants of favelas and indigenous people – in Venezuela, the Andes, Brazil and the Southern cone – rounding off more than a decade of left-wing organizing – starting with the Zapatista rising in Chiapas in 1995 and culminating in the first World Social Forum gathering in Porto Alegre in 2001, iconic moments of the alter-globalist movement. Finally, break-neck urbanization in Turkey – a country that had been sucking up financial surpluses from both the West and the Gulf states – saw its own mimesis in a revolt of the great metropolises of Istanbul and Ankara as citizens rose in the Gezi Park rebellion against the unaccountable real estate development machine around prime minister – now president and all-round strong man – Erdogan (Kuymulu, this volume).

Any discussion of this unprecedented (past or ongoing?) wave of worldwide urban mobilizations at this moment of writing – early 2017 – must happen against an inescapable and paradoxical double background. First, as the democratic movements of these years failed to conquer power or enforce serious concessions in the reigning forms of rule during their ascent – and indeed they often consciously refused to want to do so – they have left a major vacuum for a resurgent right to pick up on the widespread disillusionment, anger and anxieties among the governed, signalled so incisively by the mass popular outrage. Euro-America has turned massively rightward since then. This includes North-western Europe, Scandinavia, the Visegrad countries of Central and Eastern Europe, the United Kingdom – expressed most clearly in its Brexit vote – and indeed the United States itself, with a Tea Party morphed into a Trump show that overran the Republican establishment, liberated the politically non-correct 'alt-right' in the digital media, and has ascended against all the polls and predictions – as with Brexit – to claim the US presidency. No matter how extravagant the personal liabilities of Donald

Trump, he commanded the steady loyalty of close to half the actually voting electorate, with class in all its entanglements with race and gender as a crucial driver. In Spain, the right fought off the challenge of Podemos, a new party that emerged from the Indignados movement, which in the end had to content itself with just occupying a slot in the system next to the old social democrats of the PSOE without producing a breakthrough (indeed, it took Podemos two years to admit that it was a left-wing party in the first place) – notwithstanding important local successes in cities such as Barcelona (Suarez 2017) and Madrid. In Greece, the only country with a left-left electoral breakthrough, Northern sovereign creditors and the Troika have demonstratively dismantled any semblance of popular sovereignty and have forced Syriza into a combination of stark austerity with internal reformism. Latin America, meanwhile, has been seeing a slow moving takeover by a more or less revanchist classical bourgeois right as the programmes and fiscal resources of the left began to exhaust themselves in the wake of the end of the commodities boom, and some supporters began losing belief: this, in Argentina, Brazil and Venezuela. Bolivia and Ecuador may follow suit. Russia, China, Turkey and Egypt have each bolstered local autocratic forms of rule, combined with active claims to great power status and nationalist self-celebrations, supported by conservative and hierarchical, partly fake, political parties, congeries of brokers and rent-takers of all kind. India, in its turn, has chosen the BJP of Narendra Modi to fuse neoliberal competitiveness with explicit religious-racialized hierarchy.

As compared to 2011, the world scene has descended fearsomely fast toward nationalism and right-wing populism; towards a new-old right that is drawing up clear lines of authority and hierarchy between the deserving, the undeserving and the alien. This is, however, and not only in the Global North, a right that is at the same time cognizant of some of the obvious pitfalls of neoliberal capitalism that fuelled 2011. It is often a neo-populist and 'antiglobalist' right, playing on popular fears of failure, stagnation and decline. It works by shifting some of those concerns onto a national security-driven reassertion of national boundaries, and towards the socio-legal recalibration, indeed reinstatement, of a 'traditional' or 'natural' hierarchy that is perceived to be evaporating; that is a crucial part of the explanation of the fast rise of the new right.

The failure of the short moment of universalist counter-politics has allowed the spread and consolidation of the particularistic quasi-counter-politics of 'deserving majorities' against the establishment as well as against the barbarians in, at, and outside the gate.

Significantly, the right appears to have become the one political force ready to directly address 'the working class' – the domestic and 'white' working class, that is.

The second aspect of that double background lies in the domain of intellectual history. While popular politics ultimately, and ominously, escaped the left, and was in many places usurped by a neo-populist right, the Euro-American left did celebrate a series of intellectual victories, indeed veritable public breakthroughs against what Neil Smith called a 'dead but dominant' neoliberalism (Smith 2008). This is most obviously illustrated by the blockbuster sales of two radical, deeply scholarly and voluminous books, for which sales figures are, like the protest wave itself, all but historically unique. First, David Graeber's anarchist world historical anthropology of debt (2011) sold more than 100,000 copies in English within two years and was translated into more than twenty-five languages after its release by a minor publisher. Second, economist Thomas Piketty's *Capital in the Twenty-First Century* (2013), a rather technical, social democratic argument for high taxation of wealth – wealth that Piketty argued would always grow faster than the economy as a whole, leading therefore inevitably to plutocracy and oligarchy – sold more than a million copies and won unlikely prizes such as the Financial Times Business Book of the Year Award (2014), sponsored by the global capitalist consultancy McKinsey. These are the publicity peaks – both of them, we note, avowedly non-Marxist – among what has become a vibrant field of left-wing writing in journals, websites, books and blogs, where radical economists mingle with social scientists, philosophers, Marxists and anarchists, and where capitalism as such, in its multiple manifestations – its class inequalities, its current oligarchic and rent-taking tendencies, its plutocratic, finance-driven post-democratic forms, its recurrent resort to primitive accumulation, dispossession and disenfranchisement – is facing more serious intellectual scrutiny than at any time in the last generation. The intellectual omnipresence of neoliberalism, in short, has been broken, both from the left and from the right – though probably not quite its practical dominance and its dead weight of governmentalist ritual excess: dead but dominant, and now in many places in a rocky alliance with the populist Right.

Idealists and Realists

This is the context in which, in the field of anthropology, the subfields of political anthropology, economic anthropology and anthropological political economy have been drawing closer together. Economic anthropologists, while still indebted to Polanyi or Mauss and often more interested in circulation than in production, have started to talk about the state, austerity, inequality, labour, democracy, resistance, and even class (Hart and Sharp 2016 is perhaps the best example).[1] Political anthropologists felt they had to begin to deal with issues of capitalist crisis, austerity and neoliberalism, while continuing to engage with manipulation of political symbols in circumscribed political arenas (Alexandrakis 2016). Anthropological political economists felt compelled to turn more decisively towards urban study and social movements (recently for instance: Kalb 2009; Kalb and Halmai 2011; Kasmir and Carbonella 2014; Narotzky 2015, 2016a, 2016b; Gill 2016). Dominant neoliberal capitalism and its crises and contradictions have brought them together. Similarly, in the neighbouring field of the sociology of social movements there has arisen a belated awareness that one cannot continue to ignore the issue of capitalism and class any longer (Della Porta 2015). This issue has been pushed aside as impractical and old-fashioned during the growth and professionalization of this subfield in the last thirty years, not entirely unlike what has happened in anthropology (Kalb 2015a).

However, rather than leading to consensus, this mingling forces us to have more explicitly different things to say on roughly shared issues. One particularly important dividing line when it comes to the popular risings of 2011 and their aftermath is, obviously, how we should study and explain them. What is worth revealing and discovering? Roughly, there are two approaches in anthropology, which for heuristic purposes may be divided between a realist-materialist school and an idealist school; the first derives more from anthropological political economy, the latter more from both economic anthropology and political anthropology.[2] In anthropology, the idealists, as always in this discipline, seem to be more numerous than the realists.[3] These contrastive approaches to 'rebel cities' come interwoven with competing ideas about the place of ethnographic fieldwork, history and comparison in anthropological research, including the uses of theory. Realists or materialists incline strongly towards building history, process, spatial linkage and comparison into their ethnographic interests. Idealists tend to embrace a more exclusively ethnographic approach, driven predominantly or singularly by participant observation. This also has consequences for the mode of generalization or universalization scholars are likely to deploy. Idealists often universalize from small observations to deeply ontological or cosmological generalities – that is, towards philosophy, ontology, to 'what it is to be human', or to esthetics, ethics, affect or to basic local senses of temporality and futurity: the singularly atmospheric stuff that strikes you when you are there. Alternatively, they may generalize towards protest tactics or the use of social media or humour or music. Realists tend to universalize towards what Charles Tilly called meso-level relational mechanisms, such as class experiences and trajectories, processes of class or class-alliance formation, recurrent ideological tropes and memes, and in particular to the wider spatiotemporal conjunctures within which events, processes and outcomes take place – more in the direction of historical sociology or macro-anthropology.

Idealist work tends to draw a lot on the political anthropology of symbols, spectacles and communication – indeed, crucially, on the supposedly uniquely human capacity of the ethical and esthetical imagination (for instance Graeber 2012; Werbner, Webb and Spellman-Poots 2014; Alexandrakis 2016). Its mission in the preceding period of political turbulence can be summarized as discovering the ethical imagination at work among small groups of activists while such groups engage in a collective project to imagine other futures and engage in collective action esthetics that seek to bring change to their immediate worlds. Their ideal method has accordingly been the classic long and close-up participatory immersion among circles of activists during periods of localized fieldwork, the quintessential research mode of anthropology since Malinowski. Their key rationale: discovering alternative senses of the future, 'futurities', non-capitalist moralities, moral economies of the gift and of everyday communism as described by Marcel Mauss (2016), and alternative forms of personhood as sought by Marilyn Strathern (1992). The work of David Graeber and the new journal *HAU*, launched in 2012, both ostensibly inspired by Mauss more than by any other scholar, has given this stream a forceful jolt – even though, somewhat paradoxically, the journal itself hardly engaged with the popular risings (but see Corsin Jimenez and Estalella 2013). There is an affinity in this work with an ethical anarchism and with horizontalist forms of 'spontaneous' organizing as epitomized by Occupy and the notion of popular assemblies. Networks of activists are being followed and participated in as they claim and create 'free spaces' and new 'intimacies' against capital and the state – spaces where 'everyday communism' can flow freely and creatively, and a more relational personhood can be realized in rejection of the acquisitive individualism supposedly reigning in Western capitalist space.[4] Such experiments are sometimes seen as more consequential for imaginative social change in the long run than confrontative public engagement with the state on behalf of desired, willed and enforced social transformation. Idealists, therefore, tend to subscribe to the 'termite theory of revolution': revolutionary change will ultimately result from the growing number of people whose daily practices amount to the ongoing rejection of hegemony (James Scott is the key representative, 1987, 1992, 2014). They share in an optimistic theory of a culturally creative multitude that simply overwhelms the state through their active rejection of obedience and hierarchy, à la Hardt and Negri (2011; for a discussion of Hardt and Negri in anthropology see *Focaal* 2012, No. 64). Idealists often see the state as an almost inherently evil homogenizer of the cultural difference and freedom they cherish above all (see Graeber 2016 for example). Zuccotti Park, then, is the model and the horizontalist creative collective the practice that needs to be captured ethnographically for posterity. The style of writing is that of cultural critique.

Realists, in contrast, seem less in thrall to the moral imaginations and creative practices of small avant-garde groups or momentary gatherings. Nor do they succumb as quickly to the idea that all of this, the context, the experience, the agency, is new. Crucially, they tend to have a more historical, and in particular a structurally differentiated vision, of the wider capitalist environment of those protesting groups. For them capitalism is not first of all an objectionable expressive moral universe, a practised ideology of possessive individualism and associated forms of acquisitive personhood, for instance. Above all, capitalism is not seen as being of one cultural piece, an expression of one particular spirit. It is for them, rather, a structured relational universe with a plethora of dominant and subordinate, but always potentially competing, embodied subject positions, 'structures of feeling', 'traditions', moral codes, knowledges and practices, including, of course, the idealist rejection of hegemonic values by particular groups of actors so cherished by the idealists. For them, 'really existing capitalism' is, rather than a disliked coherent culture, a contradictory ensemble of social relationships and practices, vertical dependencies and potential horizontal solidarities, an ensemble shot through with lived contradictions that often become openly exposed as times change and are pushed to a tipping point. Realists are looking for ways to account for why large masses of people become willing to engage in risky political confrontations with capital and the state. They are interested in the changing popular sensibilities of 'common people'. For that they may use ethnographically generated intimate insights into the biographies, practices, solidarities and livelihoods of particular groups or segments, small or large – though they may be less driven towards the small political avant-gardes of the idealists, and indeed tend to have a more explicit interest in workers or peasants of all kinds than in the cultural becoming of small bohemian clubs. For that they rely on other sorts of data than just participant observation; in particular data that can be made to reveal the 'hidden histories' and lived realities of social groups and classes in situ. They will also seek to understand more in detail, and above all more analytically, the exact contradictions in a wider urban political economy, and will seek to show how such contradictions play themselves out in the histories, livelihoods, moral economies and hopes of the people they are working with. Realists, finally, spend a lot of time documenting actually existing hegemonic as well as submerged political traditions, assuming that histories of moral and political contestation continue to be available for re-articulation and re-signification – also under capitalism, despite, and often precisely against, the homogenizing capacities of the capitalist state. In short, they emphatically invest themselves in spatiotemporal process or trajectory, in addition to the gatherings and events of the moment.

In sum, and provocatively: if the imaginative capacities, ethical visions and protest practices of small experimental avant-garde groups, or larger protesting crowds, are what drives the interests of the idealists, the realists seem rather mesmerized by the historical conundrums of class and hegemony, in their existential, relational, discursive and political sense (for example: Smith 2013; Kasmir and Carbonella 2014; Carrier and Kalb 2015; Kalb 2015a; Crehan 2016; Gill 2016). It is this that the realists see as key to understanding and explaining large-scale political phenomena, such as worldwide urban insurrections, but also for understanding shifts towards and within the right, which are seen as an equally important topic for analysis, one that seems often conveniently ignored by the idealists (Kalb 2009; Kalb and Halmai 2011). Marx, Gramsci and sometimes Polanyi may serve as key inspirations.

While any good analysis combines these two approaches, this book leans, as the reader may have sensed, towards the side of realism. It builds on the anthropology of labour and class, in which both editors have been intensely involved since their early work (Kalb 1997; Mollona 2009). And it seeks to extend that subfield to the more directly political terrain of contemporary urban politics, including large-scale protest. Building among others on Eric Wolf,

David Harvey and Manuel Castells, as well as on Kalb's notion of 'critical junctions' (2005, 2011), what is ultimately at stake for us is a new gusto for urban political class analysis (see also, Epilogue).

Conundrums of Class

When we say that the realists are mesmerized by the conundrum of class, what exactly might we mean? The coded answer is that we suspect that any necessary explanation of the ongoing urban insurrections places them, concretely and analytically, within and against the forces, multi-scalar as well as situated, of a transforming global capitalism – the accumulation of capital structures and restructures, the conditions and forms of livelihoods, as well as the attendant politics of social reproduction – and it does so in particular ways in particular world regions.

But let us begin at a less elevated level. Sian Lazar, for example, has been making the timely case (2017) that supposedly 'old' class organizations such as labour unions and labour federations played a considerable role in the making, sustaining and outcomes of the worldwide urban mobilizations of 2011. Indeed, Bouazizi's self-immolation in Sidi Bouzid would not have been so consequential had it not been for the sustained support of his labour union of street vendors for the public expression of the outrage of his friends and family; and for the subsequent facilitation and translation of local popular indignation towards collective action at the national level (see among others Mason 2012; Beinin 2015; Castells 2015). Similarly, in Egypt, Greece, Istanbul and ultimately also the United States, labour organizations were in all sorts of ways important vehicles for protest articulation in 2011 and after, as well as before.

Arguably, the relatively peaceful and consolidated democratic outcome in Tunisia, as compared to Egypt and Libya, was in significant measure due to the role of labour (Beinin 2015). The dramatic shift to the right that happened during the Ukrainian Maidan rebellion in February 2013, as barricade fighters and state security police were pitched against each other, might have been channelled differently had efforts at union support for a national strike been more successful (Kalb 2015b). Even OWS was allowed to continue because of the support of local unions. Also, it can be argued that in cases where 'old' labour refused to align with new protest movements, such as in Spain and the United Kingdom, the political punch and mobilizing force of such protest was in the end severely weakened. And who would deny that the working- class vote for Trump in Ohio, Michigan, Wisconsin and Pennsylvania in the fall of 2016 – as critical for his election as the weak turnout of black voters for Clinton – was an expression of the proven powerlessness of 'old' labour in its alliance with Clintonite democrats in the face of economic globalization (combined with concerted attacks by Republican governors to weaken labour). This is one aspect of what we mean with 'the conundrum of class'.

Lazar (2017), and many others including our authors here, also emphasize that protest cultures are never created just from scratch but have longer local histories that younger participants, including the imaginative avant-gardes of the idealists, may not always be aware of. In those longer histories, 'old' labour may or may not play an important role. But where it does so, the likelihood increases of the presence of a common tradition, a public legacy, not a template, but what Eric Wolf called 'an engram' (1982), a shared, remembered and somehow practised basic script of potential common claim-making, indeed of 'commoning' as an active everyday practice (Harvey 2014).

Together with Susser and Tonnelat (2013) and Kalb (2014a), we describe working-class struggles as forms of 'commoning'. Paraphrasing Kalb (2017) – 'over time, no commons without commoning' – we could braid these historical trajectories and practices even tighter: over time, no class without commoning (with the reverse being equally and perhaps even more urgently true). While such a rapprochement seems politically savvy in light of the contemporary urban mobilizations that are the focus of this volume, we suggest also that the two forms of historical action take shape out of similar processes of laminated contradictions. In other words, commoning shares in the conundrums of class; it is, in fact, 'deeply entangled historically and in the present with formal politics, the state and capital, in antagonistic as well as collusive ways' (Kalb 2017). The following chapters address, explicitly or implicitly, these intersecting entanglements of class and commoning. Mollona (this volume) offers a stark and persuasive summary of the stakes of such a potential collusion and/or collision: 'There has always been a great deal of overlap between the struggles of the urban poor, those of civic movements and those of the industrial or postindustrial proletariat. Perhaps the biggest challenge posed by contemporary urban movements worldwide is precisely the way in which they bring together all these different components into a composite class articulation, the understanding of which is fundamental for the future of class struggle.'

Commoning practices seek to enact shared rights to livelihoods for all and embody and express a popular sense that such rights should be protected and be enforceable. They also rest in a structure of feeling that people should be entitled to claim the right to moral outrage and the right to take to the street and occupy public space if the supposed commons is systematically violated or recurrently threatened. In other words, the importance of public traditions of critical activism goes far beyond 'mere events' and beyond the political arithmetic of protest in the here and now, a point easily missed by the idealists. Of course, this popular claim to social justice can also be usurped and articulated by the neo-populist right, as Trump, the Brexit campaigners, Marine Le Pen and the Polish and Hungarian new right know all too well, and as history shows abundantly. The historical engrams of labour are real but they are also highly malleable.

When we write this, it is obviously not intended as a political defence of 'old labour' versus 'new social movements' or even 'the imagination'. We think discussions in such general terms are futile. We say this, rather, in order to work towards an understanding of 'labour' as 'a political category' (Kasmir and Carbonella 2014): as a set of practiced political claims, identities, and indeed imaginations, that prioritize the dignity and the interests of those who cannot live and reproduce themselves from profits and rents that are derived from control over substantial property and wealth, that is, from the accumulation of capital – the big majority of mankind, 'the 99 per cent'. Further, following Kasmir and Carbonella (2014): the difference between being in work, being unemployed or being practically relegated to a 'workless' surplus population is of little conceptual consequence here; indeed, on a conceptual level – though not on a practical one – it is spurious. They all face the possibility of 'wagelessness', even while their exposure to it may in practice be extremely uneven. In a similar way one should refuse to magnify the importance of the supposed boundary between production and reproduction, classically between the factory and the home – men's and women's labour under Fordism. Rather than emphasizing the separations between production and reproduction, being in labour and being out of labour, or material labour versus immaterial labour, etcetera, we are picturing whole livelihoods that are dependent on their capacity to work or care for others, or be taken care of. Their opportunities of labouring and caring are in a fundamental sense dependent upon the sale to, or exchange with, others. It is that existential dependence that is fundamental to our argument.

To them, the conditions under which that exchange happens matter vitally and immediately, as do the conditions under which they can make themselves a home or a meal or become educated and so on. So this is not about 'old labour' versus all the old-new stuff of movements or imaginations or commons, it is about the key conditions of the social reproduction of life as we live it.

Now, prioritizing these steps in the 'conundrum of class' suggests that we think a Marxian idea of class is far more to the point in the present conjuncture of forceful capitalist globalizations and class formations than a Weberian one (see Carrier and Kalb 2015 for a recent discussion). That is indeed what we argue; it is the necessary perspective, even though not necessarily sufficient. Marx did not use the concept of class a lot, and when he used it, he deployed it rather loosely. The obsession with defining classes, and layers within classes, as exactly as possible comes more from positivist sociology or economics than from Marx. What defines the Marxian vision is an idea of class as thoroughly relational; a relationality that emerges from the way the reproduction of 'classed' livelihoods is, under capitalism, fundamentally entangled with those of other classes, and with, indeed within, the accumulation of capital. Livelihoods are therefore by definition fully embedded in the particular spatiotemporal fixes – the particular regional structures– that capital produces, reproduces, transforms, devalues and discards in its quest for endless accumulation. This is often understood in terms of the 'swirl of markets', or of 'economic growth', or 'de-industrialization' or 'precariatization' etcetera. But independent from the empirical processes one sees at any place and at any one moment in time, the deeper Marxian point is that these transformations of livelihoods and the transformation of the class relations within which they are lived are recurrent, inevitable and profound, and indeed systemic. This is not to deny the usefulness of an additional and somewhat Weberian perspective on stratification, status or consumption. As Jeff Maskovsky has pointed out, '… expulsion and precariatization are not in themselves politically unifying developments' (Maskovsky 2017). There is no reason to assume that current transformative processes, even when they lead to the decline of a more encompassing hegemony and to the production of surplus populations, to Saskia Sassen's expulsions (2014), will lead to political unification. Indeed, Weberian dynamics of cultural closure may well in these supremely Marxian moments paradoxically, and as a rule, become powerful competitors to inclusive class solidarities. Szombati's (forthcoming) analysis of the rise of Jobbik in provincial

Hungary is a good example, though he leans more on Polanyi than on Weber. He explains the rise of the right precisely from what he sees as the emergence of rural Polanyian countermovements against the market seeking 'to protect society'. Polanyi never said that such movements had to be egalitarian. On the contrary, he was equivocal whether they might be on the left or the right. In the Hungarian case, one segment of society protects itself against the market via protection against another segment, the surplus population, whose rights it ostensibly takes away. And the demarcation lines between those segments are being drawn by, and through, culture, ethnicity, race and gender. Weberian hierarchies within what, theoretically speaking at least, could also have united as a class. In other words, on class we need to cast Marx and Weber into their respective roles: Marx the overarching and structuring one, Weber the politically and culturally contingent one. The dialectic is what matters. Class formation and class segmentation are the processes through which that dialectic touches the ground.

But there is more to the conundrum of class. This includes a fascination with the imagination, but one that is different from the indulgence of the anthropological idealists with the imaginative avant-gardes. As the urban insurrections went rolling in 2011, journalists were struck by how they appeared to be driven by the new social media. Typically, reporters of *The Economist* or the *Financial Times* would find one or another demonstrating software programmer working on and off for Google in Cairo or Athens who would steadily upload YouTube videos, Facebook pictures and generally Twitter his or her way around the world, calling for further outrage and action. And this is how the masses came on to the street, the story implied. The public media, but also researchers of digital communication, quickly decided that the unprecedented wave of urban protests must have been conditioned by the quick spread of digital social media in the preceding years (Mason 2012; Wolfson 2014; Castells 2015). Since they also assumed that the social media had not yet reached the global working class, or in any case that the use of them did require some digital and technical literacy, and therefore some further education, they also swiftly surmised that they were witnessing a middle-class revolution, see the Google programmer. Ergo, the logic went, these were revolutions not about bread but about ideals of freedom. Indeed, as we well remember reading of 1968, they were about the liberation of the imagination. This allowed commentators to arrive at a known and reassuring liberal figure of thought: rather than social insurrections driven by anger, failure and need, these were 'democratic revolutions' driven by the desires of the rising networked global middle classes. The founding myth of the West was at once reconfirmed. All the classic liberal, and indeed liberatory, fantasies of a virtuous circle uniting capital, technology, the Internet, the middle class, democracy and liberty that has always marked capitalism in its millennial moment were projected onto the worldwide urban mobilizations. Here was the Whig version of 2011.

Unsurprisingly, our realist and materialist approach, 'mesmerized by the conundrums of class', rejects such readings, even though it recognizes them as significant public myths in their own right. Rather, we like to take as a clue Paul Mason's (2012) quote of an operator from the British secret services, confiding in the middle of the 2011 uprisings to Mason that 'this is 1848 all over again'. It is not difficult to see how this is a point about historical class formations. '1848' summarizes nothing less than the shock appearance of the working class as a political category on the public stage: the massive Chartist mobilizations in the United Kingdom in the years preceding 1848, demanding the vote and regulation of the labour market – interpreted by Marx in the Manifesto as the historical forerunner of the exploited but organized working class that industrial capitalism was about to bring into being; the February revolution in Paris, where a working class, organized in tighter ways than the sans-culottes of 1789, appeared on the street in numbers and with a readiness to fight off state repression and defend the bourgeoisie and its claims for democracy in a way the middle classes themselves would not dare to; a bourgeoisie that was then going to betray them a few months later. In England, the working class was already an industrial one; in France, it was still mainly artisanal but it was in the process of a swift and uncertain transformation. The wider context of 1848 both in the United Kingdom and on the continent was one of uninterrupted price rises of basic food supplies, rapidly rising costs for living in the fast growing and increasingly overcrowded and dangerously unhealthy cities, steadily declining real incomes, ever rising competition for declining resources for living in a context of visibly increasing class divisions of wealth, power and prestige – sound familiar? And after Paris, the whole continent went into insurrectionary mode, after which the reactionary forces in most cases re-established themselves via repression, and prepared for another round of accumulation under the autocrat Louis Bonaparte. That was '1848'. And of course it was also Marx and Engels's 'Manifesto', and all the left learning and organizing that followed; and then 'The Eighteenth Brumaire'.

What can we surmise if we take the idea seriously that 2011 was indeed '1848 all over again'? What if we start to think about 2011 in terms of a set of territorially differentiated but deeply interconnected and interlocking longer run global social transformations of livelihoods plus the associated transformations of political and cultural frameworks; transformations that are simultaneously generating new needs, anxieties and grievances, as well as helping to assemble the collective will to articulate such needs and grievances in the form of a new common sense, or better, as Gramsci would have it, ' a good sense', and in spectacular ways (see Crehan 2016 on Gramsci's 'common sense' and 'good sense')? What if 2011 were in fact an empirically contingent but nevertheless structured concatenation of planetary social changes – call it global capitalism – with different sites and different instantiations of protest encapsulating the locally and regionally differentiated experiences of that connective larger story? How would we seek to talk about class in a crucible such as this?

Mao Mollona writes in his chapter on Brazil that the old parameters of classes do not work anymore in contemporary metropolitan Brazil. In the new class scenario, the old and 'embourgeoisefied' industrial working classes coexist with a younger and expanded cyber-proletariat, casualized service workers, and a socially mobile 'lumpen' lifted up by Lula's famous cash transfer programmes for poverty reduction. Parts of the new middle classes, meanwhile, have been proletarianized and they and their children are facing concrete threats of precariatization. The way in which the protest actions of these segments were coming together and then grew apart in these years can be read like a collective, always incomplete and provisional, effort at making some political sense of these uncertain transformations. As in 1848 these are classes and segments of classes, literally 'in the making', reaching out for a collective politics of life that might suit them, that might articulate meaningfully with their livelihoods, and respond more or less adequately to the contradictory reconfigurations of their habitats and probable futures. Mollona's sense about the contradictory uncertainties of Brazilian metropolitan life may serve as a guide for our other cases. When we talk about the conundrum of class we seek to emphasize once more the rejection of essentialism, reification, reductionism and groupism that has sometimes, rightly or not, been associated with historical versions of class thinking. Both of us, and many others, have repeatedly pointed at and rejected those errors, and have programmatically transcended such problems supposedly associated with 'class' in our earlier work on European working classes. Class, in anthropology more than anywhere else, calls for conceptual subtlety and flexibility, and for an agenda of historical and empirical discovery (Kalb 1997, 2011, 2015a).

Here is where our notion of critical junctions comes in. Operating, rather eclectically, in the space between Trotsky's 'uneven and combined development', McMichael's 'incorporated comparison' (1990), and Ernst Bloch's 'asynchronic simultaneity', it urges us to focus on the structured contingency of emergent hybrid class formations as they crystallize within the dialectics between local and global histories concatenating into the insurgencies of 2011 and after. As with '1848', we know that the urban mobilizations emerged at least partly from their mutual inspiration and transfer of personnel. As in 1848, they also developed in a now amply enlarged space of territorial and social differentiations. We should refuse to see such differentiations as contingencies based in cultural difference. These are relationally structured contingencies of combined and uneven development organized within a tightly synchronized process of global accumulation, much more tightly now than in 1848. This is not the place to work this out at length, nor does the present collection sufficiently address the full range of significant variations to require such an excursion. But we do not need a fully developed argument in order to make a suggestion: the nature of all these rebellions, the composition of insurgent groups, their claims, scripts, theatrics, discourses, actions, the histories and policy actions against which they came together can only become understandable against their common global-local contextualization; a contextualization that is realized within their particular regional histories of accumulation, development, class formation and urban change. That is, through their specific insertion into the post-1989 Pax Americana and its now accelerating push towards disentanglement. It is exactly at this point, where local rebellion, urban-regional change and global transformation meet, that our realist analyses can make a political difference.

In chapter two, Baris Kuymulu studies the Gezi Park protests in Istanbul and in Turkey at large. Kuymulu engages directly with the 'middle class' narrative taken up by the media and pundits and shows that not only a majority of participants were in fact of working-class background but also that what is usually assumed to be the middle classes are in fact much poorer, much more precarious, more downwardly regulated by the neoliberalizing state and, in particular, more indebted than is generally understood by the liberal 'commentariat'. The protesters also sought and practised forms of urban 'commoning' that cannot be captured by the stories of economic growth, private lives and rising consumer expectations associated with the middle-class narrative. Most importantly, perhaps, he traces the emergence of the massive all-Turkey protest wave of 2013 to the 'aggressive urbanism' that has been the key engine for economic growth of the AKP regime. He then goes on to show how what he calls a 'frictional heterogeneity' developed among protesters of very different persuasions, such as anti-capitalist Islamists and LGBT activists. This practice of frictional heterogeneity helped different actors to identify and negotiate their differences and commonalities in the face of violent police actions. Kuymulu's chapter is an excellent example of class analysis in the critical junctions mode we are advocating.

Stef Jansen's analytically rich analysis of the Bosnian revolt of spring 2014 continues and further refines this approach among others in a dialogue with the work of Ernesto Laclau on populism. Starting from a workers' uprising in Tuzla, demanding payment of wages, the Bosnian revolt quickly spread throughout the Muslim part of the country, including Sarajevo – where Jansen did his observations. It mobilized thousands of assumed to be 'a-political' and 'apathetic' postsocialist citizens in a protest against 'hunger'. It organized plenums against 'the politicians' who were failing 'the people'. An echo here of Kuymulu's 'frictional heterogeneity', but in this case a heterogeneity less about identity issues than about class differentiations, as more secure citizens found themselves fearing reputational contamination by aligning themselves on the streets with 'the losers of transition', a category long publicly attacked for their supposed refusal to change their purportedly 'socialist' outlooks (Kalb 2009, 2014b). Jansen explicitly deals with the wider critical junctions, both local and global, of this transformative experience, which he expects has definitely opened the window for a popular and political concern with social reproduction that seemed absent as a public discursive possibility in 'identity-scripted' Bosnia Herzegovina before. These critical junctions importantly include social memories of Yugoslav worker-managed socialism. With its emphasis on social security and vertical mobility, socialism is increasingly endorsed positively in post-Yugoslav societies, slowly turning a popular nostalgia into a potential source for political claims. This memory-production turned into political claim-making in 2014 and is feeding into a popular 'commoning' around issues of social reproduction that, during this protest wave, combined the innovation of popular assemblies with small work groups and new labour union formations in making explicit, though hard to satisfy, claims on the state. Here too, as in Istanbul, a mobilization that targets the core of the accumulation regime: in this case transnational financial linkages and the associated neo-patriarchal redistributive arrangements within the state machine.

Sian Lazar's chapter looks at political mobilizations in Argentina. She draws on Chantal Mouffe's (2005) distinction between an agonistic politics that sets adversaries against each other and respects pluralism, and an antagonistic politics where adversaries appear as enemies. Lazar explores the link between collective identities, antagonism and the moralization of politics by looking at the history of political mobilizations in Argentina from the mid twentieth century to the present, particularly focusing on the 2001 debt crisis. She identifies two types of urban protest. One is the 'self-convened', 'spontaneous' and nationalistic series of protests of the middle classes associated with a morality of outrage and exemplified by the 'cacerolazo' (people who take to the street banging empty pots and pans). The other kind of urban mobilization is that convened by organized social forces – principally trade unions and workers' confederations but also neighbourhood associations and political parties, based on explicitly specified and concrete social demands. These two different moralities of protest emerge in the different forms of, respectively, denunciation and demand-making. In line with Mouffe's analysis, Lazar argues that the political friend/enemy discrimination and the degeneration of politics from a more preferable agonistic mode to one that is antagonistic is a defining feature not only of contemporary Argentinian or Latin American politics but also of the mass mobilizations in recent years in Southern Europe. Lazar warns against mapping her typology of urban mobilizations onto a straightforward left and right taxonomy. Lines between left and right are blurred Lazar argues. Besides, for middle-class protesters each demonstration is a new beginning, she claims. But the question remains: Are these forms of protest an expression of different class interests? Perhaps by looking at the new articulations of politics and protests under Macri, a regime clearly attuned to the morality of the middle classes, we will find some answers.

Loperfido's chapter focuses on the fascist ex-militants from the 'Spontaneista groups', an extra-parliamentary group that was active in Italy in the late 70s. Loperfido starts the chapter by identifying the historical roots of spontaneism in the anti-materialist philosophy of Le Bon, Pareto, Mosca and Sorel, which was later appropriated by fascism. Besides, two common features of historically diverse experiences of spontaneism are anti-rationalism (the primacy of action and instinct over reason) and distrust of the state, which is seen as an enforcer of rationality. Loperfido then looks at the development of spontaneism in Italy in the 1970s. The cycle of political turmoil that started in 1968 led the Communist Party (PCI) to nearly win the elections in 1979. But when the PCI eventually managed to accede the governmental area by supporting a Christian Democrat-led cabinet, the well-known 'historical compromise', the expectations of left-wing young militants were crushed. Splinter groups from the extra-parliamentary left and neo-fascist groups started a self-organized movement, the so-called 'movement of 1977' against the whole political system. Such radical left-wing and right-wing groups shared a similar violent, spontaneist and identity-driven approach to politics and constituted a common front against both the parliamentary left and the parliamentary right, which they considered equally corrupted. Particularly striking was that the slogan 'neither Left nor Right' was endorsed at both ends of the political spectrum. Reflecting on the weakness of the Italian political system, Loperfido argues that the violent anti-establishment and post-ideological attitude of these radical groups of the past dangerously returns in the populist Movimento 5 Stelle (5 Stars Movement) run by ex-political satirist Beppe Grillo, which is now the second biggest party in Italy. The chapter is intended more to raise questions than give easy answers. For instance, what is the relationship, if any, between past forms of fascism and present forms of populism? And more importantly, what are the class implications of the current wave of spontaneism and anti-state posture across the political spectrum? More importantly, what can we infer in terms of class struggle from spontaneist forms of political action and philosophy?

Mollona's chapter moves the analysis to the present again. It analyses closely the so-called Brazilian 'June Revolution' of 2013. This revolt consisted of an escalating series of massive gatherings and demonstrations, initially against the looming rise in the cost of public transport, led by the Free Fare Movement (Movimento Passe Livre – MPL), which spread across 400 cities and towns, brought millions of people onto the streets and forced President Dilma Rousseff to start a process of constitutional reform. The chapter starts by engaging critically with two readings of the June events. Göran Therborn (2012) reads them as an example of cross-sectional 'bricolage socialism' or a 'movement of movements' that characterizes contemporary working-class mobilizations in Latin America. Unlike him, Saad-Filho argues that the June events are the consequence of the new democratic accountability of the Brazilian state under the Workers Party (PT) as well as of the restrengthening of middle-class power in Brazil, which had opposed the PT in a dormant form since the party first gained power. Bridging these two views, Mollona relates the demonstrations to the sudden end of the commodity boom, which had fuelled the PT's neo-developmental policy combining pro-labour and anti-poverty measures (such as a 70 per cent increase in the minimum wage and the very effective programme of poverty reduction, Bolsa Familia) with a pro-finance and pro-business stance. For Mollona the June revolution reflects, as said earlier, a complex class scenario where the old and bourgeoisified industrial working classes coexist with a younger and expanded cyber-proletariat, casualized service workers, and a socially mobile lumpen. In spite of the absence of the traditional left (the PT and CGT trade-union confederation) from the initial phases of the demonstration, the events of 2013 led to a successful rearticulation of the left towards more radical left-wing trade unions (such as CONLUTAS) and parties (such as the MPL and PSOL). In the concluding part Mollona recontextualises the 2013 events in the light of the impeachment of President Rousseff, the deep crisis of the PT, and the abrupt end of the Pink Tide in Latin America in 2016. He argues that, unlike the movement of 2013, the demonstrations against the government in 2016 – leading to the impeachment of Rousseff – were led by middle-class parties and their ideologies of austerity, anticorruption and free markets.

Analyses of political mobilizations tend to focus on those who take active part as protesters or on those who actively stand against the protests, but they rarely acknowledge the point of view of those who make a conscious decision not to care much. Based on extensive industrial fieldwork in Bulgaria, Dimitra Kofti discusses the refusal of factory workers in Pernik to join the waves of protest that took place in Bulgaria in 2013 and 2014. Workers in Pernik, an industrial town near Sofia, expressed a general distrust in any kind of political participation. They did so in the motives and claims of the 'protesters' as well. Kofti focuses especially on the second wave of protest from 2014 onwards, which was widely described as middle class and was mainly directed against the new postsocialist left-wing government. The term 'communists', or 'red trash' had come to signify those pseudo-communist governments who wildly privatized, liberalized the market, and demolished anything that was left of the welfare state over the course of the last two and a half decades of capitalism in Bulgaria. During these protests demands and slogans varied – from wanting 'real capitalism' to banning foreign investments. Besides, these protests often had deep xenophobic and nationalist undertones, showing growing hostility in particular against the Roma community, which is viewed as responsible for Bulgarians' 'negative' image in 'Europe'. The steelworkers of Pernik went through a long period of industrial decline, experiencing precaritization, informalization, worsening working conditions and increasing indebtedness. In a context of outmigration of people as well as capital, social reproduction has become a struggle in itself. They are also deeply disillusioned with trade union politics and the new post-communist establishments and have a strong sense of corruption all around. They claim to have no money and no time to think of other things than their daily sorrows. Urban commoning requires resources. Kofti describes how these structural factors affect the steelworkers Mariana and Penko. Feeling lonely and isolated, and disillusioned with communism as well as capitalism, they withdrew from all activism, which, like their workmate Ivo, they consider as 'just playing the game of the political parties'. Rather than as political apathy, though, Kofti reads their abstention as an active refusal to align with any of the modern teleologies of communism and capitalism, a sensibility explained by the particular trajectories of Bulgarian 'transition' into globalized capitalism.

Michael Hoffmann, in his chapter on ex-bonded labourers' protests in urban Nepal, reminds us of two things that the current focus on urban activists and protests in relatively developed societies tends to neglect. First, armed struggle, such as the Maoist uprising in Nepal, may still be one of the few ways for marginal people to fundamentally reform the state in the poorest developing countries (see also Feuchtwang and Shah 2017). Secondly, for them it is indeed the direct confrontation with the state, almost as a citizenship entitlement, which matters most directly. In this high-risk continual struggle, strong leadership – in contrast to the 'leaderlessness' arguments of the horizontalists – is essential. Hoffmann's activists engage in public and highly visible ritualistic confrontations with the state, among others, to gain and keep public attention for the unfulfilled promises of the new post-revolutionary state concerning the rehabilitation and compensation of former bonded labourers. That does not mean they are beholden to leaderships and cannot change them. But centralized hierarchies are crucial to plan and sustain the ritual confrontations. They also facilitate bargaining with the local state and offer a certain protection for activists. Here no populism and 'empty signifiers' of the Laclau type, as in Jansen's study of Sarajevo, but concerted bargaining about focused issues within established democratic procedures and legal frameworks. Those procedures and frameworks, however, are themselves still remarkably fluid and changeable: 'open signifiers' rather than the 'empty' ones of Laclau as it were. This is another stark contrast with the highly legalistic, security-driven bureaucracies of contemporary developed states. Hoffmann's chapter testifies to the overriding importance of contextual critical junctions in understanding and explaining specific insurrectionary practices. It also brings to the fore the uneven and combined nature of current worldwide political turbulence.

Such contextual critical junctions come once more to the fore in Luisa Steur's chapter on the tumultuous rise of the urban Aam Aadmi Party, the Common Man Party, in New Delhi in 2012–2014, which emerged from the mass protests around Anna Hazare's weeks' long, 'spontaneous' Ghandian hunger strike against corruption in central Delhi. Here we have a chapter that actually looks closely at some activists in classic ethnographic mode as they are building a city-focused political party out of the sentiments and energy generated during mass mobilizations. But rather than magnifying their imaginative prefigurative practices, Steur grounds them firmly in the actual class backgrounds, histories, relationships and expectations that bring these different people together and from which these practices arise. The Common Man Party's core tenet of 'anti-corruption' was and is a symbol highly prone to cross-class and indeed potentially class-denying populist mobilizations and alliances (as are similar anti-corruption symbolisms in the chapters of Jansen, Lazar and Mollona). Steur dissects the contradictory ideas and interests aligned around the anti-corruption symbol. She suggests that in the Indian neoliberal context anti-corruption tends to acquire an upper-class, Brahmin, strictly ethical, anti-political connotation. It deeply suspects the state, and the lower orders that are increasingly inhabiting and claiming it, of being corrupted/polluted by something as dirty as material self-interests. While left-wing activists began catering to the Common Man Party in order to secure rights to affordable utilities for slum dwellers, for example, wealthy patrons of the party, working in the stock markets, were emphasizing its useful function in teaching the poor responsibility and accountability in paying their utility dues. Working through the critical junctions behind this populist cross-class alliance, Steur shows the dynamic contradictions underlying a project that, not unlike OWS and other recent popular insurgencies, emphatically embraced practice and practical solutions over theory.

With Ida Susser's chapter we come back full circle to the New York of OWS. Susser does not focus on OWS so much but looks at the variable 'class compasses' expressed in a long trajectory of mobilizations in NYC over time, starting from the late sixties. She sees these class compasses as embedded in and responding to the ongoing political economic transformations of the city. She wonders whether OWS and the subsequent election of the democrat Bill de Blasio signal a similar sort of coming together of middle-class activists and (black) working-class protestors as in the 'public service' activism of the early 1970s, classically described by Piven and Cloward (1971). The 99 per cent of OWS and Bill de Blasio should perhaps be seen as a new class formation in this increasingly unequal world, not unlike E.P. Thompson's early nineteenth-century artisans, who began to see more commonalities than differences among themselves when they were making the English working class.

Don Kalb is professor of social anthropology at the University of Bergen, Norway. Recent books include *Financialization: Relational Approaches* (Edited with Chris Hann, 2020); *Insidious Capital: Frontlines of Value at the End of a Global Cycle* (Editor, 2024, winner of the Society for the Anthropology of Work prize); *Value and Worthlessness: The Rise of the Populist Right and Other Disruptions in the Anthropology of Capitalism* (2025); and *Backlash: The Global Rise of the Radical Right* (Edited with Walden Bello, 2026). Don is Founding Editor of *Focaal – Journal of Global and Historical Anthropology*.

Massimiliano Mollona is an anthropologist and filmmaker. He has conducted extensive fieldwork in Brazil and England around themes of class, work, racism and post-capitalism. He currently teaches at the Department of the Arts (DAR) at the University of Bologna. His most recent book is *Brazilian Steel Town: Machines, Land, Money and Commoning in the Making of the Working Class* (2020).

Notes

1. There has also been an effort to keep the focus of economic anthropology on circulation and moralities rather than production, extraction and exploitation; for example Appadurai 2015; Graeber 2011; Karatani and Bourdaghs 2014. Other works adroitly straddle the classic divides, such as: Bear 2015; Carrier and Kalb 2015; James 2014.
2. This is not a hard division. For example, Steur's chapter in this book can be seen as a combination of the two, as are many articles referred to in note 3, even though idealism clearly prevails. The opposition is made for the sake of distinguishing between competing forms of knowledge and theory, and indeed competing political sensibilities and visions. For good statements of the idealist approach see Ciavolella and Boni 2015; Graeber 2008, 2009; Melenotte 2015. See also Jansen, this book, for a similar discussion.
3. Several journals in anthropology published theme sections on the global insurrections: *Critical Inquiry* (2012) on the aesthetics of rebellion; *American Ethnologist* (2012, no. 1 and 2) on the Arab Spring and Occupy; *Critique of Anthropology* (2012) on anarchism and anthropology; *Focaal* (2015) on 'alterpolitics'. An incomplete list of articles in anthropological journals includes: Bayat 2015; Caldeira 2015; Collins 2012; Corsin Jimenez and Estalella 2013; Dole 2012; Frug 2013; Gray 2016; Hirschkind 2012; Juris 2012; Lazar 2015; Maskovsky 2013; Massad 2014; McQuarrie 2013; Narotzky 2016a, 2016b; Nugent 2012; Parla and Ozgul 2016; Philips 2014; Razsa and Kurnik 2012; Susser 2016; Tambar 2016; Theodossopoulos 2013; Thorkelson 2016; Winegar 2016. See also the excellent cultural anthropology blog 'hotspot' on Occupy: https://culanth.org/fieldsights/63-occupy-anthropology-and-the-2011-global-uprisings.
4. For an elaboration of this critique see Kalb 2014b.

References

Alexandrakis, O. (ed.). 2016. *Impulse to Act: A New Anthropology of Resistance and Social Justice*. Bloomington and Indianapolis, IN: University of Indiana Press.

Appadurai, A. 2015. *Banking on Words: The Failure of Language in the Age of Derivative Finance*. Chicago, IL: Chicago University Press.

Bear, L. 2015. *Navigating Austerity*. Stanford, CA: Stanford University Press.

Beinin, J. 2015. *Workers and Thieves: Labor Movements in Tunisia and Egypt*. Stanford, CA: Stanford University Press.

Bayat, A. 2015. 'Plebeians of the Arab Spring', *Current Anthropology* 56(11): 33–43.

Caldeira, T. 2015. 'Social Movements, Cultural Production, and Protests: Sao Paulo's Shifting Political Landscape', *Cultural Anthropology* 56(11): 126–36.

Castells, M. 2015. *Networks of Outrage and Hope: Social Movements in the Internet Age*. London: Polity Press.

Carrier, J. and D. Kalb (eds). 2015. *Anthropologies of Class*. Cambridge: Cambridge University Press.

Ciavolella, R. and S. Boni. 2015. 'Aspiring to Alterpolitics: Anthropology, Radical Theory, and Social Movements', *Focaal – Journal of Global and Historical Anthropology* 72: 3–8.

Collins, J. 2012. 'Theorizing Wisconsin's 2011 Protests: Community-Based Unionism Confronts Accumulation by Dispossession', *American Ethnologist* 39(1): 6–20.

Corsin Jimenez, A. and A. Estalella. 2013. 'The Atmospheric Person: Value, Experiment, and 'Making Neighbors' in Madrid's Popular Assemblies', *HAU: Journal of Ethnographic Theory* 3(2): 119–39.

Critical Inquiry 39: 1–88 (autumn 2012). 2012.
Critique of Anthropology. 2012. 32(2): 93–216 (Anarchism theme section).
Crehan, Kate. 2016. *Gramsci's Common Sense: Inequality and its Narratives.* Durham, NC and
London: Duke University Press.
Della Porta, D. 2015. *Social Movements in Times of Austerity: Bringing Capitalism Back into Protest Analysis.* London: Polity Press.
Dole, C. 2012. 'Revolution, Occupation, and Love: The 2011 Year in Cultural Anthropology', *American Anthropologist* 114(2): 227–39.
Feuchtwang, S. and A. Shah (eds). 2017. *Emancipatory Politics: A Critique.* London: CreateSpace Independent Publishing Platform.
Ferguson, J. 2015. *Give a Man a Fish.* Durham, NC and London: Duke University Press.
Focaal. 2012. 64: 3–68 (Hardt and Negri section).
Focaal. 2015. 72: 3–79. ('Inspiring Alterpolitics' section).
Frug, G. 2013. 'Democracy's Future: What's Left?', *Public Culture* 25(2): 311–14.
Gill, L. 2016. *A Century of Violence in a Red City: Popular Struggle, Counterinsurgency, and Human Rights.* Durham, NC andLondon: Duke University Press.
Graeber, D. 2008. *Hope in Common.* Available at theanarchistlibrary.org
———. 2009. *Direct Action: An Ethnography.* Oakland, CA: AK Press.
———. 2011. *Debt: The First 5000 Years.* New York: Melville House Publishing.
———. 2012. *Revolutions in Reverse: Essays on Politics, Violence, Art, and Imagination.* London and New York: Minor Compositions.
———. 2016. *Utopia of Rules.* New York: Melville House Publishing.
Gray, P. 2016. 'Memory, Body, and the Online Researcher: Following Russian Street Demonstrations via Social Media', *American Ethnologist* 43(3): 500–10.
Hardt, M. and T. Negri. 2011. *Commonwealth.* Cambridge, MA: Harvard University Press.
Hart, K. and J. Sharp (eds). 2016. *People, Money and Power in the Economic Crisis: Perspectives from the Global South.* New York and Oxford: Berghahn Books.
Harvey, D. 2014. *Rebel Cities: From the Right to the City to the Urban Revolution.* London: Verso.
Hirschkind, C. 2012. 'Beyond Secular and Religious: An Intellectual Genealogy of Tahrir Square', *American Ethnologist* 39(1): 49–53.
James, D. 2014. *Money from Nothing: Indebtedness and Aspiration in South Africa.* Stanford, CA: Stanford University Press.
Juris, J. 2012. 'Reflections on #Occupy Everywhere: Social Media, Public Space, and Emerging Logics of Aggregation', *American Ethnologist* 39(2): 259–79.
Kalb, D. 1997. *Expanding Class: Power and Everyday Politics in Industrial Communities, the Netherlands 1850-1950.* Durham, NC and London: Duke University Press.
———. 2009. 'Conversations with a Polish Populist: Tracing Hidden Histories of Globalization, Class and Dispossession in Postsocialism (and beyond)', *American Ethnologist* 36(2): 207–23.
———. 2011. 'Introduction: Headlines of Nation, Subtexts of Class: Working-Class Populism and the Return of the Repressed in Neoliberal Europe', in Don Kalb, Gabor Halmai (eds), *Headlines of Nation, Subtexts of Class: Working-Class Populism and the Return of the Repressed in Neoliberal Europe.* New York and Oxford: Berghahn Books, pp. 1–36.
———. 2014a. 'Mavericks: Harvey, Graeber, and the Reunification of Anarchism and Marxism in World Anthropology', *Focaal – Journal of Global and Historical Anthropology* 69: 113–34.
———. 2014b. '"Worthless Poles" and other Post-socialist Dispossessions', in A. Carbonella and S. Kashmir (eds), *Blood and Fire: Toward a Global Anthropology of Labor.* New York and Oxford: Berghahn Books, pp. 250–87.

———. 2015a. 'Introduction: Class and the New Anthropological Holism', in J. Carrier and D. Kalb (eds), *Anthropologies of Class: Power, Practice and Inequality*. Cambridge: Cambridge University Press, pp. 1–27.

———. 2015b. 'Theory from the East? Double Polarizations versus Democratic Transitions', *Baltic Worlds* VIII (3–4): 17–29.

———. 2017. 'After the Commons: Commoning!', *Focaal – Journal of Global and Historical Anthropology* 79, forthcoming.

Kalb, D. and G. Halmai (eds). 2011. *Headlines of Nation, Subtexts of Class: Working Class Populism and the Return of the Repressed in Neoliberal Europe*. New York and Oxford: Berghahn Books.

Kalb, D. and H. Tak. 2005. 'Introduction: Critical Junctions – Recapturing Anthropology and History', in D. Kalb and H. Tak (eds), *Critical Junctions: Anthropology and History beyond the Cultural Turn*. New York and Oxford: Berghahn Books, pp. 1–28.

Karatani, K. and M. Bourdaghs. 2014. *The Structure of World History: From Modes of Production to Modes of Exchange*. Durham, NC and London: Duke University Press.

Kasmir, S. and A. Carbonella (eds). 2014. *Blood and Fire: Toward a Global Anthropology of Labor*. New York and Oxford: Berghahn Books.

Khosrokhavar, F. 2012. *The New Arab Revolutions that Shook the World*. Boulder, CO: Paradigm.

Lazar, S. 2015. '"This is Not a Parade, It's a Protest March": Intertextuality, Citation, and Political Action on the Streets of Bolivia and Argentina', *American Anthropologist*

———. 2017. 'Introduction', in S. Lazar (ed.), *Where are the Unions? Workers and Social Movements in Latin America, The Middle East and Europe*. London: Zed Books, pp. 1–24.

Maskovsky, J. 2013. 'Review Essay: Protest Anthropology in a Moment of Global Unrest', *American Anthropologist* 115(1): 126–29.

———. 2017. 'Reclaiming the Streets: Black Urban Insurgency and Anti-social Security in Twenty-First-Century Philadelphia', *Focaal – Journal of Global and Historical Anthropology*, 79, forthcoming.

Mason, P. 2012. *Why it's Kicking off Everywhere*. London: Verso.

Massad, J. 2014. 'Love, Fear, and the Arab Spring', *Public Culture* 26(1): 127–52.

Mauss, M. 2016. *The Gift: Expanded Edition*, trans. J. Guyer. Chicago, IL: HAU.

McMichael, P. 1990. 'Incorporating Comparison within a World Historical Perspective: An Alternative Comparative Method', *American Sociological Review* 55(3): 385–97.

McQuarrie, M. 2013. 'No Contest: Participatory Technologies and the Transformation of Urban Authority', *Public Culture* 25(1): 143–75.

Melenotte, S. 2015. 'Zapatista Autonomy and the Making of Alter-native Politics: Views from its Day-to-Day Praxis', *Focaal – Journal of Global and Historical Anthropology* 72: 51–63.

Mollona, M. 2009. *Made in Sheffield: An Ethnography of Industrial Work and Politics*. New York and Oxford: Berghahn Books.

Mouffe, C. 2005. *On the Political*. London: Verso.

Narotzky, S. 2015. 'The Organic Intellectual and the Production of Class in Spain', in J. Carrier and D. Kalb (eds), *Anthropologies of Class*. Cambridge: Cambridge University Press, pp. 53–71.

———. 2016a. 'Between Inequality and Injustice: Dignity as a Motive for Mobilization during the Crisis', *History and Anthropology* 27(1): 74–92.

———. 2016b. 'On Waging the Ideological War: Against the Hegemony of Form', *Anthropological Theory* 16(2–3): 263–84.

Nugent, D. 2012. 'Commentary: Democracy, Temporalities of Capitalism, and Dilemmas of Inclusion in Occupy Movements', *American Ethnologist* 39(2): 280–83.

Parla, A. and C. Ozgul. 2016. 'Property, Dispossession, and Citizenship in Turkey; or, The History of the Gezi Uprising Starts in the Surp Hagop Armenian Cemetery', *Public Culture* 28(3): 617–53.

Philips, S. 2014. 'The Women's Squad in Ukraine's Protests: Feminism, Nationalism, and Militarism on the Maidan', *American Ethnologist* 41(3): 414–26.

Piketty, T. 2014. *Capital in the Twenty-First Century*. Cambridge, MA: Harvard University Press.

Piven, F. and R. Cloward. 1971. *Regulating the Poor*. New York: Pantheon.

Razsa, M. and A. Kurnik. 2012. 'The Occupy Movement in Zizek's Hometown: Direct Democracy and a Politics of Becoming', *American Ethnologist* 39(2): 238–58.

Sassen, S. 2014. *Expulsions: Brutality and Complexity in the Global Economy*. Cambridge, MA: Harvard University Press.

Scott, J. 1987. *Weapons of the Weak: Everyday Forms of Peasant Resistance*. New Haven, CT: Yale University Press.

———. 1992. *Domination and the Arts of Resistance: Hidden Transcripts*. New Haven, CT: Yale University Press.

———. 2014. *Two Cheers for Anarchism*. New Haven, CT: Yale University Press.

Smith, G. 2013. *Intellectuals and (Counter-) Politics: Essays in Historical Realism*. New York and Oxford: Berghahn Books.

Smith, N. 2008. 'Comment: Neo-liberalism – Dominant but Dead', *Focaal – Journal of Global and Historical Anthropology* 51: 155–57.

Strathern, M. 1992. *The Gender of the Gift*. Berkeley, CA: University of California Press.

Susser, I. 2016. 'Considering the Urban Commons: Anthropological Approaches to Social Movements', *Dialectical Anthropology* 40: 183–98.

Susser, I. and S. Tonnelat. 2013. 'Transformative Cities: The Three Urban Commons', *Focaal – Journal of Global and Historical Anthropology* 66: 105–21.

Szombati, K. Forthcoming. *The Revolt of the Provinces: Anti-Gypsism and Right-Wing Politics in Hungary*. New York and Oxford: Berghahn Books.

Suarez, M. 2017. *The Subprime Middle Class: Precarious Labour, Mortgage Default, and Activism among Ecuadorian Migrants in Barcelona*. Ph.D. dissertation. London: Goldsmiths University.

Tambar, K. 2016. 'Brotherhood in Dispossession: State Violence and the Ethics of Expectation in Turkey', *Cultural Anthropology* 31(1): 30–55.

Theodossopoulos, D. 2013. 'Infuriated with the Infuriated? Blaming Tactics and Discontent about the Greek Financial Crisis', *Current Anthropology* 54(2): 200–21.

Therborn, G. 2012. 'Class in the 21st Century', *New Left Review* 78: 5–29.

Thorkelson, E. 2016. 'The Infinite Rounds of the Stubborn: Reparative Futures at a French Political Protest', *Cultural Anthropology* 31(4): 493–519.

Werbner, P., M. Webb and K. Spellman-Poots (eds). 2014. *The Political Aesthetics of Global Protest: The Arab Spring and Beyond*. Edinburgh: Edinburgh University Press.

Winegar, J. 2016. 'A Civilized Revolution: Aesthetics and Political Action in Egypt', *American Ethnologist* 43(4): 609–22.

Wolf, E. 1982. *Europe and the People without History*. Berkeley, CA: University of California Press.

Wolfson, T. 2014. *Digital Rebellion: The Birth of the Cyber Left*. Urbana, IL: Illinois University Press.

– Chapter 1 –

CONFRONTING 'AGGRESSIVE URBANISM'
Frictional Heterogeneity in the 'Gezi Protests' of Turkey
Mehmet Barış Kuymulu

As the resistance of twenty-five activists to protect an urban commons met with heavy police violence in Istanbul at the end of May 2013, the cities of Turkey saw a rapid mobilization of millions that turned this small protest into an uprising at the national scale. The resistance in Gezi Park started as a peaceful sit in to stop its demolition and appeared as an entirely spontaneous mobilization. Since the protests in Gezi Park were not organized explicitly by an identifiable political organization, such as a labour union, NGO or political party, the ensuing vast and fast mobilization of millions raised a set of questions concerning the social factions and classes involved. There was a widespread tendency, both in and outside of Turkey, to dub the protestors as freedom- and democracy-searching middle classes (Keyder 2013; Surowiecki 2013; Fukuyama 2013). Although those who were deemed as middle class in these analyses were certainly in the streets and notions of democracy and freedom were not absent as important themes during the uprising, I will remain critical to such analyses. I will argue that the discourse of freedom-seeking middle classes is problematic on two grounds. First, it conceals a deep-seated and widely shared resentment among the protestors against a certain kind of authoritarian urbanism underwritten by the commodification of urban space, which leads to the enclosure of the commons, privatization of public spaces and displacement of working-class and marginalized communities from their neighbourhoods. The growth-driven class project based on the production of urban space in Turkey since the early 2000s, in other words, created a political reaction that exploded during the uprising, and it is this key aspect that gets lost in discourses that label Gezi protests as a freedom-searching middle-class mobilization. Secondly, identifying the agency of the uprising as middle class does not do justice to the diversity and heterogeneity of the people from all walks of life that crowded the streets and squares during the uprising. What I will call the 'frictional heterogeneity' that occupied urban Turkey during the uprising was made up of very diverse groups of people with various cultural, political and class backgrounds, including those that have been historically in conflict with one another. My argument is that what unified these conflict-ridden diverse social groups during the formation of the frictional heterogeneity throughout the uprising was a shared resentment towards an urbanism that dispossessed people from their cities, dovetailed with authoritarianism and required the ruling elite to carry out the process of dispossession.

Frictional Heterogeneity

I was in Istanbul in the early days of June and participated in the uprising, staying as well to attend the park forums that emerged after the heat of the uprising. I spent two months organizing, documenting and participating in the events. Although the two months spent in the streets, parks and political meetings hardly qualify as ethnography, many observations I share in this chapter on the ground rests on these two months. The intensity of political organizing and struggle, as well as my personal connections with the people who had been part of the urban social movements in Istanbul well before Gezi protests, contributed to these observations. It is this first-hand experience of the uprising that got me thinking about the formation of the frictional heterogeneity from the early days of the protests onwards.

The formation of this frictional heterogeneity in the streets was a process, albeit a quick one. As I mentioned, when bulldozers entered Gezi Park to remove the trees on 27 May, there were a handful of activists in the park to stop the demolition. The activists were mostly composed of the 'usual suspects' of Turkey's recent street politics. Leftists, students, artists, environmental activists and LGBTQ groups were joined by the anti-gentrification activists who had long been active around the Taksim/Beyoğlu area, where Gezi Park is situated. As the repeated police violence took its toll in the following couple of days, more and more activists, who were mostly organized through social media, crowded the park. The initial resistance in Gezi Park during the first couple of days did not overwhelmingly involve the 'ordinary inhabitants of Istanbul'.

However, what turned the protests into an uprising was precisely the massive participation of those ordinary urban inhabitants. The uprising that caught the governing 'Justice and Development Party' (Adalet ve Kalkınma Partisi, hereafter AKP, its Turkish acronym) off guard brought together an unlikely body of people from all walks of life for the first time in recent memory. The overwhelming majority of people who regularly took to the streets every day during the uprising reportedly did so for the first time in their lives (Bilgic and Kafkasli 2013; Yoruk and Yuksel 2014: 119). The invisible wall of fear that had kept people at home for so long seemed to be superseded by the sheer creative energy released by massive numbers of bodies on the streets. The very process of claiming and appropriating the central public space and fighting over it with heavily armed riot police for days brought about a process of forming political solidarities for people who did not share the same class position and politics. The heterogeneity of banners, colours, flags and other political symbols that occupied the space in Taksim Square was simply unprecedented in any political event in the history of Turkey. It was hard to find any oppositional political fraction, large or small, which was not somewhat represented at the square. It would be naive, of course, to think that all these groups, some of which have long been hostile to one another, simply coexisted in Taksim without any friction.

On the one hand there were Turkish nationalists, who chanted, 'We are the soldiers of Mustafa Kemal', referring to the 'founding father' and the first president of the modern, secular, and nationalist Republic of Turkey. This chant represented secular nationalists' disgruntlement with the new political regime of the Islamic AKP government and its reforms, which the former saw as a threat to the secular foundations of 'Ataturk's republic'. However, this militarist chant with nationalist overtones was constantly interrupted by the anti-war groups, anarchists and conscientious objectors, who chanted, 'We will not kill, we will not die, we will not be soldiers of anyone'. In its other variations the same nationalist/militarist slogan was humorously appropriated by the LGBTQ groups, who chanted, 'We are the soldiers of Zeki Muren', referring to the infamous queer Turkish singer of the 1960s and 1970s. On other repeated occasions, the same militarist/nationalist slogan was interrupted – this time by Kurdish groups, who chanted in Kurdish, *'Biji Serok Apo'* (Viva Leader Apo), referring to the imprisoned leader of Kurdish guerrilla groups that have been fighting for Kurdish autonomy against the Turkish army for over thirty years.

The fragility of new solidarities enacted against a common opponent during the uprising at Taksim Square was captured neatly by one incident, recounted to me later on by a participant. The usual safe distance between a socialist fraction of secular Turkish nationalists and militant socialist Kurdish groups was lost at one point due to the constant flow of people at the square. Each found the other by its side. At that moment, the leftist Turkish nationalists started to chant, 'We are the soldiers of Mustafa Kemal', which was immediately countered by 'Biji Serok Apo!' As the tension escalated, both groups exchanged curses and started to poke one another with the sticks of the banners. 'It was a matter of seconds, my friend,' the participant told me 'and we started to chant the infamous socialist slogan, '"Shoulder to shoulder against fascism" … and thank god they both joined in.'

All this happened alongside the football fans and their mostly sexist chants and slogans, which were often interrupted by socialist feminist collectives. Socialist feminists raised much attention and appreciation when they started a campaign to erase sexist slogans and graffiti off the walls, attaching a note that read, 'Removed due to its sexist content'. Those who thought that the people in Taksim Square were exclusively composed of secularists who had been anxious about the increasingly conservative and Islamist politics of the AKP government had their share of surprise when they saw a huge banner (and a large crowd underneath) that read, 'Property belongs to Allah, Capital get out of Taksim' (Altinors 2013). This was an organization called 'Anti-capitalist Muslims' and they were not alone. Further down in Gezi Park 'Revolutionary Muslims' had their banner that read, 'Trees bend before Allah, AKP bends before Capital'. Both groups were preaching how capitalism was completely in discord with the teachings of the Qur'an and were extremely influential during the uprising. 'Anti-capitalist Muslims' and 'Revolutionary Muslims' were yet another fraction standing 'shoulder to shoulder against fascism' with more pro-capitalist or socialist secularist fractions.

What was interesting with the frictional heterogeneity in Taksim Square was that all these groups and many more were united against massive police violence, and came into contact with one another to a large extent for the first time. The fact that they were necessarily united to resist police violence gave them a chance to talk and get to know one another. Resisting 'shoulder to shoulder' enabled talking face to face. For instance, after the successful campaign by the feminist collectives, more people started to hush others when they started to chant sexist slogans intending to insult the then Prime Minister Recep Tayyip Erdogan. The same went for homophobic chants and slogans. For instance, the most widely used homophobic insult in Turkish would probably be *ibne*, a derogatory term for a male homosexual, the equivalent of which would be 'faggot'. As it is one of the most favourite insults of straight men, it was widely used to insult the police, PM Erdogan or whomever the crowd was resentful and angry against during the early uprising. As I mentioned, the LGBTQ groups were very well represented during the uprising and their presence was felt strongly by many straight men, who would not otherwise spend time with the former. After a few days loaded with homophobic chants and slogans, the members of LGBTQ groups started to carry small hand-banners that read 'We're faggots, so what?!' and even further appropriated the intended insult with their chants: 'What if we're faggots, get used to it, we're everywhere!' 'What if we're faggots, freedom is all we're after!'

In one of the park forums I attended in the Beşiktaş district in late June, where people who want to speak could do so for three minutes, I heard one man confessing in front of hundreds of forum participants that during the Gezi protests he had learnt that he was such a homophobe, and he added that he probably still is (laughter from the crowd). 'But now I know better,' he said and 'I try not to use the word *ibne* for the gay folk.' He shared his experience: he was running away from a police officer in one of the dark winding back streets of Beyoğlu in the middle of the night, and as the police just caught him, a group of gay and transvestite individuals appeared out of nowhere and confronted the police. The police had to flee. 'They were just living in that building, you know, where I was just caught ... and they took me upstairs. We just sat down for a few hours waiting for the "storm" to pass.' He added, 'They weren't what I thought they were. They were great, brave guys' (crowd applauding and cheering).

There is one more crucial dimension to what I have been calling the frictional heterogeneity that emerged during the uprising. Apart from the social groups that would not come together easily, such as homophobes and transvestites, or sexist football fans and feminist collectives, this frictional heterogeneity also represented a confrontation between what could be called the old social movements and the new social movements in Turkey. As I mentioned, the protests and uprising emerged as a spontaneous eruption, and the more traditionally organized political actors, such as political parties and trade and labour unions, were latecomers to the event. It was not until the first week of protests were over that two of the largest progressive labour unions, Confederation of Revolutionary Trade Unions (DISK) and Confederation of Public Workers Unions (KESK), joined forces for a general strike (*Hurriyet Daily News* 2013a). That such labour unions and opposition parties did not jump on the bandwagon quickly enough led to their dismissal by some groups and protestors, as they were seen as too big and too bureaucratic; too well entrenched in the bigger game of politics at the state level to react to a spontaneous uprising. During the early days of the uprising, there were many calls to labour unions and political parties for support in such an unprecedented event and criticism of their dithering ensued.

However, after the first week or so, as Taksim Square was already appropriated and police had withdrawn, the arrival of the organized 'old forces' of political society created as much criticism and reaction from various groups of protestors. The old forces that had been criticized for being late to the uprising were, this time, criticized for joining the protests to co-opt 'the Gezi spirit', for it was decidedly leaderless and spontaneous, led by the principles of direct democracy and solidarity. The organized forces of political society were blamed for their presumed desire to sit behind the wheel. Such allegations continued to be a matter of contestation and dispute throughout the uprising, as there were a considerable number of protestors who valued the spontaneous and leaderless form the uprising represented. There seemed to be a conundrum. While there were some leftist groups that criticized DISK and KESK for holding the general strike for only three days and for going back to work, there were others who argued that the protests were not about political parties or labour unions with their red and yellow socialist flags, because the Gezi protest was not about 'politics'; it was only about saving the trees.

Although the confrontation between the older traditional actors and the newer less organized members of the political society did not go away completely, they cooperated and stood by each other most of the time during the heat of the uprising. None of those actors boycotted the events, for instance, or deserted the streets and squares due to the presence of the other. They simply kept on existing side by side during the uprising. In a way, the older and more organized social forces and the newer ones were the two other somewhat hostile groups that made up the frictional heterogeneity of the uprising. Nationalists, the Kurdish movement, Anti-capitalist Muslims and secularists as well as the old forces and the new forces had tensions among them, but this did not deter cooperation and solidarity during the uprising and in its immediate aftermath. One could argue, moving from Henri Lefebvre's insightful observation about the 1968 revolutionary *irruption* in Paris, that during times of revolt and uprising people are 'endowed with intense, rapid, and lucid perception of immediate possibilities', even though more often than not this may be temporally limited (1969: 113). Certain options that were traditionally seen as impossible before the uprising emerged as possibilities in the heat of it. The formation of the frictional heterogeneity, therefore, was a complex political process, driven by a dialectic between cooperation and contestation among diverse groups with many social and political backgrounds. In fact, amidst this diversity, one of the few shared attributes among the protestors was that around two thirds of them came from proletarian backgrounds – manual, non-manual and informal sector proletarians (Yoruk and Yuksel 2014: 111). Why were Gezi protests quickly labelled as a middle class mobilization, then?

'Spectre of Comparisons' and the Middle Class

The pace and spontaneity of the unprecedented collective mobilization of millions of people without the overt lead of established and organized actors took the governing AKP by surprise. However, the AKP was not the only actor that was caught off guard and many analysts, both in and out of Turkey, those who remained critical to the mobilization as well as those who celebrated it, shared AKP's shock.

This initial shock and awe was quickly translated into a search for the origins, causes and agents of the uprising. A spectre of comparisons haunted the initial analysis. Some argued that the so-called Arab Spring had finally knocked on Turkey's door. Others brought to our attention the similarities between the encampments in New York City's Zuccotti Park and Gezi Park in Istanbul and the ensuing police violence unleashed in both cities. Still others developed several arguments to place Turkey in the politically boiling southern fringe of Europe, along with Greece, Portugal and Spain.

However, the people on the streets of Turkey were not trying to topple an unelected tyrant by calling for the first free elections in recent memory, as Egyptians and Tunisians did. Nor was the reaction clearly directed at a financial elite, holding the rest of the society hostage, as in the United States; although class-based disgruntlement was very salient in the streets of Turkey. Moreover, similarities between the streets of other Mediterranean countries and Turkey's eventually hit the wall of comparison between the imposed austerity and contracting economies of Greece, Spain and Portugal and the growth of Turkey's economy in the past decade. If all this was not enough to satisfy the appetite for comparison, protests broke out in Brazil and Bulgaria roughly at the same time. Turkey's urban uprising was grabbing international media attention in June (O'Brennan 2013; Watts 2013).

There is nothing wrong, in and of itself, with the attempt to understand post-2011 urban mobilizations around the world in relation to one another, as each represents a growing dissatisfaction with the globalized capitalism that is increasingly elitist and repressive in character. On the contrary, such connections between distant and apparently unconnected urban mobilizations should be made; and the common structural mechanisms behind each of them should be carefully revealed and analysed. In the end, youth unemployment, precarious and insecure working conditions, enclosures of the commons, and rampant privatization as well as the widening gap between those who toil every day and those who speculate on the life and labour of others are hardly unique to any specific geography of contemporary global capitalism. However, this common dissatisfaction with an increasingly authoritarian capitalism seemed to get lost in comparison, as the theme of 'middle class' became salient in the media to explain the protests. Discussions around the middle class component of social unrest usually revolved around vague notions such as 'middle class militants' (Surowiecki 2013) and 'global middle-class revolution' (Fukuyama 2013).

For instance, Francis Fukuyama, in a short article he penned for the *Wall Street Journal* at the end of June 2013, argues that 'the political turmoil' that he sees 'all over the world' stems from 'one common theme: the failure of governments to meet the rising expectations of the newly prosperous and educated' (Fukuyama 2013). Fukuyama asserts that 'the rise of a new global middle class' is the theme that connects not only Turkey with Brazil but it connects them with Tunisia and Egypt as well. Citing a 2008 Goldman Sachs report that defines 'the global middle class' as those who make anything between 6,000 US$ and 30,000 US$ a year, Fukuyama attests that 'the corporations are salivating at this emerging market', since this new class will 'grow by some 2 billion people by 2030'. Moreover, if one takes the education and not just income into consideration, Fukuyama goes on, it will then be obvious that the size of the new global middle class is actually larger.

It might look futile to take issue with a political scientist who announced the end of history in 1989 but continues to comment on urban upheavals that are making history (Fukuyama 2000 [1989]). But his views were reproduced by more locally influential intellectuals in such countries as Brazil and Turkey, where the urban mobilizations were taking place. Figures like Fukuyama were largely responsible for the circulation of 'the global middle class' thesis in explaining the post-2011 urban mobilizations. I engage with this thesis here in order to make the argument that what is deemed as middle class by these commentators is largely made up of unemployed and underemployed youth, precarious labourers and underpaid, insecure professionals, most of them highly indebted. In other words, the class in formation throughout the 2013 urban uprising in Turkey is much more complicated than the proponents of 'the global middle class' thesis would have it (see also Mollona's chapter in this book; Kalb 2014).

There were certainly many among the 'two and a half million people' (according to the figures of Turkish Interior Ministry) who took to the streets during the Gezi protests that would fit in Fukuyama's generous category of educated middle class. But whether they are as 'prosperous' as Fukuyama imagines them to be is less certain. To begin with, recent research demonstrates that almost 70 per cent of those who were on the streets during the uprising were younger than thirty years old (Bilgic and Kafkasli 2013, see also Altinors 2013). Had Fukuyama looked at the youth unemployment rate in Turkey (*Hurriyet Daily News* 2013b), he would have seen that it surpassed 20 per cent in 2013 and he might have hesitated to call the demonstrators 'newly prosperous'. Although we cannot be absolutely sure that the youth in the streets during the uprising was exclusively made up of young people without jobs, the high percentage of youth participation in the events and high youth unemployment figures suggest that there may well be a relationship. What is more, the problem with Fukuyama's argument is not limited to unemployment and the growing pauperization of youth. Those who are lucky enough to have a job with a living wage are not exactly better off either. Let me try to demonstrate this with one example.

The medical doctors who work in Turkey's research universities would definitely fall into Fukuyama's global middle class category, both in terms of income and surely in terms of high level of education. However, the AKP governments over the past decade have transformed the legal structures that govern worker rights, length of the working week, pension rights, social security and many other legal structures that turned Turkey's growing population into a flexible labour force. Flexibilization of labour has been one of the key tasks of the neoliberal state around the world. This has undermined the share of labour in accumulated social value to the advantage of capital in the past four decades and this process has been highly visible and important in Turkey as well. The neoliberalization of the medical sector in Turkey has historically been achieved by the privatization of almost every state hospital and by introducing tax cuts for new private investment in the sector. Moreover, the AKP government initiated a series of structural transformations by introducing a new law, effective January 2011, which now dictates that doctors should be paid according to a 'performance evaluation system' (*Hurriyet Daily News* 2011). The Turkish Medical Association (Türk Tabibler Birliği) and the faculty of various university hospitals repeatedly protested the new law and explained that it threatens scientific research, the healthy working conditions of doctors as well as the wellbeing of patients. The 'performance evaluation system' poses such multifarious threats, according to the medical association, because it ties the amount of money doctors could earn to the number of patients they examine, and to the number of surgeries they perform during the working day. The more one examines, the more 'prosperous' one gets. By doing so, it takes precious time away from scientific research, which is what the primary function of university doctors is supposed to be. It also threatens the wellbeing of patients (*Hürriyet* 2011).

I intentionally chose my example from the flexiblization of medical research doctors because they belong to one of the most privileged strata of wage labourers in Turkey. Arguments like Fukuyama's do not even consider the labour conditions under which people produce; the alienation they experience; the rights violations they have to endure; and the growing insecurity and precariousness workers experience. That is to say, Fukuyama and others (Bohn and Bayrasli 2013; Deen 2013; Yueh 2013) make such claims about 'the global middle class' only by looking at the income figures or consumption patterns and without even considering the material conditions under which people live and work.

By questioning how the Gezi protests were identified as a middle class mobilization I do not mean to argue middle classes were absent in the protests. Instead, I argue that the frictional heterogeneity in formation throughout the uprising was much more complicated than simply being about middle class demands. However, there is a good reason why such broad-based mobilizations around the world are labelled as middle class movements. Ideologically, this comes in handy for the ruling elite and for its media pundits, since middle classes are imagined to demand more of something that already exists. This can be more democracy, more freedom or more purchasing power, but such movements are thought to exclude a demand for the wholesale transformation of the social and economic structure that enables such demands. That is to say, the ideological function of representing the agency of such mobilizations as 'middle class' is to imply that the contemporary capitalism is working just fine except an issue here and a trouble there, and these problems could be reformed with a few minor touches (see Kalb 2014).

The middle class card is especially handy in an explosive situation like Gezi protests because it also appears to quickly explain why such a grand mobilization took place in a country like Turkey, which was deemed a star student of the IMF, with relatively healthy growth rates in the past decade, unlike, say, the contracting economies of Greece, Spain and Italy. It is often argued by the liberal commentators who subscribe to 'the global middle class' thesis that while the recent urban mobilizations in the latter stem chiefly from the austerity measures that inhibited economic growth, the protests in Turkey happened precisely because there was such growth, which ostensibly uplifted people's living standards and expectations (Keyder 2013; Deen 2013; Yueh 2013). Therefore, in order to interrogate the ideological function of postulating a freedom-searching newly prosperous middle class as the agent of social mobilization in Turkey, it is necessary to unpack Turkey's so-called economic success.

The 'Construction' of Growth in Turkey

Caglar Keyder, one of the most prominent urbanists and social theorists of Turkey, argues in his piece 'Law of the Father', published during the uprising in the *London Review of Books*, that the protestors in Istanbul were the 'beneficiaries of economic growth and greater openness to the world' accomplished by the AKP government. Furthermore, Keyder argues, economic growth was coupled with the AKP's policies that allocated 'more money for education', which led to some 200 universities in total, and 2.5 million new graduates have been added to the population since 2008. Therefore, greater investment for education powered by economic growth under the AKP's decade-long rule gave rise to a new middle class, according to Keyder, that is more open to the world and demands the standards of its global counterparts (Keyder 2013).

Much has been made of the growth-based economic success of the AKP government in the past decade. It is lamentable that Keyder's account remains uncritical of this success story and simply offers a local version of Fukuyama's 'global middle class' argument. It is true that Turkey's GDP grew by an average of 5 per cent per year, fluctuations notwithstanding, throughout the early and mid 2000s. To equate such growth rates with the increase in purchasing power of the population and with the rise in its general standard of living and welfare, however, is to assume that the extra wealth was distributed equally across society.

There were also serious fluctuations in Turkey's growth rate, in synchrony with the systemic global capitalist crisis. This makes sense, considering the long process of neoliberalization that Turkey has gone through since the early 1980s. However, the vulnerability of the Turkish economy to external shocks was further exacerbated by the highly financialized economic regime the AKP government has built. The AKP's so-called economic success rested on high foreign capital inflows into Turkey's economy. The first ten years of AKP rule witnessed an unprecedented 421 billion US$ flowing into the country, 340 billion of it being in the form of debt (Sonmez 2013a). The economic vulnerability caused by foreign debt is only aggravated by Turkey's account deficit, as the currently growing private sector debt is exclusively in foreign currency (Savran 2013; *Financial Times* 2015). However, in complete accord with neoliberal orthodoxy, foreign capital inflow – even though it mostly comes as debt or speculative short-term investment – is still lauded as the most important sign of a healthy and growing Turkish economy. Yet, barely one third of the 421 billion dollars' worth of this foreign capital landed in Turkey as foreign direct investment. And most of this came to buy existing assets, such as state economic enterprises and banks that were put up for sale (Sonmez 2013b).

Foreign debt is only part of the problem with the debt-infused growth economy during the last decade. The figures on internal debt are as worrying. The 9.2 per cent growth in Turkey's economy in 2010, and 8.8 per cent in 2011, which the AKP government is so proud of, and which is constantly applauded in international liberal circles, relied heavily on household consumption within the domestic market. The share of household consumption in the total growth of Turkey's economy in this two-year period was 70 per cent (Sonmez 2012; The World Bank 2016b). According to the 'Financial Stability Report', published in May 2012 by the Central Bank of the Republic of Turkey, disposable household income is estimated to be 487.2 billion Turkish Liras. Household debt figured as 51.7 per cent of this amount, around 252 billion Turkish Liras (2012: 25) and rose further to 55 per cent the following year (Ewing and Arsu 2014). In 2003, in the early days of AKP rule, the share of household debt in disposable household income was just 5.5 per cent. The 1,000 per cent increase in household debt is a staggering testament to the fact that the much-celebrated economic growth of Turkey and the ostensible rise in people's standard of living has been based on intensifying indebtedness. 1.6 million people are apparently unable to pay their credit card debts (Rutledge 2015). This should not come as a surprise, as the amount of debt from credit cards rose more than 50 per cent in the two years after 2011 (Ewing and Arsu 2014). Note that official household debt figures only reflect formal household debt based on credit card debts and consumer credits obtained from banks. The figures exclude informal debts from friends and family, or from the informal underground institutions, which have proliferated in Turkey.

The Central Bank of the Republic of Turkey seems to be unconcerned with the explosive increase in household debt in the last decade. Its 'Financial Stability Report' announces in a favourable tone that 'the ever increasing use of credit and debit cards, which plays an important role for the registered economy, and consumption expenditures of households via credit cards, continue to increase' (Central Bank of the Republic of Turkey, 2012). This is the core reason why I began examining Turkey's growth-based 'economic miracle', by challenging the analyses that hastily labelled the agency behind Turkey's urban uprisings as 'middle class' (Keyder 2013), and the process as part of 'the global middle class revolution' (Fukuyama 2013). Considering the indebtedness and precarious working conditions of Turkey's so-called middle classes, it is not tenable to argue that two and a half million 'newly prosperous and educated' members of the 'global middle class' participated in Gezi protests in order to demand the consumerist advantages of their global counterparts.

At this point let me go back to the issue of foreign debt, as it provides a joint that connects to another pillar of AKP's so-called economic success. As I mentioned, foreign capital inflow during the AKP decade was unprecedented in the history of Turkey's economy. It is not surprising that this was accompanied by an equally unprecedented privatization of public assets. Although the early attempts at privatization go back to the mid 1980s, it was not until the end of 1990s that it became systemic. Turkey privatized its decades-long accumulated social wealth for 54 billion US$ in twenty-nine years. More than 40 billion US$ of this privatization, that is 78 per cent of it, has taken place during AKP rule in the last decade. Just in the first half of 2013, the AKP government privatized 8 billion US$ worth of public property, which is a testament to the ongoing accelerated privatization under AKP's rule (Sonmez 2013c).

Dovetailing with the foreign capital inflow and vast privatization of public wealth, including urban public lands, one of the chief sectors that gained a new prominence during the AKP decade was the construction sector (Baysal 2010: 39; INTES 2013: 1–2). Powered by state-driven urban redevelopment schemes that have been chiefly about privatization of urban public lands and their redevelopment, the construction sector became one of the driving motors of Turkey's economy under the AKP rule. Imperative in this process has been the transformation of the 'Housing Development Administration of Turkey' (popularly known as TOKI, its Turkish acronym) from a state institution established to serve the housing needs of urban working classes into an almost autonomous institution with extraordinary powers. Directly answering to the Prime Minister, TOKI is indeed acting as a proper ministry. However, TOKI became more independent and powerful than any regular ministry in Turkey, with the introduction of new legal adjustments. For instance, even though TOKI is still formally a state institution, it can work independently with foreign capital and act as an investor both in the construction and finance sectors (Baysal 2010: 40). Moreover, TOKI can change land use patterns, without consulting with the Ministry of Environment and Urbanism or conferring with the Ministry of Culture and Tourism, or Ministry of Forest and Water Resources, which are allegedly responsible for the protection of cultural and natural wealth and heritage in Turkey. TOKI has become the absolute authority over public land, and is able to singlehandedly determine land use patterns, and to make necessary changes in zoning plans to expropriate any piece of land that it can valorize (Adanali 2011: 10; Deniz 2013).

With such centralization of power, TOKI became the chief institution that has been orchestrating the production of urban space in Turkey. It is a hybrid institution that blurs the usual categories through which neoliberal urbanism is usually understood. On the one hand it is a state institution, and seems to be the chief institutional actor of Turkey's state-led urban development. But, on the other hand, it is an autonomous market actor that borrows from international financial institutions, partners with global construction companies, and buys and sells land and real estate. If we are to understand neoliberalism not as a set of political economic practices that exclude the state in favour of private market actors but as a 'class project' (Harvey 2005, 2012) that aims to raise the share of capital at the expense of labour and uses the state to produce that outcome, then TOKI and AKP's authoritarian urbanism seems more neoliberal than any of its predecessors. The AKP government in general, and TOKI in particular, form the vital institutional link between public property and domestic as well as global capital, transferring the former into the latter.

Debt-infused privatization and redevelopment, especially of urban land, together with the steady inflow of foreign capital have been the pillars of AKP's political and economic power in the last twelve years. In this period, the AKP transformed Turkey's urban spaces into one gigantic construction site. It is no coincidence, then, that the largest spontaneous social protest in Turkey's history emerged, precisely, to rescue a small public park in the heart of Istanbul from the AKP's redevelopment mania. Just like the accumulation of capital in one place brings about the accumulation of the working class, and hence of the possibility of workers' resistance, as Marx reminds us, the primary engine of capital accumulation in Turkey – that is, the redevelopment and gentrification of urban land – led to a massive resistance in Taksim Square on a scale unlike anything the AKP or any preceding government has ever seen. The frictional heterogeneity in formation during the uprising, in other words, had very much to do with large- scale investment in the transformation of urban space and the political resistance occasioned by the threat urban inhabitants felt vis-à-vis their social spaces. To demonstrate that the uprising was about much more than simply middle class demands, I suggest taking a look at what the protestors attempted to set up in the urban spaces that were temporarily secured from police incursion during the uprising. The social practices in these liberated spaces give us a clue about why the protestors hit the streets in the first place, and what the protests were about.

The Collectivization of Frictional Heterogeneity

What started as a small protest to protect a tiny public park in the heart of Istanbul quickly escalated into a country-wide uprising in a couple of days, as discussed at the outset. In the case of Istanbul, after heavy clashes with the police for three days and nights over the control of Taksim Square, on 1 June the police forces finally had to withdraw and Taksim Square was claimed by hundreds of thousands of people. Thus began the Taksim Commune. In fact, the attempts towards practising self-management through forming collectives and volunteer groups were already in place in Gezi Park from day one. Many groups, such as 'Our Commons' *(Müştereklerimiz)*, the Taksim Solidarity Platform *(Taksim Dayanışması)* and many others, played significant roles in organizing 'a free medical center, food center and library'. They organized workshops, help centres and information desks 'that aimed to produce a database of oral testimonies and visual records of the protests and police violence' (Gokariksel 2013).

However, the withdrawal of the state and its services from the Taksim area led to a process of 'commoning' (Susser and Tonnelat 2013), which amounted to an unprecedented experiment with self-management. Along with the police, garbage collectors and street cleaners were now absent, for instance. Every little errand was run collectively, first very spontaneously, and then in more organized ways. Every morning began with the collective garbage collection. Protestors set up volunteer teams to distribute the food that was sent to the park by hundreds of anonymous people. Others served food, while some others set up and ran a free library – 'the Looter Library' *(Çapulcu Kütüphanesi)* – sustained by book donations from anonymous individuals as well as from publishing houses.

What is more, for over two weeks money almost lost its significance in the park. The commune set up what they called 'the Revolution Market' *(Devrim Market)*, where various goods, ranging from clothing to gas masks, from snacks to garbage bags, were there to be taken freely by those who were in need. In the absence of money, the market was not sustained by the infamous supply and demand either. As Lefebvre (1969: 7) observed during the French upheaval of 1968, 'events upset the structures which made them possible'. When such structures as commodified market relations or the supply and demand mechanism are upset, the new elements of social life suddenly 'become briefly visible in luminous transparency', to put it in Lefebvre's words (ibid.). What became briefly visible in Gezi Park was the possibility of organizing exchange without the hegemony of exchange value. In the absence of money and the formal market, those who volunteered to undertake required tasks made 'lists of needs' and attached them on the tents and desks of organizations and political fractions situated in the park. These lists were a heavy presence in the social media as well, constantly circulated and updated according to the flow of goods in the park and their consumption pace. Protestors set up a kitchen where people cooked and they kept it open for over two weeks. The makeshift hospital, where volunteer doctors treated the wounded early in the resistance, was kept open for 24 hours, where many homeless received treatment for the first time in their lives (Turan 2013: 70). Volunteers even established a firefighter squad, since many trees and tents had caught fire in the early days of resistance due to countless tear gas canisters launched by the police. That is to say, the organization of solidarity-based self-management was one of the most significant practices that defined Gezi Park.

It is important to note that the process of commoning was not confined to Gezi Park and the Taksim Square. When the Taksim Commune was evicted from the park on 15 June by the heaviest police blow until then, people turned to the neighbourhoods and organized park forums, which turned many parks into a Gezi Park across the country. One major difference was the absence of tents to spend the night, as there was no need to guard the trees. Instead, most park forums gathered around 8pm and dispersed after midnight. The commoning that rendered money irrelevant was still effective in park forums, sustained by people who cooked and brought to the park more food than they would need in order to share with others who did not or could not undertake such a task. For instance, in Abbasağa Park Forum of Beşiktaş/Istanbul, where I attended the assembly several nights, cigarettes, snacks, alcohol as well as other beverages were stashed in the middle of the park and sustained by the 'leave or take freely' logic. The communal solidarity was not confined to the collective consumption of material goods either. In Abbasağa Park as well as in others, after the first few days in which people mostly talked about the police violence of 15 June, participants started to set up workgroups and workshops. Topics and dates were decided upon collectively. Workgroups served as platforms where experience, information and knowledge of individual participants were circulated and shared. Some of the problems discussed in these workgroups included 'communication and media', 'urban renewal and displacement', 'agriculture and ecology', 'women and law' and 'animal rights'. As many people voiced their enthusiasm for learning more and getting organized vis-à-vis specific issues, certain volunteers who had a professional background in such issues stepped up to share their knowledge and experience. Doctors offered brief first-aid workshops, for instance.

Lawyers explained how to deal with the police in the event of an arrest. Such workgroups and workshops proved to be functional for connecting different park forums with each other, as those who wanted to do deeper political organizing on similar subjects in different forums formed alternative workgroups such as 'Inter-forum Workgroup on Resistance to Urban Renewal'. Therefore, the park forums, like the Taksim Commune in Gezi Park, emerged as significant spaces of communal solidarity, where the famous 'another world' was experienced and practised daily.

Conclusion

The narratives that label Turkey's 2013 urban uprising a middle class mobilization rest on a set of claims about the AKP's economic successes since 2002. I have tried to show that both the economic growth – inconsistent and fluctuating, heavily dependent on the stability of the world market – and the purported increase in people's standard of living have been based on intense private indebtedness. The growth-based economic strategy of AKP rule has been a class project from the beginning, benefiting the economic and political elite at the expense of the working population. When the AKP came to power in 2002, the share of the top 1 per cent in Turkey's total wealth was 39.4 per cent. While GDP growth fluctuated wildly during AKP rule, the upward trend in the share of the 1 per cent was never interrupted. It increased every single year, from 45 per cent in 2009 to 54.3 per cent in 2014, laying bare the exacerbating inequalities during the AKP period (Güney 2015). If we look at the income distribution data of 2011 – the latest figures that were released by the state – we see that 61.2 per cent of the households live by 400 US$ a month or less (around the poverty threshold), while only 5 per cent of the households earn more than 1,000 US$ or more. Let us add that 300 US$ is the bare minimum for a family of four in Turkey with respect to food security (Güney 2013). These figures not only put Turkey in third place among the OECD countries with the highest income inequality, with a Gini coefficient of .41 in 2011 (OECD, 2016). They also suggest that debt has become the primary engine behind the growth of household consumption – given that more than half the households have incomes around or below the poverty threshold. From this standpoint, it looks like the only social class that was able to uplift its standard of living is the actual grand bourgeoisie, rather than the people who see themselves as middle class.

Since the AKP came to power in 2002, these worrisome figures have also been inscribed into the layout of urban space. The privatization of public lands, enclosures of the commons, displacement of the working class and massive urban redevelopment projects across the country have been the norm. Such an aggressive urbanism, which benefits capital at the expense of the urban working population, could only be sustained by a hyper-assertive authoritarianism. The way the AKP government and its heavy-handed riot police responded to protestors' demands to safeguard Gezi Park was only a simple manifestation of this authoritarian urbanism. People responded by appropriating central squares and parks in many cities. They set up tents, put up banners, embellished the trees and set up a solidarity economy, where money, the universal form of power, was almost irrelevant. They cleaned the streets and parks together, sang, cooked and ate together. They did not only occupy urban spaces but transformed them into social laboratories where they experimented with an alternative urban commoning at the local scale. The experiments with self-management, direct democracy and solidarity economy reveals, in my view, how deeply the resentment towards authoritarian urbanism was shared within the frictional heterogeneity across urban Turkey. The analyses that reduce the agent of the uprising to the freedom-and democracy-searching middle classes have a hard time capturing the diversity of the protestors, the actual condition of urban life in Turkey, and the underlying resentment towards the AKP's authoritarian urbanism.

Mehmet Barış Kuymulu has a PhD in social anthropology from CUNY Graduate Center and is an assistant professor at the Department of Sociology at Middle East Technical University. Based on ethnographic fieldwork in New York, Boston, and Istanbul, his work seeks to develop a theoretical framework for analyzing diverse urban politics articulated through the "right to the city." He is interested in integrating the conceptual and theoretical insights from Marxist geography and urban studies into the field of disaster studies, with a specific focus on earthquake processes, spatio-temporal frameworks, and the production of space.

References

Adanali, Y. 2011. 'Despatialized Space as Neoliberal Utopia: Gentrified Istiklal Street and Commercialized Urban Spaces', *Red Thread* 3, NP#.

Altinors, G. 2013. 'Misunderstanding the Gezi Movement: Secularism Strikes Back?'. Retrieved 20 January 2016 from http://adamdavidmorton.com/2013/07/misunderstanding-the-gezi-movement-secularism-strikes-back/.

Baysal, C.U. 2010. 'Istanbul'u kuresel kent yapma araci olarak kensel donusum ve ardindaki konut hakki ihlalleri: Ayazma(n)'dan-Bezirganbahce'ye tutunamayanlar', Ph.D. Dissertation. Istanbul: Istanbul Bilgi University, Faculty of Law, Department of Human Rights Law.

Bilgic, E.E. and Z. Kafkasli. 2013. *Gencim, ozgurlukcuyum, ne istiyorum? #Direngeziparki anketi sonuc raporu*. Istanbul: Istanbul Bilgi Universitesi Yayinlari.

Bohn, L.E. and E. Bayrasli. 2013. 'Why Gezi Park isn't Resonating in the Rest of Turkey', *The Wall Street Journal*, 28 June.

Central Bank of the Republic of Turkey. 2012. 'Financial Stability Report', May, vol. 14. Ankara.

Deen, T. 2013. 'Are Middle Class Protests Fallout from Poverty Alleviation?', *International Press Service: New Agency*, 17 June. Retrieved 20 January 2016 from http://www.ipsnews.net/2013/07/are-middle-class-protests-fallout-from-poverty-alleviation/.

Deniz, E. 2013. 'The Politicizing of Dikmen Valley Residents by the Right to Shelter Movement', *Contentions against Neoliberalism: Reconstructing the Social Fabric in the Developing World Conference, 27–28 June*. Oxford: Oxford University.

Ewing, J. and F. Arsu. 2014. 'Credit Card Debt Threatens Turkey's Economy', *The New York Times*, 28 February. Retrieved 20 January 2016 from http://www.nytimes.com/2014/02/28/business/international/credit-card-debt-threatens-turkeys-economy.html?_r=1.

Financial Times. 2015. 'Turkey's Current Account Deficit Widens', 15 February.

Fukuyama, F. 2000 [1989]. 'The End of History?', in P. O'Meara, H.D. Mehlinger and M. Krain (eds), *Globalization and the Challenges of a New Century: A Reader*. Bloomington, IN: Indiana University Press, pp. 161–80.

_____. 2013. 'The Middle-Class Revolution', *The Wall Street Journal*, 28 June.

Gokariksel, S. 2013. 'Speaking of Resistance, the Gezi Park Forums have Spread Across Turkey', *Occupy*, 12 August. Retrieved 20 January 2016 from http://www.occupy.com/article/speaking-resistance-gezi-park-forums-have-spread-across-turkey#sthash.JoluA3eK.dpbs.

Güney, M. 2013. 'Ekonomi kimin için büyüyor: Türkiye'de gelir dağılımı adaletsizliği', *Davetsiz Misafir*, 26 May. Retrieved 21 January 2016 from http://davetsizmisafir.org/2013/05/26/ekonomi-kimin-icin-buyuyor-turkiyede-gelir-dagilimi-dengesizligi/.

_____. 2015. 'Ekonomi kimin için büyüyor: Türkiye'de servet bölüşümü adaletsizliği', *Davetsiz Misafir*, 19 May. Retrieved 21 January 2016 from http://riturkey.org/2015/05/ekonomi-kimin-icin-buyuyor-turkiyede-servet-bolusumu-adaletsizligi-k-murat-guney/.

Harvey, D. 2005. *A Brief History of Neoliberalism*. Oxford: Oxford University Press.

_____. 2012. *Rebel Cities: From the Right to the City to the Urban Revolution*. London, New York: Verso.

Hürriyet. 2011. 'Performans Sistemine Protesto', 1 February. Retrieved 4 January 2018 from http://www.hurriyet.com.tr/performans-sistemine-protesto-16896785.

Hurriyet Daily News. 2011. 'Turkish University Doctors Decry Plans to Tie Payment to Performance', 31 January.

_____. 2013a. 'More Unions to Join in General Strike amid Turkey Unrest', 5 June. Retrieved 20 January 2016 from http://www.hurriyetdailynews.com/more-unions-to-join-in-general-strike-amid-turkey-unrest.aspx?pageID=238&nid=48197.

_____. 2013b. 'Joblessness among Young Turks Surges', 16 May. Retrieved 20 January 2016 from http://www.hurriyetdailynews.com/joblessness-among-young-turks-surges.aspx?pageID=238&nid=46944.

INTES (Turkiye Insaat Sanayicileri Isveren Sendikasi). 2013. 'Insaat sektoru sorunlar ve cozum onerileri'. Istanbul: Nisan.

Kalb, D. 2014. 'Class', in D. Nonini (ed.), *A Companion to Urban Anthropology*. Oxford: Wiley Blackwell, pp. 157–77.
Keyder, C. 2013. 'The Law of the Father', *London Review of Books Blog*, 19 June. Retrieved 20 January 2016 from http://www.lrb.co.uk/blog/2013/06/19/caglar-keyder/law-of-the-father/.
Lefebvre, H. 1969. *The Explosion: Marxism and the French Upheaval*. New York and London: Modern Reader Paperbacks.
O'Brennan, J. 2013. 'The Spirit of Protest in Brazil and Turkey Has Now Swept into Bulgaria', *The Guardian*, 25 June.
OECD. 2016. 'Income Distribution Database'. http://www.oecd.org/social/income-distribution-database.htm.
Savran, S. 2013. 'The Future of the Revolt and the Fate of Turkey's Strong Man', *New Left Project*, 27 June. Retrieved 20 January 2016 from http://www.newleftproject.org/index.php/site/article_comments/the_future_of_the_revolt_and_the_fate_of_turkeys_strong_man.
Sonmez, M. 2012. 'Ailelerin gercek borcu ne kadar?', *Cumhuriyet*, 22 October.
_____. 2013a. 'AKP'nin dis destegi cokerken...'. Retrieved 20 January 2016 from http://mustafasonmez.net/?p=3412.
_____. 2013b. 'Ten Years of Turkish Capitalism and Tendencies', *Perspectives—Political Analysis and Commentary from Turkey* 5(13): 18–22.
_____. 2013c. 'What Left to Sell after $54 Billion of Privatization', *Hurriyet Daily News*, 27 July.
Surowiecki, J. 2013. 'Middle Class Militants', *The New Yorker*, 8 July.
Susser, I. and S. Tonnelat. 2013. 'Transformative Cities: The Three Urban Commons', *Focaal – Journal of Global and Historical Anthropology* 66: 105–21.
Rutledge, N. 2015. 'Turkey Leads Europe in Credit Card Debt', 19 January. Retrieved 4 January 2018 from https://www.lowcards.com/turkey-leads-europe-credit-card-debt-29986.
Turan, O. 2013. 'Gezi Parki direnisi ve armagan dunyasi', *Toplumsal Tarih* 238: 62–73.
Watts, J. 2013. 'Brazil Protests Erupt Over Public Services and World Cup Costs', *The Guardian*, 18 June. Retrieved 20 January 2016 from http://www.theguardian.com/world/2013/jun/18/brazil-protests-erupt-huge-scale.
World Bank. 2013. 'GDP Growth (Annual %)'. Retrieved 20 January 2016 from http://data.worldbank.org/indicator/NY.GDP.MKTP.KD.ZG.
_____. 2016a. 'GDP Growth (Annual %)'. Retrieved 20 January 2016 from http://data.worldbank.org/indicator/NY.GDP.MKTP.KD.ZG.
_____. 2016b. 'Household Final Consumption Expenditure, etc. (% of GDP)'. Retrieved 20 January 2016 from http://data.worldbank.org/indicator/NE.CON.PETC.ZS.
Yoruk, E. and M. Yuksel. 2014. 'Class and Politics in Turkey's Gezi Protests', *New Left Review* 89: 103–23.
Yueh, L. 2013. 'The Rise of the Global Middle Class', *BBC News*, 18 June. Retrieved 20 January 2016 from http://www.bbc.com/news/business-22956470.

– Chapter 2 –

RECONFIGURING 'THE PEOPLE'?
Notes on the 2014 Winter Revolt in Bosnia and Herzegovina

Stef Jansen

Winter 2014

On 4 February 2014 a few hundred workers took to the streets of Tuzla to demand, once more, that the government of Canton Tuzla, one of the dispersed organs of government in the semiprotectorate of 'Dayton' Bosnia and Herzegovina (BiH)[1], secure payment of their salaries and social security contributions, as well as a strategic solution for investment in and ownership of their firms. In addition to a long industrial tradition, Tuzla by now also had an extended postindustrial record of unrest by factory workers, many of whom had gone without pay and associated contributions for years. By 2014 Tuzla's demonstrations were increasingly bringing together workers from different firms. Like elsewhere in Dayton BiH, the town's industries had been decimated by the 1992–1995 war, the disintegration of Yugoslav networks and shady (semi)privatizations, but, atypically, Tuzla had seen a combination of relatively strong syndical activity (mostly without support from the higher echelons of the trade unions) and increasing co-ordination with other local left-leaning initiatives. Still, when yet another protest occurred there on 4 February 2014, this hardly made any headlines. I had no inkling that something special had started and my day in BiH's capital Sarajevo unfolded as usual.

Things changed the next day, when several thousands joined a demonstration at the seat of the government of Canton Tuzla, housed in the former offices of an industrial enterprise. This unusually large crowd included many people who had no direct links with the town's factories. Slogans targeted the cantonal government and political elites more generally, denouncing privatization, unemployment, violations of workers' rights and corruption. Skirmishes with police, injuries and arrests ensued. That evening a few dozen people held a solidarity demonstration in Sarajevo. Over the next days thousands joined protests in towns across the Federation of BiH (one of Dayton BiH's two 'Entities'), condemning police interventions in Tuzla and expressing their fury at political elites and their mismanagement of socioeconomic concerns. Injuries and arrests marked clashes between police and some protestors who stoned and partly burned some government and other public or party buildings in several towns. On 8 February, having cleaned up debris first, Tuzla protesters had organized the first 'plenum': a participative-democratic citizens' assembly to discuss their concerns and to formulate demands for political and socioeconomic measures. In other towns in the Federation too, hundreds, and sometimes thousands, continued to gather on the streets to demand the release of those who had been arrested and to show dissatisfaction with the situation in the country. There too plena were organized. In Sarajevo, the first plenum attracted such a large crowd that it had to be cut short until a larger venue was found. Almost a thousand people attended that plenum at the second attempt on 14 February.

Within days, resignations were tendered by four out of ten cantonal governments, mostly consisting of the conservative Bosniak-nationalist Stranka demokratske akcije (SDA) and the nominally centre-left Socijaldemokratska partija (SDP). Media controlled by those parties sought to close ranks by expressing outrage at the protestors' 'hooliganism', evoking widespread fears of chaos. Some hand-wringing understanding for the 'legitimate' concerns of 'the people' was heard too, but patience was called for. BiH's foreign 'supervisors' likewise focused on denouncing violence. They spoke of the democratic right to non-violent protest and urged domestic elites to 'listen to citizens'. Fahrudin Radončić, the BiH Minister of Security, used his newspaper to position himself in support of the protests, even claiming to have put them in motion himself. This tycoon, who had made his fortune under SDA wings during the war, had founded a new party, Savez za bolju budućnost (SBB), before the 2010 elections. He was now quickly removed from his post by his coalition partners. While his activists were present (largely incognito) on the streets and in the plena in Sarajevo, banners and demands targeted *all* politicians, including SBB, which did have its share of power.

What had started as a workers' protest in a single town thus gained momentum and, over the next two months, congealed, affectively if not institutionally, into one revolt under a universalist banner of 'social justice'.[2] This was the largest mobilization in BiH since the war. Street protests, decreasing in size, continued. Plena sessions provided platforms for the formulation of demands, on stage or in written form. Working groups went through thousands of such demands to articulate sets of them to be voted on and then to be presented to acting cantonal governments (and, later on, aggregated ones to Federation organs). Many demands focused on socioeconomic issues, such as a revision of privatizations, social protection, an employment strategy and implementation of workers' legal entitlements. Others focused on the judicial system and public institutions of care, education and government, particularly demanding a curtailing of corruption, of the privileges of political functionaries and of the influence of party apparatuses. There was an overarching call to finally put 'the state' in order.

As a part-time inhabitant of Sarajevo, then on unpaid leave from the University of Manchester, I put aside my anthropological work to join the revolt as a participant. I did not conduct ethnographic research on the events. Yet, as it happens, the scholarly work that I suspended in order to join in was an ethnographic study focused on political reasonings around shared concerns with 'normal lives' and 'the state' in Dayton BiH, culminating in a book that was, appropriately, delayed as a result (Jansen 2015). In light of calls for 'affirmative ethnography', this text relies on that earlier work to locate the 2014 revolt in its historical conditions of existence.

Affirmative Ethnography

Much recent anthropological work focuses on activist self-organization to reveal innovative alternatives to neoliberal capitalism and to institutional representative democracy. In line with Graeber's call for studying anarchism as an ethics of revolutionary practice (2008), many such studies foreground egalitarian, anti-statist practices and imaginings of particular sets of activists. Empirically, they tend to zoom in on processes internal to activist practices that authors consider to prefigure desirable alterpolitical possibilities (see e.g. Krøijer 2010; for examples and critical discussion see *Critique of Anthropology* 2012; *Focaal* 2015). Thus, they largely leave aside the concerns and practices of these activists at times and in spaces where they are not primarily preoccupied with political interventions, and they pay little attention to questions of the embedding and resonance of that activism in the social formation where it unfolds. Theoretically, their focus on 'becoming' often evokes Deleuze as a source of inspiration (see Jansen 2016), particularly through references to Hardt and Negri (2005). Much of this work exemplifies what Maple Razsa has called 'affirmative ethnography' of 'movements centred on the radicalisation of democracy' (2012: 35). With Andrej Kurnik, Razsa himself (2012) has provided a fine example of such an approach in a study of the politics of 'becoming' in Occupy mobilization in Ljubljana.

I too want to develop an 'affirmative' take on the 2014 revolt in BiH here. However, I will not do so through a focus on internal processes of becoming amongst activists. There are two main interrelated reasons for this.

A first reason is empirical. Horizontal, open-ended self-organization was a crucial dimension of the 2014 revolt in BiH and in that way the plena constituted avenues for the reimagining of politics beyond the tired institutions of parliamentary representation. Yet this existed alongside strongly opposed calls for 'putting the state in order'; for caring, fair and efficient institutions, all embedded in a broader desire for order and predictability. Reading an otherwise insightful article on assemblies, I was therefore not a little surprised to see the plena in BiH listed as one of several 'cases' of recent mobilizations that 'have largely stopped expecting changes from government institutions and have rather focused on envisioning and establishing new forms of horizontal decision-making' (Boni 2015: 14). Ethnographic research provides a good insurance policy against such summoning of cases to confirm a received model, and indeed against positing an either/or choice between direct democracy and 'expectations from government institutions' in the first place. In that way, much as it grates with their own anarchism, Razsa and Kurnik do in fact note that 'the state' remained a key addressee even in the more self-selected 'radical' Occupy movement in Slovenia (2012: 249–50). They decided not to follow this through in their analysis. Approaching the 2014 revolt in BiH, I too could have foregrounded internal processes of anti-statist, open-ended becoming through a selective focus on certain activities by certain persons in the interstices of the events. I will trace dominant empirical patterns instead.

The second reason for taking this alternative route is of a political nature. Razsa's call for an 'affirmative turn' states:

> While we must not shy away from the limits and contradictions of these emergent direct democracies, we must *also* attend to their potential contributions to a radically re-imagined politics. In some sense, such an affirmative turn would be a return to anthropology at its best: the exploration of ways of being human that are at odds with what appears natural and inevitable from the vantage point of the present. (Razsa 2012: 35, emphasis in original)

I agree. Yet, I want to extend Razsa's 'also' to the second sentence in this quotation. Anthropology, I contend, can *also* be 'at its best' (in terms of politically affirmative potential) through critical analysis of the constellation in which mobilizations occur and of their target: the functioning, legitimation and reproduction of a status quo. In that way this text seeks to extend my attempts during the revolt in BiH to evoke resonances between some concerns that animated it and certain yearnings shared amongst many people in BiH who did not participate.[3] My priority at the time was to join others in attempts to increase the revolt's efficacy as a counter-hegemonic project focused on social justice. We tried to maximize the revolt's short-term impact (i.e. to see the fulfilment of some of its publicly formulated demands). Additionally – and, for some of us, especially – we sought to force questions of social justice onto public agendas, and to create a register for a maximally radical politics of distribution with maximal resonance amongst the population of BiH. We wanted to redefine the terms of political struggle and to mobilize – making social justice a legitimate parameter of debate beyond circles who already shared such political convictions. And while the articulation of such a counter-hegemonic discourse can perhaps be combined with direct democracy, their relative prioritization is always shaped in specific ways. In the particular case of the 2014 revolt in BiH a focus on its internal processes of becoming would lead me into a conflict between my scholarly and political engagements. Good ethnographic analysis and good political action are not necessarily incompatible, but their primary objectives and modes of operation may sometimes clash. Any half-decent ethnographic account of internal processes of the 2014 revolt in BiH would have to address challenges and tensions within it (on the Zapatista example, see Melenotte 2015). Yet whether such an analysis can be affirmative depends not only on pure intentions by the anthropologist. It also hinges on the relative robustness and viability of the mobilization that she/he studies in the specific constellation in which it occurs. Here and now, I feel unable to formulate a good ethnographic account of the internal processes of the revolt in BiH – warts and all – that would manage to be affirmative of its politics of social justice both actual and potential. And it is in this latter domain that my primary political commitment ultimately lies, more so than in the ethics-in-action of our experimentation with direct democracy and its prefigurative potential for a politics of my liking. So in this text it is precisely my desire for affirmative engagement with the revolt that drives my analytical turn away from the internal processes of becoming.

Instead, through a focus on widely resonant concerns with social reproduction, I want to locate the revolt in local-global processes in which it shaped up: those of a divided, supervised, postwar, postsocialist, semiperipheral BiH on the Road to Europe.

Populist Reason and Political Subjectivity

To my knowledge, no data were collected on the sociological profile of participants in the revolt. Moreover, the lack of reliable population statistics in Dayton BiH at the time renders it difficult to identify categories according to income, property or employment status. On the streets and at the plena in Sarajevo[4] I found that the crowds were unusually varied for BiH protests, bringing together employed and unemployed people, and pensioners, with diverging sets of economic, social and cultural capital. Unlike in Tuzla, where synergy between syndical and academic activists had been nurtured before the revolt, in Sarajevo there was only limited involvement by students or professional academics. Highly educated activists on casual contracts in the para-academic scene were more prominent. Amongst some of them I noted a marked shift from NGO-cultivated liberal-civic concerns to more leftist ones.

Rather than trying to map protestors' backgrounds as independent variables, it therefore seems more interesting to trace how the revolt *forged* a subject. So 'becoming' after all – only from another angle. Inspired by Ernesto Laclau's political theory treatise *On Populist Reason* I will explore this question through a focus on demands, distinguishing between 'democratic' and 'popular' ones (2005: 72–77). An example of Laclau's 'democratic' demands can be found in the initial requests of Tuzla workers for solutions to their employment and social protection status, and for strategic interventions in their firms. As Laclau points out, authorities may incorporate such demands institutionally into the existing order in a differential manner – in isolation from other such demands. This was a common elite strategy in Dayton BiH. Yet if such 'democratic' demands remain unfulfilled, Laclau explains, people may become alert to similarly unsatisfied demands by others, elsewhere. Different demands can then be articulated in 'a chain of equivalence', giving rise to 'popular demands': 'a plurality of demands which, through their equivalential articulation, constitute a broader social subjectivity' (Laclau 2005: 74). So we could say that when the winter 2014 mobilizations rippled out from Tuzla workers equivalential chains expanded, 'democratic demands' were articulated into 'popular demands' and, while retaining their plurality, they were symbolically unified through the construction of a popular political subject. While the category of 'citizens' was also used, the key rhetorical 'we' device for doing so was *narod* ('the people').

A collective subjectivity-in-revolt was thus named with the affectively charged term 'the people' and conceived of in a dichotomous relation to an institutional system, here referred to mainly as *političari* ('politicians'). Characteristically, as the chain of equivalence grew, with ever more and ever more heterogeneous demands, the 'reason' of the revolt was difficult to pin down as 'right wing' or 'left wing' (Laclau 2005: 87; cf. Kalb and Halmai 2011). What remained relatively stable was the affective investment in an 'antagonistic frontier' (Laclau 2005: 77–83), signalled with two ultimately empty signifiers – 'the people' and 'politicians' – and continually confirmed as constitutive and irreducible.

Laclau refers to the logic described here as 'populist reason'. I now trace the emergence of a particular form of incipient 'populist articulatory practice' (Laclau 2005: 73) in the conditions of existence of Dayton BiH.

Politics and Anti-politics in the Dayton Meantime

The 1995 Dayton Peace Agreement, of which the constitution of BiH is an annex, ended the military violence and safeguarded the country's sovereignty as an internationally recognized state. It also established foreign supervision and cemented territorial division and ethnonational institutional representation of three 'constitutive peoples' (Bosniaks, Croats, Serbs), thus allowing the key protagonists of the war to maintain their dominance in newly enshrined subpolities. As many studies have documented, alongside continuous ethnonationalist contestation, this resulted in a kind of marriage de raison whereby political elites can demobilize most unrest amongst 'their' respective (ethnonationally circumscribed) 'peoples' with a combination of identitarian fear-mongering and party clientelism (see e.g. Donais 2005; Bojičić-Dželilović 2013; Kurtović 2016). This entailed depoliticizing calls for closing ranks in the face of outside threats to constitutionally enshrined ethnonational 'vital interests' (see e.g. Mujkić 2007) and, within their own fiefdoms, elites also selectively provided certain (often minimal) conditions for social reproduction, especially through the party-channelled allocation of public sector jobs and war-related allowances. This ethnonationalist-clientelistic machine reproduced domination and inequality and, to a large degree, it set the register through which politics could be waged. Support for and contention of the ruling elites could almost exclusively be framed in identitarian terms or, within the respective fiefdoms, in terms of supplication for clientelistic paternalism (Roseberry 1994). Identitarianism and clientelism thus combined into a depoliticizing, demobilizing machine, attuned to the Dayton institutional set-up and sanctioned by a foreign supervision that had long retreated into empty mantras of ever-postponed Euro-Atlantic integration as an overall, non-political remedy without alternatives. It was extremely hard to establish non-identitarian parameters for political action, because elites could force almost any contention into the terms of the (identitarian) legitimacy of the state's existence and its Dayton territorial-institutional set-up.[5] If concerns with social justice appeared, they were ignored in favour of 'vital' identitarian issues or deflected in ethnonationalist blame games. At best, solutions were promised *after* the settling of priorities in terms of statehood and Euro-Atlantic integration. 'The people' (i.e. 'the Peoples') were continuously told to be patient.

Protest was not absent from Dayton BiH. By 2014, the country had seen many smaller particularist mobilizations; for example, by former soldiers or workers of particular firms, usually organized around 'democratic demands' for the implementation of legal entitlements. These often included denunciations of elites as well as calls upon their patronage. I had also participated in bigger protests in 2008 and 2013, mainly of formally educated urbanites organizing themselves as 'citizens' around issues of accountability. Still, BiH was perceived by inhabitants and outsiders as mired in apathy. This was particularly so with regard to questions of social justice, for which no legitimate political register seemed to exist at all. With my friends, I too became exasperated with the tendency of people to quell their dissatisfaction with resignation, as exemplified in the notorious phrase *šuti i trpi* ('shut up and suffer/endure').

In a 2008–10 ethnographic study in a Sarajevo apartment complex (Jansen 2015) I found much impatience but not much action. My interlocutors worried especially about the lack of conditions for the transgenerational reproduction of projected household trajectories of 'normal lives'. On the societal scale, too, they felt that since the end of the war, nothing in BiH had 'moved from the dead point'. These shared concerns amounted to a sense of living in continuous suspension between a war that had not quite ended and a future – widely held to be related to EU accession – that had not quite been embarked upon. In this 'Dayton Meantime',[6] my interlocutors were particularly anxious about the absence of 'a normal state'. Institutionally dispersed and captured by party elites, the actually existing state of BiH left them feeling dispossessed, cheated and both over-governed by predatory 'politicians' and abandoned in a mess that provided no conditions to (re)launch 'normal lives' (see also Jansen, Brković and Čelebičić 2016). At the time, many of my interlocutors cherished a degree of hope that SDP, then in opposition in most places, could bring improvement. Yet by 2014 such hopes were increasingly considered untenable, since, after a resounding 2010 electoral victory, SDP had now been part of various ruling coalitions and failed to move things from the 'dead point'. If anything, it was now perceived to be just as bad as the rest. This further strengthened already intense and widely shared scepticism towards *all* political engagement, governmental or non-governmental, domestic or foreign, parliamentary or insurgent (see Helms 2013; cf. Kofti, this volume). This stance combined beliefs that all political activities are *always* orchestrated by parties, embassies, secret services, NGOs, etc., and that the *only* real motivation for people to participate in them is for personal or household material benefit. This image of politics as exclusively populated by cynical players, large and small, was accompanied by a defeatist sense that all genuine attempts to organize for change could only fail anyway.

Three Refusals

Against this background it is unsurprising that, while the popular demands formulated at the plena were presented under the banner of the 'empty, not abstract' signifier 'social justice' (Laclau 2005: 96), the fledgling political subject of the revolt was articulated as much by refusals to engage on particular terms as by positive identification. Again, this is typical of populist reason. Let me identify three dimensions of such negative self-positioning.

First, mobilization involved a radical 'no' to fear-induced patience. In Dayton BiH scepticism regarding political mobilization merged with fear of disorder, widely associated with war memories. Many people recoiled at any threat of violence, chaos or mere instability (and change, of course, requires instability). Despite widespread dissatisfaction with the 'abnormal' status quo, for many the phrase 'just let there be no shooting' remained powerful during the revolt too. Elites continually stirred this fear ('hooliganism'!) and kept many potential waverers from joining protests and plena. In a more insidious pattern, since the mobilization involved explicit evocations of poverty and inequality, many sceptics also seemed anxious to distance themselves from the 'losers of transition' they associated with the revolt (cf. Repečkaité 2011).[7] Struggling to make ends meet themselves, many retained aspirations to middle-class dignity that they could not afford anymore. Fear of instability, I suggest, was thus wedded to fear of contamination. In defiant response, the 2014 revolt included a self-presentation not just of 'the people' having risen up to fight for 'social justice', but of them having *finally* risen up to fight for it in the face of widespread fears and of long-term depoliticizing pacification by political elites. This time calls for patience would not do.

Second, compared to other mobilizations, the revolt included remarkably few attempts to enlist the help of the so-called 'International Community'. While some protestors did seek audiences with foreign functionaries, these were aimed more at changing their perspectives than at supplication. Also, Dayton BiH's supervisors were not considered likely allies in a struggle for 'social justice'. They were instead seen as part of the problem, due to ongoing intimate entwinements with domestic elites, due to their role in the semiprivatization processes that were considered key to current predicaments, and due to their implication in the increasing hold of IMF and EU conditionality on policies. In addition, there was a marked desire to set the revolt apart from 'civil society' (i.e. NGOs that in BiH are strongly associated with foreign supervision). Some NGO activists were involved but, as with party members, their presence was on the whole incognito. Strikingly, some speakers on the Sarajevo plena started out by specifying 'I am not a member of any political party, nor of any NGO'. Many saw 'civil society' as a trans-border, Western-promoted, professionalized, snobbish variety of politics. The term 'citizens', widely employed in 'civil society', was frequently used, particularly at the plena and in supportive media reporting, but this was limited compared to earlier universalist mobilizations. More than before it was subsumed in a collective subject that could be more effortlessly associated with a struggle for 'social justice': 'the people'.

This brings us to a third form of self-positioning through refusal. In the divided polity of Dayton BiH, shaped by 1992–1995 'ethnic cleansing', the empty signifier of 'the people' was already omnipresent in public: in ethnonationalist elite claims to legitimacy. Much work, therefore, went into repelling any capture of the 2014 revolt in an identitarian frame. Yet there was not much trans-ethnonational solidarity organized around shared dispossession that some sympathetic commentators claimed to detect (especially outside of the country, see e.g. Žižek 2014). Two corrections to this wishful thinking are in order. First, almost no mobilization occurred outside areas of the Federation of BiH inhabited by a majority of people that can be identified ethnonationally as Bosniaks. The revolt's chain of equivalence did not transcend war-produced borders into areas controlled by Serbian or Croatian nationalist parties, who dismissed evocations of social justice as merely a disguise for a Bosniak nationalist campaign. Second, crucially, I believe that seeking to detect a trans-ethnonational dimension in the 2014 events asks the wrong questions, mired in identitarianism even if seeking to counter ethnonationalism. True, when protestors had to engage with the Dayton BiH set-up, they did so largely through the civic register of 'the people of BiH', not in ethnonational categories. Yet, much more importantly, a key dimension of the revolt's political significance consisted of relatively successful attempts to remain *oblivious* to the identitarian matrix that pervades the institutional configuration of Dayton BiH. Most, no doubt, considered this configuration, and its ethnonational-territorial form, a key obstacle to improvement. But formulating concerns in those terms would invite elite invocations of identitarian questions of statehood, resulting in more calls for closing ranks and for patience. Indeed, attempts by some participants to reconfigure the stakes around such 'Dayton' parameters were resisted in favour of a strategic focus on cantonal governments, and later on Federation institutions. This selection of main addressees for the plena's popular demands also chimed with the emphasis on social justice, since cantonal (and federal) institutions governed most domains of employment, social protection, education, health care, etc. To be sure, in Dayton BiH, all government is to a degree inflected by ethnonational categories, but the revolt mostly avoided being sucked into *any* debates on ethnonational matters and constructed 'the people' largely without reference to *any* identitarian concerns, whether ethnonational or trans-ethnonational.

'Normal Lives' and Concerns with Social Reproduction

With those three refusals in mind, let us now return to the demands that shaped the 2014 revolt in Dayton BiH. The uprising came to be framed as a struggle for social justice with universalist aspirations, not limited to democratic demands for implementation of legally guaranteed arrangements for particular groups. Initially, many protestors focused on the release of youngsters who were arrested in the skirmishes of the first days. This remained important, but increasingly crowds joined the Tuzla initiators in decrying poverty, inequality and misgovernment across the board, articulating an antagonistic frontier between 'the people' and 'politicians' through the formulation of popular demands. Pace Laclau, these retained their plurality. There were demands for the reduction of privileges of functionaries; for judicial prosecutions of corruption; for depoliticized, technocratic government; for transparency and accountability; for democracy beyond institutional representation; for an orderly state; for welfare provision and redistribution; for secure employment and social protection; for revision of privatizations; and so on. The rhetoric of 'hunger' was omnipresent, as the revolt thrived on performative evocations of the contrast between 'the people's' conditions for social reproduction and those of 'politicians'. Whereas many protestors felt they could not even aspire to 'normal lives', they pointed out that the latter's high salaries, perks and corruption reinforced privilege and inequality. In the process, the empty signifier of 'the people' was articulated both morally (as the virtuous 'part as the whole' (Laclau 2005: 86), fighting for social unity)[8] and positionally (as those who had been dispossessed, mistreated and abandoned by predatory politicians and who now demanded their part). An anti-political focus on the privileges of politicians (decrying limousines, nepotism, mobile phone accounts, etc.) thus combined with broad socioeconomic indignation, facilitating an emerging politicizing articulation of a universalist concern with social justice.

Crucially, this involved a marked awareness of contingency. The revolt saw explicit attempts to reason in political-economic terms about how the current situation had come into being, with reference to the 'critical junctions' (Kalb and Tak 2005) of war and of postwar, supervised, semiperipheral, postsocialist state formation, and, particularly, of (semi)privatizations under foreign auspices as key mechanisms through which elites had accumulated and solidified positions and fortunes. Yearnings for 'normal lives' clearly shaped up in 'wider landscapes of power that structure local capacities for action and critical memory' (Kalb and Tak 2005: 6). In this sense, an anthropological analysis must account for the importance of prewar lives in Yugoslav socialist BiH as a central resource in the 2014 revolt (and beyond). People recalled secure lives with comparatively high living standards, limited social inequality and, crucially, built-in aspirations to biographical and transgenerational upward mobility. 'Normal lives', thus understood, are above all lives in which the reproduction of trajectories is securely gridded in institutional arrangements of 'a normal state' (Jansen 2015). Dayton BiH was seen to fail to deliver on all these accounts. By now, for over two decades its UNDP Human Development Index had been one of the lowest in Europe, with 26 per cent of the population living on 2.5 to 5 dollars a day.[9] Data assembled for 2012 (Mujanović 2013) show that the country had one of Europe's lowest activity rates of the working age population (47.4 per cent). Although unemployment had been a major problem in Yugoslav BiH too (Woodward 1995), this exploded in the 1990s, especially amongst young people, leading to the highest youth unemployment rate (54.3 per cent) in Europe. The overarching concern in the revolt, then, was that social reproduction was continuously endangered even at the much lower level to which people had fallen with the war. Let me give two more figures to index the intensity of that experience of regression and dispossession. First, in absolute terms, the 2014 average salary in BiH for those who were in registered employment was some 30 per cent higher than the 1990 average. With sharply increased living costs and unemployment, and much reduced social protection, this represents a vertiginous drop in real living standards. Second, BiH's latest available Gini coefficient of income inequality is 0.33 (2006), well above the European average and up dramatically from 1990 (0.26).

In this context, apart from remittances, one of the few channels available to secure social reproduction was the party clientelistic machine. Relative security was widely associated with employment in public institutions. These were controlled by elites through party structures and, in Laclau's terms, were geared at meeting ('democratic') demands 'differentially'. While many had long been excluded, I would argue that up to 2014 the Dayton clientelistic machine had succeeded to do so (or succeeded in *appearing* to do so) for a sufficient number of people to a sufficient degree to avoid the creation of an 'antagonistic frontier' *within* BiH's ethnonationalized fiefdoms (see also Mujkić 2014). The revolt can then be read as a sign that, in addition to the many who had long struggled for basic social reproduction, many others now lost hope that the Meantime machine would allow such reproduction in the future, and ever more people increasingly feared they might lose the security they did currently have. For the first time in two decades of Dayton BiH, the 2014 revolt thus articulated universalist popular demands in terms of social reproduction, refracted against widely shared, if unequally experienced, downward household social mobility from prewar conditions. The register of precarity, not used explicitly, seems appropriate here. In terms of material livelihoods precarity was a sustained experience for many and a looming threat for others. In terms of biographical continuity of normative trajectories it was a predicament that was shared much more widely.[10]

The articulation of concerns with social reproduction was also inflected by the lived, institutional experience of Yugoslav socialist self-management. In addition to state and private property, self-management had distinguished 'social property'. This encompassed enterprises and other institutions that were officially collectively owned by all members (e.g. all workers in a factory were also its owners, all inhabitants of a municipality owned some of its institutions, etc.). During the 1992–1995 war, social property had been turned into state property. Later, under foreign auspices, much of it had been converted into private property and asset-stripped, while mostly worthless vouchers were allocated to workers (Pugh 2005; Begić 2014). Yet in Dayton BiH, much was officially retained as 'state' property and served as the material base for the reproduction of domination by political parties and their tycoon allies. These mutations of property, and the dispossession they entailed, were prominent matters of resentment in the revolt, with people demanding back 'what they had built' and 'what they had paid for'. Then too, of course, in socialist Yugoslavia, they had been 'the people'. While some referred explicitly to self-management, I think this should not be read as actual valuation of its practice in Yugoslav times. Studies from those days show that, on the whole, workers in self-managed enterprises did *not* feel or act as if they were owners (e.g. Županov 1985 [1969]).[11] Indeed, this is echoed in a text about the 2014 revolt by a prominent Tuzla trade unionist (Busuladžić 2014: 12). While self-managed social property was thus not usually recalled as an instance of some kind of 'commons' (Nonini 2007), its memory was, in some ways, integrated into a fledgling politics of 'commoning' (see Susser and Tonnelat 2013) several decades later. Partly this occurred through a mere awareness of contingency: people knew first-hand that things had once been different.

Within the mixed bag of demands that shaped the revolt (with calls for solidarity, egalitarianism, liberal-democratic proceduralism, democratic renewal, welfare-statist paternalism, etc.), I now turn to an ingredient that sits uneasily with the desire to inscribe the 2014 BiH events in leftist projections of worldwide mobilizations: demands for transparency, technocratic management, accountability, lean administration and a reduction of political-deliberative decision-making. If a major preoccupation, reflecting broader shared concerns in Dayton BiH, was to put 'the state' in order, this included a focus on eradicating corruption and making institutions work properly. But in a context where so many people considered *any* politics to be tainted, and *any* mobilization for an alternative politics doomed, it also included much sentiment, and not a few demands, that resonated with neoliberalizing measures usually referred to as 'structural adjustment' outside of Europe, and as 'reforms' in Southeast Europe.[12] This is a paradox proper to the postsocialist European semiperiphery, where even those who wish to mobilize politically must accept that this is a politics after disappointment with politics (Greenberg 2014), a politics that is reflexively aware of the impasse it is condemned to operate in (Kurtović 2012). Hence, while it certainly contained antineoliberal dimensions, we cannot characterize the revolt in BiH in 2014 as an antineoliberal mobilization per se. In fact, I contend that the dominant governmental rationality within Dayton BiH is not best understood as 'neoliberal' in the first place, by any of the understandings of that term (Mujanović 2014; Mujkić 2014; Jansen 2015). Some 'reforms' certainly have 'neoliberalized' the country, such as the (foreign-enforced) 2006 introduction of one of the few flat VAT rates in Europe (17 per cent), and the 2009 establishment of a flat income tax rate (10 per cent), now fairly common in postsocialist Europe. Yet BiH also retains high social security contributions on labour,[13] a tightly regulated formal labour market, many 'barriers' to foreign investment, and a massive public sector. It counts a large number of inhabitants plugged into welfare arrangements that could be called cruel in their shortcomings, selectivity, inefficiency and corruption, but that are nowhere near a punitive model of 'workfare'. The revolt could therefore not really be targeted against 'neoliberalism', because there is not that much of it within BiH.

Yet nor can we grasp this mobilization *without* reference to neoliberalizing processes, such as EU conditionality and global dynamics of financialization, with different elites in BiH allied to players in the EU, Russia, the Gulf, the United States, Turkey, etc. BiH's elite has come into being as part of a war-driven, ethnonationalist, party-political pattern of semiperipheral incorporation into neoliberalizing global capitalism. And so has the dispossession of 'the people' which, in the Dayton BiH machine, relies less on private ownership and exploitation than on clientelism and rent-seeking through foreign-enforced channels of an institutionally ethnonationalist Dayton BiH that is, presumably, on the Road to Europe.

Epilogue

Faced with denunciation, appeals to reason and patience, and political elites prepared to 'outwait' the protestors, the revolt nevertheless retained much of its momentum until mid April. Catastrophic floods in May 2014 provided a new focus of attention, partly approached through channels forged during the revolt. Some concrete demands were fulfilled; for example, some cantonal governments reduced 'white bread' (ongoing payments to politicians after they have left their posts). In June 2015 a Tuzla trade union and its bankruptcy manager agreed on restarting some production lines of the chemical firm Dita, accompanied by a social-cum-patriotic campaign to buy their goods. Tuzla's cantonal government also announced a revision of the privatization process of several enterprises. Other promises were made, but no improvement in conditions for social reproduction ensued. In 2015 a new labour law was rushed through under foreign pressure. At the time of writing in mid 2017, the unemployment rate has remained roughly the same and new restrictions made even fewer people eligible for unemployment allowances (maximum 300 KM, for maximum of two years). War-related allowances – more attuned to party clientelism – were left more or less untouched. Average net wages have been almost stagnant since 2009 at 800–850 KM across the Federation, with intensified inter-cantonal and inter-sectoral disparities (for example, wages in the building industry and in hospitality are a third of those in party-controlled telecommunications and energy). Pensioners, some 15 per cent of the population, saw their average pensions rise slightly to 371 KM, but more than half of them continue to receive the minimal pension (326 KM). The consumer basket for a four-member household, as calculated by trade unions, requires 1,800 KM.[14]

If any of the protestors had hoped to seriously affect the composition of the political elite and its clientelist machine through the October 2014 elections (I think few did), this did not materialize either. SDA, since 1990 the dominant coalition partner in almost all the cantons where the revolt occurred, regained much of the votes it had lost in the 2010 elections. In some areas it returned to its earlier status as by far the strongest party with over 30 per cent. In the race for the Bosniak member of the three-headed BiH presidency, the incumbent SDA candidate, son of the first president of BiH and heir to SDA's empire, attracted almost a third of the vote to beat SBB's frontman. Compared to 2010, both lost proportionally but gained in absolute terms. In the parliamentary vote SBB made gains in most places (not in Sarajevo) but perhaps less than expected, with about 14 per cent overall. Demokratska fronta (DF), newly created by former SDP members, attracted a similar proportion. The main loser was SDP, which had gained many votes in 2010 with a promise of a 'normal state' but which soon lost credibility in acrimoniously confrontational coalitions, mainly with SDA. It now dived under 10 per cent in many areas. As usual, turnout was in the mid 50s and the number of invalid votes only rose minimally. So in legislative and executive institutions and, crucially, in party headquarters and in semiprivatized firms, the 2014 elections brought a slight reshuffle of the cards and essentially more of the same.

This sobering balance in terms of concrete effects should not lead us to conclude that the revolt had no significance. Even the most enthusiastic participants did not expect to revolutionize Dayton BiH when, at its height, at most a few thousand people gathered on the streets and in plena, and many Bosnians never considered joining it. Yet few would dispute, I believe, that the revolt resonated with broader anxiety about social reproduction and accumulated resentment with elites that relied on dispossession and identitarian posturing to reproduce their privileges in the face of widespread hardship. While such widely shared diagnoses had previously never led to universalist mobilization, winter 2014 saw the creation of discursive space to articulate questions of social justice into legitimate matters of public debate for the first time since the early 1990s. Notably, unemployment, poverty, inequality and privatization became items for media coverage outside of inter-party smear campaigns.

The prevalence of a specific form of populist reason in the 2014 revolt in BiH that I have identified here was absent from most sympathetic readings of the events. Some instead focused on evoking equivalence with other uprisings (Maribor, Istanbul, Madrid, New York ...), conceived of as antineoliberal and radical-democratic. I contend that any such equivalence should be elucidated rather than assumed (see also the chapter by Kuymulu). This is *not* to argue for a focus on exclusively local, let alone 'cultural', specificities. Instead, wary of both wishful applications of travelling templates *and* of exceptionalist representations of BiH, I suggest we need grounded analysis of concerns with structural contradictions of social reproduction within Dayton BiH and of their articulation with ultimately global political-economic dynamics – a 'class' analysis in the terms of Narotzky and Smith (2006: 9) and Kalb (2005: 114; 2009; Kalb and Halmai 2011). This allows for sophisticated understanding of the revolt (including of seemingly aberrant patterns such as the co-presence of antineoliberal and neoliberalizing tendencies). It also facilitates an 'affirmative' strategy in support of this and similar mobilizations, not through a focus on internal processes but by accounting for specific experiential memories of relative security of livelihoods and biographical continuity, as well as of alternative political-economic arrangements. This complicates attempts to frame the 2014 events in BiH alongside recent 'alterpolitical' mobilizations elsewhere and approaches the emancipatory potential of current key words such as 'precarity' and 'commons' through understanding their situatedness in critical junctions.

Crucially, such an analysis reflects an important dimension of the revolt itself: what we could call a leftward swing of the populist register in BiH. Some participants in the revolt were clearly destitute and, in relation to them, others reflected on their relative degree of economic (in)security in a broader framework of social inequality. This was a new experience for many and informed efforts to forge solidarity amongst people who had not previously been aligned in any political sense. Oblivious to identitarianism, without illusions of foreign benevolence, and in defiance of fear and calls for patience, the revolt forced open a window to articulate concerns of social reproduction – that is, of dispossession, of property, labour and redistribution, explicitly understood in a particular conjuncture: semiperipheral European Dayton BiH's incorporation in global neoliberalizing transformations of capitalism. That window is now open, and some ongoing, small-scale, networked mobilizations work to keep it so. To me, a key political question lies in the temporal dynamics of hope-at-work: will the revolt's longer-term legacy be demobilizing disappointment after yet more evidence of the resilience of the Dayton status quo, or mobilizing reinvigoration of a politics of social justice?

Stef Jansen is a social anthropologist, professor at the University of Sarajevo (Bosnia and Herzegovina) and honorary professor at the University of Manchester (UK). His ethnographic studies in the post-Yugoslav states – among others *Yearnings in the Meantime: 'Normal Lives' and the State in a Sarajevo Apartment Complex* (2015) - have focused, amongst other things, on questions of home, hope, the state, borders, political subjectivity, social transformations and everyday geopolitics. For more information, see https://stefjansenweb.wordpress.com/.

Notes

Parts of my 2008–10 research in a Sarajevo apartment complex were financially supported by the British Academy and by the Leverhulme Trust. I thank Nejra Nuna Čengić, Andrew Gilbert and the participants of the 2015 Graduate Conference 'Hope and (Im)mobility in the Pursuit of Change', Central European University, for constructive criticism of earlier versions of parts of the argument.

1. Following local use, I refer to contemporary BiH as 'Dayton' BiH after the Peace Agreement signed in Dayton (United States), which brought an end to the 1992–1995 war over BiH statehood.
2. https://bhprotestfiles.wordpress.com is an archive of day-to-day reporting and commentary, compiled and translated into English by sympathizers. Arsenijević (2014) brings together real-time testimony and analysis by participants and sympathizers. Kurtović (2016) offers a particularly insightful retrospective analysis of the political-economic dynamics of the protests.
3. See Jansen (2014). On my use of the term 'yearning', see Jansen (2015: 54–57).
4. My account is based on my participant experiences in Sarajevo. Yet my analysis focuses on what I detected as equivalent dynamics across different towns, thus establishing much common ground with Larisa Kurtović's account formulated from the perspective of Tuzla (2016).
5. Many foreign-supported liberal multiculturalist and 'transitional justice' interventions may in principle be directed against ethnonationalism, yet do not provide an alternative to this logic.
6. If I write this description in the past tense, this is an expression of my own yearning rather than a reflection of the Dayton Meantime being over.
7. While there were some dismissals of people stuck in socialist habits, unlike in Repečkaitė's (2011) case of 2009 riots in Lithuania, this was not framed in ethnicized terms, nor in the discourse of 'European-ness'.
8. In Laclau's words: in populist reason, 'the people' emerges as an attempt to name a lacking continuity and unity of the social: an 'absent fullness' (2005: 85).
9. In BiH everyday geopolitics, as well as in supervision assessments, Europe is always posited as the legitimate category of comparison (see Jansen 2009).
10. 'Normal lives' as projected in BiH are supposed to be anything but precarious, and I know of no attempts to date to turn precarity itself into an alterpolitical form of political subjectivity.
11. Yugoslav communists committed to the ideals of self-management were all too aware of this and fretted much about how to remedy it.

12. The revolt saw calls for blocking any new IMF loans. This was legitimated as avoidance of further imperialist bondage, and/or as a way to hit those 'tucked in' in state bureaucracy, and/or as an austerity-style admonition to 'live within one's means'.
13. Employees pay over 31 per cent social security contributions; exact rates vary by sub-polity.
14. Monthly figures taken from the Federal Office for Statistics (www.fzs.ba). As part of a currency board arrangement, the Bosnian Convertible Mark (KM) is pegged to the Euro at a fixed rate of €1 = 1.955830 KM.

References

Arsenijević, D. (ed.). 2014. *Unbribable Bosnia and Herzegovina: The Fight for the Commons.* Baden-Baden and Zagreb: Nomos.
Begić, Z. 2014. 'War, Peace and Protests', in D. Arsenijević (ed.), *Unbribable Bosnia and Herzegovina: The Fight for the Commons.* Baden-Baden and Zagreb: Nomos, pp. 35–43.
Bojičić-Dželilović, V. 2013. 'Informality, Inequality and Social Reintegration in Post-War Transition', *Studies in Social Justice* 7(2): 211–28.
Boni, S. 2015. 'Assemblies and the Struggle to Diffuse Power: Ethnographic Examples and Contemporary Practices', *Focaal* 72: 9–22.
Busuladžić, E. 2014. 'Why?', in D. Arsenijević (ed.), *Unbribable Bosnia and Herzegovina: The Fight for the Commons.* Baden-Baden and Zagreb: Nomos, pp. 11–26.
Critique of Anthropology. 2012, 32(2). Special Issue 'Anthropology and Anarchy'.
Donais, T. 2005. *Political Economy of Peacebuilding in Post-Dayton Bosnia.* London: Routledge.
Focaal. 2015, 72. Theme Section 'Inspiring Alterpolitics'.
Graeber, D. 2008. *Hope in Common.* Available at theanarchistlibrary.org. Accessed April 2017.
Greenberg, J. 2014. *After the Revolution: Youth, Democracy and the Politics of Disappointment in Serbia.* Palo Alto, CA: Stanford University Press.
Hardt, M. and A. Negri. 2005. *Multitude: War and Democracy in the Age of Empire.* New York: Penguin.
Helms, E. 2013. *Innocence and Victimhood: Gender, Nation and Women's Activism in Postwar Bosnia-Herzegovina.* Madison, WI: University of Wisconsin Press.
Jansen, S. 2009. 'After the Red Passport: Towards an Anthropology of the Everyday Geopolitics of Entrapment in the EU's Immediate Outside', *Journal of the Royal Anthropological Institute* 15(4): 815–32.
_____. 2014. 'Re-booting Politics? Or, towards a <Ctrl-Alt-Del> for the Dayton Meantime', in D. Arsenijević (ed.), *Unbribable Bosnia and Herzegovina: The Fight for the Commons.* Baden Baden and Zagreb: Nomos, pp. 89–96.
_____. 2015. *Yearnings in the Meantime: 'Normal Lives' and the State in a Sarajevo Apartment Complex.* New York and Oxford: Berghahn Books.
_____. 2016. 'For a Relational, Historical Ethnography of Hope: Indeterminacy and Determination in the Bosnian and Herzegovinian Meantime', *History and Anthropology* 27(4): 447–64.
Jansen, S., Č. Brković and V. Čelebičić (eds). 2016. *Negotiating Social Relations in Bosnia and Herzegovina: Semiperipheral Entanglements.* London: Routledge.
Kalb, D. 2005. '"Bare Legs Like Ice": Recasting Class for Local/Global Inquiry', in D. Kalb and H. Tak (eds), *Critical Junctions: Anthropology and History beyond the Cultural Turn.* New York and Oxford: Berghahn Books, pp. 109–36.

———. 2009. 'Conversations with a Polish Populist: Tracing Hidden Histories of Globalization, Class, and Dispossession in Postsocialism (and Beyond)', *American Ethnologist* (36)2: 207–33.
Kalb, D. and G. Halmai (eds). 2011. *Headlines of Nation, Subtexts of Class: Working Class Populism and the Return of the Repressed in Neoliberal Europe*. New York and Oxford: Berghahn Books.
Kalb, D. and H. Tak. 2005. 'Introduction: Critical Junctions', in D. Kalb and H. Tak (eds), *Critical Junctions: Anthropology and History beyond the Cultural Turn*. New York and Oxford: Berghahn Books, pp. 1–27.
Krøijer, S. 2010. 'Figurations of the Future: On the Form and Temporality of Protests among Left Radical Activists in Europe', *Social Analysis* 54(3): 139–52.
Kurtović, L. 2012. 'Politics of Impasse: Specters of Socialism and the Struggles for the Future in Postwar Bosnia-Herzegovina', PhD dissertation. Berkeley, CA: University of California.
———. 2016. '"Who Sows Hunger, Reaps Rage": On Protest, Indignation and Redistributive Justice in post-Dayton Bosnia-Herzegovina', *Southeast European and Black Sea Studies* 15(4): 369–59.
Laclau, E. 2005. *On Populist Reason*. London: Verso.
Melenotte, S. 2015. 'Zapatista Autonomy and the Making of Alter-Native Politics: Views from its Day-To-Day Praxis', *Focaal* 72: 51–63.
Mujanović, E. 2013. *Youth Unemployment in Bosnia and Herzegovina: Current Situation, Challenges and Recommendations*. Sarajevo: Friedrich-Ebert-Stiftung.
Mujanović, J. 2014. 'The Baja Class and the Politics of Participation', in D. Arsenijević (ed.), *Unbribable Bosnia and Herzegovina: The Fight for the Commons*. Baden and Zagreb: Nomos, pp. 135–44.
Mujkić, A. 2007. *Mi Građani Etnopolisa*. Sarajevo: Šahinpašić.
———. 2014. 'The Evolution of Bosnia and Herzegovina's Protests in Five Theses', in D. Arsenijević (ed.), *Unbribable Bosnia and Herzegovina: The Fight for the Commons*. Baden-Baden and Zagreb: Nomos, pp. 119–33.
Narotzky, S. and G. Smith. 2006. *Immediate Struggles: People, Power and Place in Rural Spain*. Berkeley, CA: University of California Press.
Nonini, D. (ed.). 2007. *The Global Idea of 'The Commons'*. New York and Oxford: Berghahn Books.
Pugh, M. 2005. 'Transformation of the Political Economy of Bosnia since Dayton', *International Peacekeeping* 12(3): 448–62.
Razsa, M. 2012. 'Toward an Affirmative Ethnography', *Anthropology News* 53(9): 35.
Razsa, M. and A. Kurnik. 2012. 'The Occupy Movement in Žižek's Hometown: Direct Democracy and a Politics of Becoming', *American Ethnologist* 39(2): 238–58.
Repečkaité, D. 2011. 'Austerity against the Homo Soviéticus: Political Control, Class Imaginings and Ethnic Categorization in the Vilnius Riots of 2009', *Focaal* 59: 51–65.
Roseberry, W. 1994. 'Hegemony and the Language of Contention', in G.M. Joseph and D. Nugent (eds), *Everyday Forms of State Formation: Revolution and the Negotiation of Rule in Modern Mexico*. Durham, NC: Duke University Press, pp. 355–66.
Susser, I. and S. Tonnelat. 2013. 'Transformative Cities: The Three Urban Commons', *Focaal* 66: 105–21.
Woodward, S. 1995. *Socialist Unemployment: The Political Economy of Yugoslavia, 1945–1990*. Princeton, NJ: Princeton University Press.
Žižek, S. 2014. 'Anger in Bosnia, But this Time the People Can Read their Leaders' Ethnic Lies', *The Guardian*, 10 February.
Županov, J. 1985 [1969]. *Samoupravljanje i društvena moć*. Zagreb: Globus.

– Chapter 3 –

'SOFIA 2014, FEELS LIKE 1989'

Abstention from the Protests and Declining Market Teleology in Bulgaria

Dimitra Kofti

Political protests in Bulgaria took place from the winter of 2013, until the summer of 2014. There were two main waves of protests. In February 2013, the 'winter protests' against austerity took place in Bulgarian urban settings. Protesters initially underlined their dispossession and their inability to cover basic living costs. Their demands were mainly against austerity and for nationalization of the energy sector. Very soon, demands took a more general form and became against 'politics' and 'the politicians' and against corruption in general (Medarov 2014). These events became accelerators of governmental change, as the central right-wing government resigned a few weeks later. The second wave of protests began in the summer, after the May 2013 elections and the formation of the coalition government led by the central-left Bulgarian Socialist Party (BSP). This time, political demands were mainly directed against corruption and the basic one was the new government's resignation, which eventually occurred in the summer of 2014, after a year of continuous protests mainly in front of the parliamentary building in the capital. While both protest waves gathered various voices, political orientations and approaches, almost everyone agreed that these were the biggest political mobilizations since the winter of 1989–1990. The parallels people drew with those protests from the past did not only focus on participation numbers but also underlined that both periods of mobilizations criticized current hegemonic politics and teleologies of the period of communism and of the market economy respectively, and demanded political reforms.

My fieldwork in Pernik (2013–2015), an industrial town close to the capital, began during the second wave of protests and focused on industrial workers' lives and families. Having previously studied new production practices, work, unemployment and privatization in Sofia (2007–2010), I was familiar with workers' experiences of dispossession and daily struggles and I had assumed that my new study would include workers' political participation in the ongoing events. Despite my initial expectations, I hardly met any people in Pernik who participated in the protests, especially in the second wave. Nevertheless, the ongoing political events generated mass daily discussions about political processes and about participation among people who abstained. My research was initially focused on Pernik's steel industry but soon came to include people working in several sectors, as well as the unemployed. Therefore, my previous expectation that perhaps only steelworkers might have abstained were not proven either, as most of the people I met did not participate in the protests. Given that Pernik is one of the most impoverished Bulgarian urban industrial places, abstention from protests against austerity and impoverization seemed like a paradox, leading me to this ethnographic inquiry.

Political mobilizations are often at the core of scholarly attention, as they constitute periods of social crescendos that may bring change; they challenge previous ideas and forms and suggest different future perspectives. As such, studies often focus on those who take active part in the mobilizations as protesters and on those who actively stand against the protests, such as political parties and state apparatuses. However, abstention and non-participation are often neglected. While there might be several reasons for this overlooking, two of them are related to some methodological concerns: first, studying action is more concrete and attractive than non-action. Moreover non-action is not easily definable. I was wondering, why would I expect Bulgarian workers in Pernik to protest? However, workers in Pernik initiated discussions about the protests and underlined that their non-participation was not a stance of indifference but a thoughtful decision. Second, participants to a political event may be defined as a group, despite its diversity. However, non-participation might constitute a much wider category of people and may include various social groups with a wide range of responses, varying from non-participants who are sympathetic to the protests to others who might be completely indifferent or in opposition. In this Bulgarian case, I focus on workers who, in their great majority, sympathized with many of the ideas and demands expressed in the protests but still abstained. I tend to describe their action as abstention, rather than as non-participation, because I view abstention as a stance that requires a relatively more active decision.

There are several implications related to the overlooking of abstention and non-participation in studying social movements and political mobilizations. By neglecting non-participants, who often constitute a great majority, we tend to ignore their political stances and views. Moreover, we might run the risk of reproducing dichotomies of resistance versus passivity and of political participation versus nonparticipation (Greenberg 2010), images also often reproduced by politically engaged activists. Taking a close look at non-participants, who often constitute a vast majority of the population, may add to our understanding of political mobilizations. Given that one of the goals of political movements is to reach wider audiences and to bring more people to their side, then it is of particular interest to take into account the study of non-participation. Furthermore, it might offer insights about the potentialities of their future active involvement (Scott 1976). I view this as a timely task, given that participatory democracies are characterized by high levels of non-participation and abstention, in both political activism and elections. Here, one should be careful not to pair the lack of political activism with abstention from elections. However, they are both current phenomena of participatory democracies. Workers in Bulgaria often mentioned their abstention from both, to demonstrate their disillusionment with 'politics' due to 'corruption', to tell stories of dispossession and to underline their class-related powerlessness. In current conditions of global condemnation of the 'politics' and the 'politicians', it is worth taking a close look at such responses.

From Anti-austerity to Anti-corruption: The 2013–2014 Protests

The protests in 2013–2014 in Bulgaria occurred in a period where there was an intensification of political mobilization in the neighbouring countries of Turkey, Greece and Bosnia (see Jansen, this volume), after a period of apparent absence of contentious politics (Karakatsanis and Herzog 2016: 199). The first wave, in February 2013, was against austerity and high energy prices. It also included clear demands for nationalization of the energy sector.

Unbearable domestic bills brought many people out into the streets to protest against high prices of living expenses and low salaries. During these days, people from various backgrounds from all over the country, including marginalized groups such as ethnic Roma, took to the streets to protest (Medarov 2014). Moreover, a new phenomenon in the country – that of self-immolation as a form of protest – marked the new period. There were at least seven cases of self-immolation during and shortly after the winter 2013 protests. Some of them clearly stated their protesting character, choosing public spaces, such as in front of the town's municipality. This protest wave was represented by the media, but also by participants, as a working-class mobilization against austerity. The dominant slogans for better living standards very soon changed into more general ones against 'politics', 'the politicians' and against corruption. The anti-corruption demands, paired with discussions about morality in politics, endured during the whole period of protests in Bulgaria, cutting across left- and right-wing voices. This seemed to be enabled by a strong postsocialist condemnation of corruption and by the wide range of meanings that corruption may include (see also Jansen, Lazar, Mollona and Steur, this volume).

The centre-right prime minister resigned a few days after the start of the 'winter protests'. This strategic move sent a message that his government took criticism seriously and provided the ground for the dominant slogan 'Resign' used during the next protest wave. After the election of the new government in May 2013, the new wave of summer protests took place, this time almost exclusively in Sofia. The new government was a coalition of the Bulgarian Socialist Party (a successor of the Communist Party, which is a centre-left, pro-market economy party), the right-wing nationalist party ATAKA, and the party of the Turkish minority (DPS) – quite a contradictory combination that did not last long (until July 2014). These protests were broadly supported at the beginning, but the number of protesters involved dwindled rapidly, though they did continue on for months on a daily basis. Sometimes, a few hundred protesters in front of the Bulgarian parliament were enough to appear in the headlines and become part of daily talks among people.

The second wave of protests began after a media mogul was appointed as the head of state security by the new government. This new wave of protests was characterized by a strong rhetoric against 'the communists', as the then ruling Bulgarian Socialist Party was viewed as 'communist' by a large part of the population. Based on previous research, I have argued that the term 'communist' has come to mean almost anyone who holds power in postsocialist Bulgaria, and it is associated with alleged practices of corruption. While one could indeed find people in key positions who had connections with previous forms of power in the communist past, this was not always the case. The 'communists', or 'red trash', became a metonym for people currently in power who took decisions related to privatization, liberalization of the market and the demolition of the welfare state over the course of the last two and a half decades after the new era of capitalism in Bulgaria (Kofti 2016). In parallel to the generalization of the term 'communists', 'politicians' became almost similar to corruption and resulted in a broader negation of 'politics' that was strongly expressed by both protest waves.

This second wave of protests was often self-represented as an urban middle-class political movement. Along with discourses on anti-corruption and anti-communism, there was a strong rhetoric against 'brain-drain' mobility abroad, attributed to corrupted politics. Although migration cuts across classes and professions in Bulgaria, emphasis now was put on the mobility of those considered educated and 'creative' (Nikolova 2014). This time, a large amount of protesters emphasized individual responsibility by stating that they would pay their bills, in variance with the winter protesters. It was becoming clear that these protests were taking a middle-class rhetoric, in opposition to winter's working-class rhetoric. This was also strengthened by media representations about the class differences of the two waves (Ivancheva 2013; Smilov and Vajsova 2014). Nevertheless, the class synthesis of the protesters was far more unclear and many of the protesters were people with higher education degrees working at precarious and often underpaid white-collar positions in various companies (Nikolova 2014). Yet, the strong representations reproduced also by Bulgarian and international media that this time the protesters were distinct from the winter's working class did have an effect. This was an added reason for workers in Pernik to not join forces.

In terms of economic demands, the protests in both periods were not always clear or unified. However, there were strong voices throughout the two periods for a more transparent market, a 'real capitalism' versus a 'wild capitalism', less 'corruption' and less state intervention. There were also strong voices against foreign investments in the country, which mostly drew from popular nationalist discourses in similar ways as in other countries in Eastern Europe (Kalb and Halmai 2011). There were also strong voices for a more 'real' and 'free' market that would allow foreign investments. While these ideas cut across the two periods, voices for a stronger state intervention mostly characterized the winter protests, and voices for further liberalization of the market and/or for a less corrupted free market mostly characterized the summer protests. Given that the winter protests took place during the central-right government and the summer protests during the central-left one, these were also dominant discourses of the respective oppositions.

The rhetoric against the 'politics' and 'politicians' became so strong that many people questioned every political act, including the protests. A plethora of Bulgarian media representations about both waves of protests adopted this language of corruption, which, similar to other places, came to include the protests, and reported that there were many protesters who were paid by political parties in opposition. In this context of mutual accusations and of strong suspicion, workers in Pernik otherized themselves from the protests. Interestingly, even those who supported the central-right party, which was the opposition party during the summer political mobilizations, did not see a point in taking part. Following this volume's editors' suggestion for a long-term and class-informed understanding of political processes, the next section will focus on the daily lives of precarious workers, in Pernik, some kilometres away from the centre of the protests in Sofia, in an attempt to understand socio-historical aspects of this kind of working-class abstention.

Flexibilization of Labour, Debt and Migration

> I do not think that any protests will erase my debt ... I need to work in two jobs in order to repay them and to support my family ... Perhaps I could change this situation and repay my debt if I migrated abroad. But I cannot leave my children alone in Pernik.
>
> —Nadia, a 47-year-old worker

Nadia worked in a factory that produced sweets in Pernik. She would do some additional shifts as a shop assistant. Her husband, a laid-off miner, migrated seasonally to France to pick fruit. Her husband got a loan for maintenance work on their house, which he was unable to pay back after he lost his job. This resulted in another bank loan to repay the first and in deepening economic hardship for Nadia's family. She would often say how she was too preoccupied with her indebtedness to dedicate time to political action. Moreover, she would express doubt for the effectiveness of such practices as well as describe protesters as possibly corrupted. Nadia's take on political mobilizations was far from being exceptional. A set of economic conditions and beliefs on politics contributed to such responses.

Workers in Pernik have similar experiences with most workers in Bulgaria; they have gone through impoverishment since the early 1990s and they have lived through successive economic crises since the late 1980s. Flexibilization of labour, indebtedness and the potentiality of migration in Pernik contributed to people's responses to political non-participation. Narotsky and Smith (2006) have argued that there is a link between political oppression, dispossession and lack of political response. Similar to workers in Spain (ibid.), Bulgarian workers have experienced growing political alienation, which is strongly connected to dispossession. Yet, one could suggest that these conditions might result in mobilization instead. In this and the next section, I discuss how this was not the case in Pernik in 2013–2014 and how this was also related to both economic conditions in their entanglement with images of corruption as well as a wider disappointment about the promises of the market economy, which once might have offered hope for the future.

Pernik is an industrial town that used to be a strong symbol of industrial modernization but it gradually became an icon of industrial decline in Bulgaria. A mine was founded there in the late nineteenth century and attracted workers from the Bulgarian countryside. The steel industry, machine-making factories and a variety of other industries that were exporting products to other socialist countries were founded in the 1950s and flourished until the late 1970s. After the collapse of the socialist regime and successive economic crises from the 1980s and throughout the 1990s, most of the factories closed down. Some of them were privatized and were significantly restructured towards more flexible production by downsizing their staff and focusing on core production. This was accompanied with large-scale lay-offs.

For example, the steel plant Stomana was first bought up by a Bulgarian investor, in 1997. This investor restructured the plant mainly by lay-offs and by breaking the company into many smaller companies, and then it was sold to a Greek steel company in 2001. From approximately 9,000 workers in the 1980s, the ex-'Lenin', now 'Stomana', steel plant employed approximately 1,500 people in 2014. From those 1,500, 900 were employed with company contracts, whereas another 500–600 were 'external' ones and with a higher turnover compared to the company workers. The gender proportion in 2015 was 70 per cent male, 30 per cent female, while in 1992 the proportion used to be approximately 55 per cent and 45 per cent respectively. The casualization of work and the feminization of poverty and unemployment among steelworkers were in accordance with the changing working lives throughout the region and the country. Most of the workers, and many of their family members, had worked in Stomana for decades, and lived in the 'Lenin' neighbourhood, now 'Iztok',[1] built gradually since the 1950s for the steelworkers and their families. Workers in Stomana enjoyed services such as housing, childcare, education, healthcare and vacation. The experience of work significantly changed after the lay-offs and the cuts in services. The ex-'Lenin' district, like the whole town, is semi-abandoned and many people commute to Sofia or have migrated abroad.

Out migration is a central aspect of life in Pernik.[2] Even those who were not planning to migrate would mention the reasons why they would not like to migrate; to a great extent living in Pernik is discussed and justified in relation to migration. Migration or the prospect may further add to one's detachment from active political participation. Discussions about Bulgaria's brain-drain during the second wave of protests did not attract workers in Pernik, as most of their relatives abroad worked in seasonal agriculture or in the care sector. Rather, in making a statement about the entanglement of class and ethnicity, they would bitterly mention that things would change for them 'when people from Western and South Europe migrate to Bulgaria to take care of Bulgarian elders'. In such commentaries, they accentuated the class distance they felt from other people in Europe but also from self-proclaimed middle-class protesters in Sofia's central square.

Moreover, during the same period, two important events related to people's mobility further raised issues of nationalism and ethnic conflict: on the one hand, thousands of Syrian refugees who arrived in the country were not welcomed by a large amount of people, who saw them as an economic and even moral threat; on the other, discussions about whether migrants from Bulgaria and Romania would be allowed into the United Kingdom resulted in growing hostility against the Roma, as they were largely viewed as responsible for Bulgarians' 'negative' image in the United Kingdom and in 'Europe'. Given that Roma people had joined the protests in February 2013, very soon the demands against lower bills were attributed, by opposing voices, to an alleged 'Gypsy culture' than to working-class needs. This further added to workers' abstention; workers would rather not be identified with the Roma minority, as anti-Roma ideas are strong in Bulgaria and cut across classes and political orientations.

The ongoing impoverization and the indebtedness raised workers' fear of job losses and strengthened family dependencies. These conditions echoed Streeck's description of the broader economic downward trends of current capitalism – in economic growth, social equality and financial stability (Streeck 2014: 47). The lack of social welfare strengthened family ties and dependencies (Deneva 2012). Workers had to support unemployed[3] or underemployed family members as well as pensioners under low pension schemes. As a result, there were strong relationships of dependency inside households and among members of extended families. The shortage of jobs gave significant power and added responsibility to employed family members, while unemployed and casually employed members became more dependent. As a result, many workers were afraid of losing their job, as this would result in an immediate lack of cash for their household. This added pressure made them vulnerable to managerial decisions towards harsher work conditions and more hesitant to participate in protests.

Moreover, daily work life became significantly harder, as tasks were now fulfilled by significantly fewer people. Some positions that had been filled, for example, by four people, were now occupied by one worker and required more concentration. While workplaces were sometimes conspicuously overstaffed before privatization, in many cases they were now conspicuously understaffed. The casualization of labour enabled companies to employ workers through subcontractors and to fill some positions 'temporarily'. A more precise description of this temporariness would be that of permanently temporary. Casual workers would often work on short-term contracts and were paid on piece-rates, a method that intensifies labour exploitation and exerts constant pressure for acceleration of production (Haraszti 1978; Burawoy 1979). Therefore, exposure to health risks among workers in Pernik grew bigger, as doctors in Pernik would also confirm. Regular workers were often under stress because of threatened lay-offs and casual workers were under constant pressure to perform in order to renew their contracts. The intensification of work not only raised the probability of accidents, even in places where the machinery had been modernized, but also raised the percentages of high blood pressure, strokes and other health problems.

Harder working conditions were not followed by better payment. Rather, they were accompanied with economic hardship and indebtedness. Many households took on loans to cope with daily needs or housing projects. Moreover, while consumption prices rose, salaries remained low, especially after 2008, as a result of the financial crisis. Workers who mostly got loans before 2008 estimated initially that they would pay the loans back, according to previous salaries and prices. According to my survey, the great majority of workers (80 per cent) were indebted to a bank. Loan-free exceptions were mostly young people below the age of thirty who did not have children, and casual (mostly Roma) workers, whose income did not allow them to get a bank loan, as they were not considered credit-worthy. However, those not able to get a bank loan got loans from microcredit companies with high interest rates. There were also cases of people who were indebted to both banks and microcredit companies. The latter often offered a quick solution to repay a bank-loan instalment, positioning borrowers in a vicious circle of multiple debts and staggering interest rates, including blackmailing practices on behalf of the loaners.

Many workers, especially those casually employed, would have secondary jobs or seasonal work abroad, in order to add to their low salaries and to cope with debt. Mariana, a 46-year-old laid-off worker from the steel plant Stomana since 2007, worked as a shop assistant in Pernik. She would work every day for the entire day, from 9AM to 9 PM, besides Sundays. She would also occasionally get a day off during the week. When not at work, she would undertake housework in her apartment, where she lived with Giorgi, her 17-year-old son, and Penko, her 53-year-old husband. Although she worked long hours, her income was low. Moreover, she was not regularly paid, as the shop was not making profit every month. The owner would pay her less or not at all during periods when sales were down. Mariana's income did not allow her to cover basic living expenses but it added to the family budget, which was mainly supported by Penko's income. As Mariana put it, her income managed to almost cover the high energy bills in the flat. Penko was a security guard at Stomana. Previously he worked at a machine production factory that was gradually liquidated and eventually closed down in the early 2000s. He often complained about his tight time schedule. He would work three-day twelve-hour long shifts, with a rotation of night-time and daytime. During his two days off in between the shifts, he worked as a construction worker in Sofia whenever an opportunity arose. He would also spend some time working on their family garden in a nearby village of his origin, where he grew fruit and vegetables for self-consumption.

Mariana and Penko's yearly schedule allowed little time to do other things than work. They lived at the steelworkers' district in Pernik, in a flat that Mariana inherited from her father, who used to be a steelworker as well and who had acquired it in the 1980s. Although they did not have to pay rent, their total income hardly covered their family's expenses. While basic needs such as bills, food, travelling and education expenses could be covered on a monthly basis, they had taken a bank loan in 2012 in order to cover less regular expenses. Pipes in the bathroom had broken and they needed to change them all. This took place during their summer vacation, as they mostly did the work themselves. Working on housing maintenance during vacation was a common practice among workers in Pernik. Getting loans to buy building material for the repairs was also common. Practically their whole yearly schedule included various types of work and very limited time for other kinds of activities. Mariana would take a rest and sleep for a bit longer than usual when she had some time for herself. She said that she felt so tired that she could not go to the protests in Sofia during the little time she had off work.

One then wonders why people like Mariana and Penko, who did not take part in these urban protests, did not take part in union activism? A central topic of discussion among workers during work was their feeling of being 'lonely' and 'isolated'. They would often connect this 'loneliness' with flexible work conditions. At workplaces, less people fulfilled the same tasks and were often unable to spend time talking to each other, compared to the past. Outside work, many would be further busy with fulfilling several other tasks and not be able to socialize as much as they wished, or as much as they would claim they had been doing in previous times. Moreover, they connected 'loneliness' with their lack of participation in the work of labour unions. Workers often complained that they would love to have strong unions, but they described them as powerless and corrupted and they did not see any point in unionizing. The great majority were not members of unions, which were largely seen as 'corrupted', similarly to political parties. Furthermore, many mentioned that they were afraid of losing their job because of political activism or unionism, as it had happened with several workers after privatization.

Less than a fourth of the steel company workers were members of the two unions (180 in total, out of 900), while before privatization almost everyone was a member. This change is not necessarily indicative of a weaker participation today compared to the past.

As many narratives suggest, most workers did not view their past participation as effective either. Rather, they would draw continuity between 'corrupted unions' in the past and today. They would claim that union leaders were working in favour of the management in both epochs. However, many workers quit the unions after privatization, not only out of mistrust but also out of fear of losing their job. After privatization, unions sometimes would attempt to fight against wage reductions or to mediate between workers and managers, and managers threatened workers that if they participated they would risk their posts. However, workers would also claim that union leaders were actually paid by the management, in order to avoid clashes with the workforce. Both reasons sometimes coexisted in a worker's narrative about ceasing their union membership. It was considered dangerous to be a member, especially an active one, but also there would be no point in being one, as unions were seen as being secretly in favour of the management. The discussion about lack of unionism goes beyond the limits of this chapter. However, the point I aim to make here is that a general mistrust of politics along with a strong fear of job loss in a context of shortage of work and workers' growing indebtedness, which intensified their fear of job loss, prevented participation. Iskra, a 43-year-old crane driver in Stomana, said: 'How can we unionize? We are all indebted; there is no way to react to anything.'

Nevertheless, this did not fully answer my inquiry, given that, though they did not unionize, they could still protest along with other protesters at the urban centres without risking their jobs. Non-participation in political mobilizations was further motivated by a language of corruption and a general disillusionment of both communism and capitalism.

Disillusionment and Modern Teleologies in Decline

During the period of protests, a significant number of my correspondents expressed a general disappointment for the economic and political systems they had experienced in their lives. This was particularly prominent among middle-aged people, although it was also sometimes expressed by younger ones. Dimitar, a 52-year-old miner, summarized this widespread sense:

> There was some belief among the people: 'Better times will come'. Maybe they lied. They tell you: 'Socialism is coming, many things are changing, all people equal. All will have'. And you believe, as this was indoctrinated.

Then 1989 came. Another wave: 'Change is coming. Democracy is coming. You may freely travel in Europe'. And you believe.

Now, there is nothing to believe in.

An expressed sense of general disappointment for both the teleological discourses of socialism and of capitalism was relatively new in Bulgaria in 2013–2014. While disappointment with politics was a common postsocialist phenomenon in different countries (Greenberg 2014), this kind of direct disbelief in the politics of the new capitalist era seemed new. When I first conducted research in Sofia in 2003, there was another much heard phrase that accompanied workers' narratives about economic hardship: 'we will make it' *(shte se opravim)*. Interestingly, in 2013–2014 this had been replaced by another one 'we will not make it' *(niama da se opravim)*. There are several ways to understand this kind of disappointment. The previous section tells a story of ongoing impoverization of workers in Pernik, which contributed to an attempt to understand this disillusionment. While the protests initially motivated thousands of people to fight for a change, it also kept large numbers of the dispossessed population absent from the mobilizations. Far from being an apolitical reaction, this disappointment might be seen as indicative of a perplexity brought about by the disbelief that existing dominant ideas about the market economy could lead to a better life.

Dimitar's narrative on successive ideologies of modernity that are based on teleologies pointed to the political character of future narratives. He further remembered how in the early 1990s there was not only widespread uncertainty but widespread hope that the market economy would bring prosperity. He was now describing how, two and a half decades later, he experienced the teleology of the new era in similar ways that he experienced the hegemonic teleology of the previous one. It was as if all the future promises remained unfulfilled, from both eras. If political ideas and participation is about suggesting ideas and practices for the future, then the abstention of people who shared the view that 'now there is nothing to believe in' perhaps makes sense.

The collapse of socialist regimes in postsocialist Europe opened up space for renegotiations of the past and dynamic relations with visions of the future (Haukanes and Trnka 2013). Anthropological studies have pointed out that idealized images of the socialist past are often shaped by the experience of the present and become critical commentaries on current politics (Berdahl 1999; Creed 2010). While my previous ethnographic experience in Bulgaria (2007–2010) suggested similarly, this most recent period of research that coincided with the protests pointed out that there was also another, perhaps emerging, past-future dynamic. Although idealized images of the socialist past still existed, there was another one that expressed generalized disappointment from both the socialist past and the more recent postsocialist period. This topic requires further research on the works on memory. I view this new periodization as an indication of a strengthening narrative that, similarly to the previous disconfirmed socialist teleology of the past, the ideas of future prosperity via the market economy was severely challenged. This temporal critique is based on a profound disillusionment about current politics and economic conditions in ways that were not necessarily expressed by protesters and by mainstream media.

Narratives that included criticism on both socialist and capitalist eras were not always as clear as in Dimitar's example. There were also ideas against both socialist and neoliberal ideologies along with nationalist discourses. Ivo, a 52-year-old worker, underlined the importance of a national economy and he also expressed a more general concern about the main hegemonic ideologies of socialism and market capitalism experienced during his life-course: in the early 1990s he thought that with 'this market economy, things would get better'. Nevertheless, after twenty-five years, things did not get 'any better', as he said. Ivo supported the demands expressed during the protests, as he was 'against corruption', but he did not support 'the protesters', because they were 'just paid' and 'just playing the game of the political parties'. He viewed them in a similar way that he viewed the labour unions, from which he ceased his membership in the late 1990s, because he reasoned that they were 'only bribed' and 'did not actually support the workers' rights'. Similar ideas of union leaders being 'corrupted' and in strong cooperation with political parties and business owners were common among workers. As such, both unions and political parties were viewed as inefficient modes of political representation. Ivo used to be a miner in Pernik but he was laid off after privatization. He then started working sporadically as a casual construction worker. Although he accused the 'communists', he also talked about how things were better 'before', when his production unit was state-owned both during the communist times and throughout the 1990s. Those two aspects of his narration were not contradictory in his view, as 'we', the nation, were responsible for positive outcomes of the past:

> We used to have a house (the Bulgarian state), which had bad quality windows. Instead of changing the windows, those communists demolished the whole construction. And they gave all assets to foreigners to rebuild the house. The Bulgarian nation is only losing from this.

Ivo mentioned various benefits he had had as a worker during the previous era and stated that he supported the central right-wing party, which was the opposition party during the second protest wave. Ivo had clear suggestions for a stronger national economy and he described corruption as a phenomenon against the nation.

'They are all corrupted', was a continually repeated phrase among workers that would be mentioned in relation to politicians, union members and protesters. The protests were often thought to be driven by political parties and were part of the same problem they were addressing – that is, 'corrupted politics'. There was a widespread opinion that the February 2013 protesters were to a great extent 'paid' by the party in opposition, as the summer ones were believed to be 'paid' by the party that had just resigned from the government. This belief kept Ivo away from the protests. There were also rumours about the amount of bribe one would get for a day of protest. Almost everyone had heard about this but none of the people I spoke with knew someone who had been targeted with this. This belief of paid protests, which was strengthened by regular media reports, significantly discouraged people from participation, although they themselves would often express ideas similar to those of the protesters. People who abstained were not necessarily against 'politics' in general, but they were against 'corrupted politics'. However, those two became almost tautological, given the over-generalization of the corruption accusations.

The topics of 'corruption' and 'informal networks' in Bulgaria have been the subject of sociological discussions (Chavdarova 2001b, 2001a; Tchalakov et al. 2008) and of strong public debates. The latter are often based on the assumption that corruption is almost a cultural characteristic, external to the current political system. Daily talks about 'corruption' have been dominant among different people.[4] Similarly, workers in Pernik would often mention 'corruption' as one of the most important phenomena of both socialist and postsocialist times. This strengthened the general disappointment that cuts across the eras. No matter whether 'corruption' exists or not among the protesters or among union members, discussions about it have strong effects on people's stances about politics and active participation. Suspicion, disappointment and abstention seemed to be closely linked with the strong belief of an omnipresent power of informal networks of power.

Epilogue

The Bulgarian 2013–2014 political mobilizations raised claims against austerity, corruption and political representation and opened up vivid political discussion in the country, including discussions about political participation, abstention and change. The first wave was massive at the beginning and took place in various urban centres. The second wave began with large participation; it was mainly in the capital and, despite its dwindling participation, lasted long. The protests initiated vivid political discussions among the non-participants, who talked extensively about their abstention. I have approached Pernik workers' abstention as a refusal to participate rather than as an act of indifference or political apathy. There are several factors for this refusal. First, they did not see themselves in accordance with the middle-class rhetoric that was dominant during the summer protests. No matter whether those who were protesting belonged to the 'middle class' or not, the dominant middle-class rhetoric put off precarious workers, who openly described themselves as working class. Moreover, popular nationalist discourses against the Roma underlined that the working class, including the Roma shared the same claims during the February protests. This further put off workers from the protests, as they also wanted to avoid being identified with the Roma. Workers' abstention took on class and ethnic characteristics that I was able to grasp by focusing on their non-participation.

I took abstention into account, in order to understand both the resonance of the protests and current political ideas about contentious politics, ideology, and alternative political ideas and practices. Ideas against corruption along with ideas against communism and with some more recent ideas about the failure of the market economy contributed to political disillusionment. Abstention from the protests is partially related to workers' experience of dispossession in the context of the demise of the welfare state and their deepening indebtedness. Physically exhausted, largely indebted and in familial relations of economic dependency, workers would often say that they did not protest because they did not think there would be 'any actual change', both in the wider politico-economic context and in their lives; they faced having to repay unbearable bank loans while worrying about potential job loss. They would also say that for similar reasons they chose not to vote. The nearly 50 per cent abstention from the country elections in October 2014, after a year of regular mass mobilization, is an indicator of this phenomenon.

Besides people's time scarcity and suspicions of corruption, it seems that an important reason for not participating is a general lack of trust in activism, including union activism, and a more general lack of an alternative ideology for the future, which seems to be linked with the ongoing experience of economic decline in workers' lives. Although the Bulgarian protests have shown that activism may be catalytic for some political changes, it seems that for a significant part of the population, which is impoverished and disillusioned, there is lack of vision for a better future and the sense of inability to react to the demands of the global economy, which keeps many people away from active political participation. Bulgarian workers' mistrust of political mobilization and political representation reveals their criticism that the market is ruling politics in similar ways that it is ruling their lives. Some would say, 'Once it was the Party; now it's the market that dictates'. Streeck (2014) has suggested that we 'learn to think about capitalism coming to an end without assuming responsibility for answering the question of what one proposes to put in its place' (p. 48). Bulgarian workers, who often describe politics with irony, repeated the following joke to demonstrate how there is currently a sense of disbelief and decline, similar to the end of communist times:

Chicago -20, feels like -40.
Sofia 2014, feels like 1989.

Dimitra Kofti is Assistant Professor of Social Anthropology at Panteion University in Athens. She has a PhD from Goldsmiths and held postdocs at the Max Planck Institute for Social Anthropology in Halle, Germany. Her research interests include historical anthropology, economic anthropology and the anthropology of work. She is the author of *Broken Glass, Broken Class: Transformations of Work in Bulgaria* (2023). She continues to do fieldwork in Bulgaria and Greece.

Notes

This chapter is based on fieldwork conducted 2013–2015 in the industrial town of Pernik, Bulgaria. This project is part of the Max Planck Institute for Social Anthropology group project on 'Industry and Inequality in Eurasia'. It also draws material from my previous doctoral research in Sofia (2007-2010). All names of people in this text are pseudonyms.

1. Iztok means Eastern and refers to the geographical position of the district.
2. In a household survey I conducted among fifty steelworkers, half of them had a household member who migrated abroad.
3. The official unemployment figure in Bulgaria was 1.7 per cent in 1990, 12.5 per cent in 1991, 18 per cent in 2000 and 11.2 per cent in 2014. The official rate in Pernik was 13 per cent in 2014 but local social scientists estimated that it was much higher and undocumented, as many underemployed people do not register. Moreover, those who migrate abroad are not classified as unemployed.
4. Kremakova (2012) has documented discussions about corruption among Bulgarian maritime workers in the late 2000s.

References

Berdahl, D. 1999. *Where the World Ended: Re-Unification and Identity in the German Borderland*. Chicago, IL: University of California Press.

Burawoy, M. 1979. *Manufacturing Consent: Changes in the Labor Process under Monopoly Capitalism*. Chicago, IL: University of Chicago Press.

Chavdarova, T. 2001a. 'Corruption in the Bulgarian Postcommunist Transformation', *South East Europe Review for Labour and Social Affairs* 3(3): 9–18.

———. 2001b. *Neformalnata Ikonomika (Informal Economy)*. Sofia: Lik.

Creed, G. 2010. 'Strange Bedfellows: Socialist Nostalgia and Neo-Liberalism in Bulgaria', in M. Todorova and Z. Gille (eds), *Post-Communist Nostalgia*. New York and Oxford: Berghahn Books, pp. 29–45.

Deneva, N. 2012. 'Transnational Aging Careers: On Transformation of Kinship and Citizenship in the Context of Migration among Bulgarian Muslims in Spain', *Social Politics: International Studies in Gender, State, and Society* 19(1): 105–28.

Dunn, E. 2004. *Privatizing Poland: Baby Food, Big Business, and the Remaking of Labor*. Ithaca, NY: Cornell University Press.

Greenberg, J. 2010. '"There's Nothing Anyone Can Do about It": Participation, Apathy and "Successful" Democratic Transition in Postsocialist Serbia', *Slavic Review* 69(1): 41–64.

———. 2014. *After the Revolution: Youth, Democracy, and the Politics of Disappointment in Serbia*. Stanford, CA: Stanford University Press.

Haraszti, M. 1978. *A Worker in a Worker's State*. New York: Universe Books.

Haukanes, H. and S. Trnka. 2013. 'Memory, Imagination, and Belonging across Generations: Perspectives from Postsocialist Europe and Beyond', *Focaal* 66: 3–13.

Ivancheva, M. 2013. 'A Vicious Cycle? Some Notes on the Bulgarian Protests from the Summer of 2013', *LeftEast*, 26 June.

Kalb, D. and G. Halmai (eds). 2011. *Headlines of Nation, Subtexts of Class: Working-Class Populism and the Return of the Repressed in Neoliberal Europe*. New York and Oxford: Berghahn Books.

Karakatsanis, L. and M. Herzog. 2016. 'Radicalisation as Form: Beyond the Security Paradigm', *Journal of Contemporary European Studies* 24(2): 199–206.

Kofti, D. 2016. '"Communists" on the Shop Floor: Anticommunism, Crisis, and the Transformation of Labor in Bulgaria', *Focaal* 74: 69–82.

Koycheva, L. 2016. 'When the Radical is Ordinary: Ridicule, Performance and the Everyday in Bulgaria's Protests of 2013', *Journal of Contemporary European Studies* 24(2): 240–54.

Kremakova, M. 2012. 'What Market Mechanisms Mean? Transforming Institutions and Livelihoods in Bulgarian Maritime Employment', Ph.D. dissertation. Coventry: University of Warwick.

Medarov, G. 2014. 'Legitimating Neoliberalism in Times of Crisis: The Bulgarian Protests in 2013', *Chronos* 10.

Mollona, M. 2009. *Made in Sheffield: An Ethnography of Industrial Work and Politics*. New York and Oxford: Berghahn Books.

Narotzky, S. and G. Smith. 2006. *Immediate Struggles: People, Power, and Place in Rural Spain*. Berkeley, CA: University of California Press.

Nikolova, M. 2014. 'The Bulgarian "Creative Class" and the Reproduction of Neoliberal Ideology', *LeftEast*, 16 May.

Scott, J.C. 1976. *The Moral Economy of the Peasant: Rebellion and Subsistence in Southeast Asia*. New Haven, CT: Yale University Press.

Streeck, W. 2014. 'How will Capitalism End?', *New Left Review* 87: 35–64.

Smilov, D. and L. Vajsova (eds). 2014. *#The Protest: Analyses and Positions in the Bulgarian Press, Summer 2013*. Sofia: Iztok-Zapad. (In Bulgarian: Смилов Д., Вайсова Л., (eds). 2014. *#Протестът: Анализи и позиции в българската преса, Лято 2013*. София:Изток – Запад.)

Tchalakov, I., A. Bundzulov, I. Hristov, L. Deyanova, N. Nikolova and D. Deyan. 2008. *Mrezhite Na Prehoda: Kakvo Vsushtnost Se Slutsi v Bulgaria Sled 1989 (The Networks of Transition: What Actually Happened in Bulgaria after 1989)*. Sofia: Iztok-Zapad.

Tsoneva, J. 2013. 'Real Power Directly to the People', *LeftEast*, 7 March.

– Chapter 4 –

SPONTANEITY, ANTAGONISM AND THE MORAL POLITICS OF OUTRAGE
Urban Protest in Argentina since 2001
Sian Lazar

Mass urban mobilizations are relatively frequent in Buenos Aires, and have been important features of the political scene since the mid twentieth century at least. In this chapter, I identify two types of urban protest that have taken place since 2001, making a distinction between mass, 'self-convened', 'spontaneous' protests that are associated with a morality of outrage and those convened by organized social forces – principally trade unions and workers' confederations, but also neighbourhood-based associations and political parties. I suggest that different moralities of protest are evident in each form, identifying them respectively as denunciation and demand-making. A focus on protest events of the first type highlights the importance of a moral politics of outrage in contemporary Argentina. Analytically, this kind of moral politics is complementary to the moral politics of government, which is revealed by more state-centric ethnographies of the field (e.g. Fassin 2012, 2015).

In Argentina, and more specifically in the city of Buenos Aires, the moral politics of outrage is both consequence and cause of an increasingly antagonistic political culture, in which the friend/enemy distinction comes very strongly to the fore, and pits protesters against politicians; most recently, the president Cristina Fernández de Kirchner (2007–2015). Here, I draw on Chantal Mouffe's discussion of Carl Schmitt (Mouffe 2005). Schmitt (1996 [1932]) claimed that the friend/enemy distinction is constitutive of the political more broadly, and Mouffe developed this theory to propose a distinction between an agonistic politics that sets adversaries against each other and respects pluralism, and an antagonistic politics where adversaries are replaced by enemies. For Mouffe, this is as damaging as Anglo-American 'Third Way' politics based on consensus and individual autonomy; indeed, she argues that it is the outcome of those neoliberal political developments, at least in Europe. Argentine experiences of neoliberalism did not suppress collective identities quite to the extent that Mouffe saw in Europe. Nonetheless, recent mass urban mobilizations provide a good ethnographic case study of the links between collective identities, antagonism and the moralization of politics.

The following section of the chapter outlines a brief history of some key mass mobilizations in Buenos Aires, from the mid twentieth century onwards, focusing in particular on the December 2001 debt crisis. I then give some details of the two (broad) types of mobilization I wish to identify. Subsequently, I assess the distinction between types of mobilization on the grounds of class and spontaneity, which I then link to moralities of outrage. These are contrasted with mobilization on behalf of particular social and economic projects that can be encapsulated in a set of demands (the second type of mobilization described here). I conclude by assessing the implications of this moralization of (middle class) politics for how we understand urban mobilizations in Argentina, and perhaps also elsewhere.

Histories of Protest in Argentina, from the Mid Twentieth Century to the Present

Antonius Robben (2007) has argued that mass street demonstrations have punctuated Argentine political history and changed its course at several significant moments; especially when demonstrators were subjected to violent state repression. The archetypal example of influential street mobilization is the 17 October demonstration that secured Juan Perón's release from prison in 1945, when the Plaza de Mayo was filled with Perón's working-class supporters, famously photographed bathing their feet in the public fountains. Other key moments were the demonstrations and strikes in Cordoba in May 1969,[1] the mass greeting of Perón at Ezeiza airport on his return from exile on 20 June 1973 (which became a massacre), the protests against the Falklands War in 1983, which toppled the dictatorship, and the riots of December 2001 in response to the financial crisis. All of these events shape how Argentines interpret day to day mobilization on the streets, with the last set being especially influential today.

Sarah Muir (n.d.) suggests that the story of December 2001 holds a contemporary status as something of an origin myth. She says that 'it was in the December 2001 street protests that participants and observers alike discovered a newly cohered national public, defined by the self-conscious and generalized experience of material loss and social disintegration' (Muir n.d.: 1). The crisis was the result of the period of neoliberal structural adjustment overseen by Carlos Menem in the 1990s, when Argentina had been the poster child for the IMF and proponents of the Washington Consensus (Blustein 2005). Particularly associated with that period was the policy of maintaining 1:1 parity between the Argentine peso and the US dollar. This economic policy proved unsustainable, leading to enormous levels of public debt and eventually a three-year long recession and consequent increase in poverty levels throughout the population. As political tensions grew during the second half of 2001, especially after Congressional elections in October, a run on the banks developed, and the intensified capital flight prompted President de la Rúa to limit bank account withdrawals to $250 a week at the beginning of December. Although the peso still held 1:1 parity with the US dollar, that situation was clearly not going to last long, and so this measure, known as the 'corralito', prompted widespread protests as people attempted to withdraw their money before the parity was dissolved. As Muir points out, the corralito not only affected those middle-class people with savings accounts but also drastically reduced the amount of currency in circulation, severely affecting workers in the informal cash-mediated economy as well. Protests spread, including lootings and road blockades; and on 19 December, De La Rúa spoke on TV to declare a state of emergency, including a curfew. Marina Sitrín has recorded the words of 'Pablo', who described how in response to that speech people banged pots and pans in their houses, 'until one point, when the people banging pots began to walk' (2006: 22). People took to the streets of the capital with their empty pots and pans, in a form of protest known as 'cacerolazos'. The protests lasted two days, and were subject to police repression that resulted in thirty-nine deaths ('La causa por la represión sigue sin definiciones', 2007). On the night of 20 December, President de la Rúa resigned and fled the presidential palace by helicopter. He was followed rapidly by three other interim presidents, until on 2 January 2002, the Peronist Eduardo Duhalde took office.

Testimonies of the December 2001 cacerolazos abound (e.g. Sitrín 2006, 2012; Barros 2013), having in common an emphasis on both spontaneous 'auto-convocación' (self-convening) and an outraged rejection of the whole political class, summed up in the famous slogan: *'Que Se Vayan Todos, Que no quede ni uno solo!'* (They must all go, Not one should remain!). As Muir (n.d.) illustrates, one of the products of the December crisis was the development of forms of solidarity-based social and economic action, such as barter networks, factory occupations, popular assemblies and so on (see also Dinerstein 2003, 2007; Atzeni and Ghigliani 2007; Schaumberg 2008; Sitrín 2012). However, in this chapter I want to pause the story of 2001 at the point of the December cacerolazos and explore their heritage in subsequent protest action in the city of Buenos Aires. For, as I have also argued elsewhere (Lazar 2015), Muir (n.d.: 5) suggests that the crowd that took to the streets in December 2001 was signalled as a particular kind of crowd, 'through the medium of the cacerolazo as a doubly marked event – as both national and middle-class'.

Similar 'national and middle-class' crowds have taken to the streets of Buenos Aires relatively frequently in recent years, despite the economic recovery that began in 2003. The recovery was fuelled by the debt default and devaluation that caused so much initial economic hardship domestically, followed by the boom in commodity prices in the sectors of agriculture and other natural resources, driven by Chinese demand. It enabled Néstor Kirchner's government (2003–2007) to pay off the country's debts to the IMF in 2005 and negotiate the restructuring of most of the rest of the public debt. However, the government was not able to return to international capital markets to borrow money in order to ameliorate the effects of the economic slowdown that began to show from around 2010.[2] The result was high inflation, although exact levels were a source of contestation between the government and private think-tanks.[3] Indications of real inflation levels might be gleaned by wage increase negotiations between governments and unions: the governments of Cristina Fernández de Kirchner (2007–2015) consistently agreed to wage increases in the formal sector of well above 20 per cent, while official inflation rates remained at c. 12–15 per cent per year. Other forms of social spending were also characteristic of both Kirchner governments, in programmes such as the 'Plan Jefes y Jefas de Hogar' (Plan for heads of households) and, from 2009, the Universal Child Benefit. This distributionist policy led some commentators to include Kirchnerista governments in their roll call of Latin American 'post-neoliberal' regimes (Grugel and Riggirozzi 2007). The victory of the right-winger Mauricio Macri in the 2015 presidential elections marked a swing back to economic orthodoxy; to the point even of reaching agreement in early 2016 with debtors – the so-called 'vulture funds'– who had refused to accept Néstor Kirchner's restructuring terms.

As Cristina's second term drew to a close, the combination of inflationary pressure, economic slowdown and the effects of being shut out from international capital markets gradually created strain in the Argentine economy. Orthodox policymaking would have responded with austerity measures, but the Kirchner government attempted a more heterodox approach, including price controls on some key consumer items and control over foreign exchange to try to limit capital flight. Inflation did not reach Venezuelan levels, but was also not pulled under control; and people found themselves unable to buy (and therefore save in) more stable currencies, especially dollars; while their income did not keep pace with price rises in basic foodstuffs and other resources. This economic insecurity was matched by a feeling of personal insecurity and outrage against government corruption, stoked by media opponents of the Kirchners, both of which I discuss below.

In part as a result of all these strains, mass street demonstrations have remained a regular feature of the Buenos Aires political landscape in the years since 2003. Table 4.1 gives a roster of some notable events in the city – and my first list of mass urban mobilizations – in chronological order.

This is not an exhaustive list, and is complemented by constant routine mobilizations and demonstrations explicitly organized by trade unions, political parties, and other civic groups. These happen almost constantly throughout the year, with political rallies of course focusing on electoral campaigns, which take place in odd-numbered years, and every four years for presidential elections. Union demonstrations are often connected to wage and minimum salary negotiations – which usually take place around the months of February–March and July. When I conducted fieldwork with two public sector workers' unions in 2009, I followed the protest cycle of the Asociación de Trabajadores del Estado (Association of State Workers, ATE). That year, they took to the streets for multiple reasons, including specific workplace conflicts, such as the restructuring and refurbishment of the Colón Opera House (Lazar, 2016b) or the Buenos Aires City audit office. They also repeatedly protested against what they saw as the government takeover of the national statistics office, INDEC, and the consequent manipulation of inflation figures, with an 'abrazo' (embrace) circling the square outside the office each time the monthly inflation statistics were released. With their parent organization, the CTA (Central de Trabajadores de la Argentina, Argentine Workers Centre), they also protested against the reduction in the age of criminal responsibility, the closing of a children's cultural centre, high energy tariffs, and in favour of universal child benefit. In 2015, CTA marches mostly focused on salary negotiations, but also included mobilizations against violence against women, by and in solidarity with indigenous women to protect women's bodies and territories, in solidarity with Venezuela, and against the criminalization of protest.[4] A recurrent demand from 2009 to the present has been for the '82% móvil' for pensioners, namely that

Table 4.1 Some key mass mobilizations in Buenos Aires city since 2001

2004	Demonstration of around 100,000 people against 'insecurity', led by Juan Carlos Blumberg, the father of a kidnap victim murdered by his assailants. Two further but smaller demonstrations were held in 2004, and a final one in that cycle in 2006.
2008	Mobilizations and counter-mobilizations over government proposals to increase the rate of export duty on soya, wheat, maize and sunflowers in line with international commodity prices. This provoked a country-wide strike led by agricultural exporters, and multiple demonstrations in cities including Buenos Aires (and including cacerolazos, held in the centre and wealthy northern neighbourhoods of the city).*
2009	March: anti-insecurity demonstration organized partly through Facebook. April: wake and funeral of Raúl Alfonsín, president from 1983 to 1989 and associated especially with the transition to democracy after the military dictatorship of 1976–83.
2010	November: wake and funeral of Néstor Kirchner.
2012	Cacerolazos held in September and November, and organized through Facebook and other social and mainstream media. A further cacerolazo in this sequence was held in April 2013.
2015	January: mass demonstrations in the wake of the death of the prosecutor Alberto Nisman.

* (see 'The Kirchners v the Farmers', 2008 and also 'Cristina's Climbdown', 2008). The partisan tone of The Economist's reporting hints at the toxic nature of this debate. The second report shows that discursive tropes decrying the Kirchners' 'autocratic' styles of government were common, even in 2008. They were to become important in later demonstrations, as I discuss below.

the amount of state retirement pensions should be set at 82 per cent of their final salary, but increasing as the salary of workers in their old job increases.[5] ATE is especially associated with a proclivity to demonstrate, but their more powerful but pro-government rival, UPCN (Unión del Personal Civil de la Nacion, Union of National Civil Servants), is also not averse to mass protests if necessary. UPCN informants were especially proud of the protest they organized in 2005 when 30,000 members took to the streets to demand that Néstor Kirchner reopen collective bargaining negotiations.

'Middle-Class' Protests?

I want to draw a distinction between the second list of union-, party- or civic group organized protests and the mass mobilizations I listed first. Most of the mass mobilizations in the first list are commonly understood in Argentina as 'middle class', 'national' and, importantly, 'spontaneous'. Of course, all three of these descriptive terms are *highly* contested, and depend very much upon the social and class position of the person reading each one of these mass events. The possibility of reading them as 'middle class', for example, relies less on a materialist analysis of the protesters' class position than upon an interpretation of their motivations, such as the fear of crime and the desire for a strong state to counter that insecurity, or the objection to capital controls that limit the purchase of US dollars; as well as the reading of cues such as skin colour, clothing, hairstyle, location of the protest (in the centre of the city, in the wealthy neighbourhoods), and the use of specific protest techniques like the cacerolazo (Lazar 2015; Muir n.d.). In the wake of the cacerolazo held on 8 November 2012, for example, my pro-government informants read it as 'middle class' and atomized, arguing that the popular classes had stayed at home. This reading enabled the government and its supporters to feel confident about continuing with little change because, they argued, their 'national popular' project was supported by the popular classes, even if the wealthier middle classes opposed some aspects.

Whether or not the protest was in actual fact majority 'middle class', the gatherings on 8 November visually and physically cited the previous mass protests prominent in Argentine history in the twentieth century, with which I opened this chapter. In doing so, protesters laid a claim to be the Argentine 'people', and not merely one subsection, the 'middle classes'. To successfully label a given demonstration as 'middle class' was to delegitimize it in the eyes of many, not least because of the continuing strength of the imaginative pull of mass working-class demonstrations from 17 October 1945 onwards.[6] The November cacerolazo looked like them in the sense of the massing of bodies and the occupation of space. Yet it was also seen (by some) to be fundamentally different, because on the whole it consisted of people who were rather wealthier and whiter than the earlier protesters. These cues were extremely important for political debate among my informants, who were unionists, and, on the whole, government supporters. As civil servants, many would consider them middle class, but they thought of themselves as workers. One delegate at a workshop on leadership at the union school summed up the issue by saying that 'el pueblo' (the Argentine people) took to the streets in 2001, whereas in September 2012 it was just 'gente' (people) on the streets. In fact, Sarah Muir points out that at the time of the 2001 cacerolazos the crowds were named precisely as 'gente' and not 'el pueblo'. Then, the Argentine nation was 'gente', because of the association of 'el pueblo' with populist Peronist rhetoric (Laclau 2005). In the post-crisis era, among pro-Peronist circles, the signifiers of the crowd had flipped.

In both cases what was important was to signal the crowd as national, whether 'gente' or 'pueblo'. In November 2012, that was signalled by the prevalence of the national flag among the demonstrators. Most of them carried flags and empty pots and pans in preference to placards; and there were certainly no overt signifiers of belonging to particular political parties. Many of the protesters knew to wear white t-shirts or shirts, and if they had forgotten to bring along an Argentine flag, they could buy one on the streets surrounding the mobilization. They sang the national anthem and occupied key national spaces for mobilization in the city, namely the Obelisk and the Plaza de Mayo.[7] White tops and national flags have become relatively common in these 'middle-class' demonstrations, and featured also in the March 2009 insecurity march and the demonstrations condemning the murder of Alberto Nisman in January and February 2015.[8]

Spontaneity

Beyond the signalling of the crowd as 'national' and 'middle class', what seemed to be really contentious for my interlocutors was the extent of spontaneity in the mobilization. In late 2012, most people I knew appeared to agree that the September cacerolazos had been fairly spontaneous, and their extent had even surprised the organizers, who had called for protest on Twitter and Facebook. However, by 8 November, spontaneity had become a more contested question. When I arrived at a UPCN delegation office the day after, people were animatedly discussing an earlier issue of 'El Argentino' that purported to detail the connections between the organizers of the cacerolazo, oppositional parties, and the media groups Clarín and La Nación ('Los grupos detrás del cacerolazo del 8N', 2012). By painting the protests as not quite spontaneous, this very progovernment newspaper had further reduced their power in the eyes of my Kirchnerista interlocutors; just as much as their own readings of the protesters as middle class did. Spontaneity was a very important criterion for them when reading the cacerolazos, in large part because of the importance of spontaneity in narratives of the famous mobilizations that the 2012 cacerolazos had been attempting to cite or recreate. This was especially true for the protests of 2001–2, as I described above.

The importance of the extent of spontaneity in mobilization is not unique to Argentina, as Dalakoglou (2012) attests. In a discussion of the June 2011 occupation of Syntagma Square in Athens, he repeatedly stresses the importance of its spontaneous nature, and affirms that 'In the case of Syntagma there was *no* initial conscious leadership by a pre-existing organisational apparatus, but many, diverse historical material and contextual factors contributing towards the particular political event. This grew spontaneously into a social movement, without the Party leadership that Lenin and Gramsci had in mind' (2012: 535–36, emphasis in original). For him, the crucial aspect was that of 'post-spontaneity'– that is, the ability of social movements to organize collective action once the initial spontaneous mobilization has taken place. Moving to a different continent, Martin Webb has shown how spontaneity was considered to be a key element of the Indian anti-corruption protests of 2011 led by Anna Hazare. Yet, he argues, the narrative of spontaneity overlooks the hard work put in by anti-corruption activists prior to the spectacular mobilizations, which he describes as 'a hidden archaeology of sustained, less visible activism' (Webb 2014: 193). Spontaneity of protest is an important trope worldwide, commonly indicating a kind of authenticity that is somehow assumed not to be quite so present among protesters who have been told to take to the streets. This is certainly the case in Argentina; perhaps in part because of familiarity with the routine organized protests that comprise my second list.

To provide a counterpoint to the narrative of authentic spontaneity in the November 2012 cacerolazo, government supporters in Argentina turned to discussions of media conspiracy. Most of my UPCN informants blamed the media for at the very least stoking up opposition to Cristina Fernández de Kirchner because of her attempts to implement the media law of 2009. This law included provisions that reduce the market share that can be owned by a single media company, and they particularly affected the Grupo Clarín, whose flagship newspaper had moved into increasingly fierce opposition to Cristina since her 2008 confrontation with agribusiness (or the rural oligarchy, or farmers, depending on your point of view) over taxation of agricultural exports.[9] The Grupo Clarín 'controls 60% of the cable market, 25% of the internet market, Argentina's second most popular TV channel, three provincial channels, and 10 radio stations, as well as six other papers, a news agency and a printing works', according to The Guardian newspaper (Watts 2012). The legislation capped corporate ownership of the broadcast market at 35 per cent, and, crucially, applied to cable, meaning that Clarín's broadcasting licences would be cut from 158 to 24, by means of a forced sale. Clarín opposed this legislation both through the courts and through its media outlets. It also strongly supported the cacerolazos, and its main open-air TV channel, El Trece, famously hosted the Sunday evening programme 'Periodismo Para Todos', anchored by Jorge Lanata. This programme began airing in April 2012, and subsequently enjoyed steadily growing audiences, all the while attacking the president, her government, her late husband and her supporters in investigative reports and satirical sketches, accusing them all of corruption and incompetence. The TV programme became so popular that the rival state-owned TV channel scheduled soccer matches for the same time slot.

The Lanata show points to a further set of associations, which link spontaneity of mobilization to discursive tropes based on the morality of indignation, or outrage. This is also a question for European countries, such as Greece and Spain. Theodossopoulos (2014) shows the importance of indignation *(aganáktisi)* in the June 2011 occupation of Syntagma Square in Athens; the occupation that Dalakoglou (2012) assures us was entirely spontaneous. The Greek occupiers were influenced by the Spanish indignados; and both appear to express a morality of outrage that resonates with the Argentine 'Que Se Vayan Todos' position of the 2001 crisis. This is not a flippant connection to make: the 2001 upheavals in Argentina are very well known in European activist circles, and there have been significant connections between Argentine, Spanish and then Greek activists. In Spain and Greece, the stance of active indignation is heavily associated with the young, especially those precariously employed graduates who have an affinity with social-media organized networking and mobilization, and who are prepared to occupy squares. That said, Theodossopoulos (2014) also shows that the trope of indignation and disgust with the established political class travelled across Greek society; as it did in 2001 in Argentina.

Recently in Argentina, indignation and outrage was, it seems, directed at particular politicians, especially the former president herself. My pro-K informants were horrified at placards in the 2012 demonstrations that denounced Cristina as a 'yegua', that is, mare – and also slang for prostitute; and in early 2015 demonstrators accused her directly of murdering Alberto Nisman, with placards announcing 'Cristina Asesina'. Jorge Lanata publically accused one of Cristina's business associates of money laundering, and another one of involvement in murder (the latter, three days before the first round of the election), but it is hard to gauge the full truth of these accusations when they were combined with sketches on his show that routinely presented her as preening, overly made-up and aggressive. Social media memes accused her of an intemperate love of expensive clothes, watches and jewellery. Even publications such as The Economist repeated stories that purport to show her dictatorial and abrasive tendencies (Cristina's Climbdown', 2008).

The at times highly personal and of course utterly gendered invective was perhaps balanced out by equally personal and equally gendered protestations of love for Cristina – and especially for her late husband Néstor – by supporters particularly in pro-K youth groups like La Cámpora and Kolina. At an act honouring Néstor Kirchner on the second anniversary of his death, one very tearful young UPCN delegate declared that while some had lost a political figure when Néstor died, he and other young people had lost a father. One afternoon I walked into a discussion about Cristina's beauty in the UPCN delegation office, and one friend asked me if I thought she was beautiful. Without thinking, I said that I did not really think so, not least because she wears a lot of make-up, and the slightly frosty atmosphere after made me realize that I should not have given that response. Supporters of Cristina also sometimes balanced the invective against their president with equally crude language and personal slurs against her opponents; for example, the Secretary of Commerce was reported to have said in September 2012 that the protesters should 'stick the saucepans up their arses' (meter las cacerolas en el orto), phrasing that was frowned upon by my informants and in the mainstream media ('Guillermo Moreno: "Que se metan las cacerolas en el orto"', 2012). I assume that it was supporters of Cristina who circulated pictures of Alberto Nisman with prostitutes and sex toys a few weeks after his death (Faulk 2015).

During her second presidential term, opponents seemed to become more firmly entrenched in a direct critique of her as a person, with a consistent undercurrent of disgust at a woman with political power and strength of personality and opinion. She was constantly seen as having been influenced by her husband (for good or ill), part of the 'matrimonio K' ('K marriage') who made considerable money as a result of their real estate investments in the rather murky Santa Cruz property market. (That said, since Néstor's death in 2010, Cristina has never lost an opportunity to ally herself to his popularity among their supporters and to present her own actions and what is actually considerable political acumen as really just following in his footsteps).

Aside from the insults and accusations of corruption, opponents focused in particular on a set of criticisms that associated her with dictatorial methods of government. They suggested, for example, that she only listened to a very small set of advisers, and failed to consult broadly over policy measures.[10] Although this particular critique was not explicitly gendered, there was a complex dynamic whereby on the one hand she was concentrating too much power in her own hands for a woman in politics, but on the other, as a woman this limited set of advisers was a problem, because she would be expected to follow the advice of those men who surrounded her, rather than having her own views. At any rate, critiques of her were always filtered through her gender. In 2012, demonstrators and the media picked up on moments such as her abrupt treatment of a student who had asked her a challenging question about her economic policies during a talk she gave in Harvard or a time when she said that her ministers should be afraid of her. Showing how contested these things are, one pro-K friend insisted to me that she had been deliberately quoted out of context, since she had actually said that those ministers who were corrupt should be afraid of the fact that she would ensure due process of legal investigation and punishment. Later, in 2013, measures to institute elections for judges were interpreted by many as a means for the Executive to gain control over the judiciary via the operations of party politics. The accusations of presidential involvement in the murder of a prosecutor (Alberto Nisman), who was about to criticize the government, and the reaction to her subsequent measures to control the Security Services in early 2015, also created uncomfortable resonances with the experience of dictatorship.

Back in November 2012, my pro-K informants scoffed at demonstrators' placards that denounced a Kirchnerista dictatorship. Just over a year previously, they pointed out, Cristina had won the election with 54 per cent of the vote; and they insisted that people were in fact perfectly at liberty to say what they wanted about the regime. Indeed, they thought that part of the problem that had given rise to the November cacerolazo was ineffective opposition in conventional political spaces. They denounced the chaos of leaderless protest and the lack of organization, but at the same time they sought out any evidence they could find that there was an organizational structure behind the cacerolazos and that it was linked either to oppositional political parties or to specific media corporations. After all, somebody was producing the posters that called protesters to the obelisk on 8 November; somebody had set up the first website, Facebook page and Twitter account, surely. Nobody really knew what was going on or what people wanted when they took to the street, other than to express their outrage at the president.

Insecurity

The one issue raised by the protesters in 2012 that government supporters found hard to disregard was that of 'insecurity'. Argentina has been suffering from the region-wide increases in violent crime over the last twenty-five years. Kessler (2011) cites a report on small arms proliferation to give the following shocking statistics for Latin America: 'with only 14% of the world's population, [and] less than 4% of global arms in civilian hands, the region concentrates 40% of the homicides committed worldwide with firearms' (2011: 83, my translation), although Bonner (2014) suggests that figures for gun homicide may include police killings. However, surveys also show that 30–40 per cent of the region's population report having been victims of a crime in any one year, which is more than double the 15 per cent average in Western Europe (Tudela and Van Dijk et al., cited in Kessler 2011: 83). The rate of those who fear becoming a victim of crime tends to be about double the rate of those who actually were victims, giving figures of 60–70 per cent in Latin America, which, as Kessler notes, makes the European figure of 25 per cent pale in comparison (2011: 83).

In Argentina, Auyero, Burbano de Lara and Fernanda Berti (2014: 96) report that 'Official data for the province of Buenos Aires show a doubling of crime rates between 1995 and 2008, from 1,114 to 2,010 criminal episodes per 100,000 residents and from 206 crimes against persons (i.e. homicides, assault, and battery) to 535 per 100,000 residents'. Relative to other countries in Latin America, the figures for Argentina are actually very low.[11] Still, in 2006, a survey of populations in forty-two countries that measured fear of crime put Argentina second only to South Africa. Fear of crime stood at 18 per cent in Latin America, 24 per cent in Argentina and 7 per cent in the rest of the world (AC Neilson study, cited in Kessler 2011). Kessler's own survey research conducted in 2009 showed that 80 per cent of those surveyed considered insecurity to be the first, second or third most important problem in the country; and he estimated that comparable figures for the 1980s and 1990s were 20 per cent and 40 per cent respectively (Kessler 2011).

The combination of growth in rates of interpersonal violence and the fear of crime, increasingly framed as a problem of 'insecurity', has prompted significant mass protests in the country.[12] The targets of these protests are both concrete and diffuse. Protesters denounce two sets of actors: first, the perpetrators of violent crime, and second the (implicitly corrupt) police forces that fail to bring them to justice, or who engage in violent and repressive policing themselves. However, the dominant emotion is a sense of outrage at the fact of living in a situation of insecurity, of fear of violent crime. The first major anti-insecurity demonstration in Buenos Aires occurred in April 2004, a week and a half after the death of 23-year-old Axel Blumberg at the hands of kidnappers. Around 100,000 Argentines responded to his parents' call for a demonstration to demand government action on violent crime (Gotkine, 2004). Juan Carlos Blumberg, Axel's father, then spearheaded two further but smaller marches in 2004 and set up a foundation to document kidnappings and violent crime and campaign in favour of tougher penalties for criminals. He advocated 'mano dura' (iron fist) policies that would increase police powers, even though, as Ari Gandsman (2012) points out, the situation of his son's murder could have led him to join forces with human rights organizations demanding police reform.[13] Support for him faded as his political stance became more overt and his link to party politics grew stronger and more obvious: a demonstration in August 2006 saw him link up with opposition figures, and in 2007 he stood on behalf of the opposition for election to the position of Governor of Buenos Aires, gaining around 1 per cent of the vote (Gandsman 2012).

In March 2009 another demonstration against insecurity took place at the Plaza de Mayo and in other cities across the country, drawing together celebrity victims of crime and ordinary citizens. The demonstrations were partially coordinated through Facebook and Twitter, one of the early examples of this kind of mobilization.[14] Discussions in the media betrayed concerns about its spontaneity similar to 2012 – for example when newspapers reported that it had been organized by an NGO headed by Constanza Guglielmi, an ally of the anti-Kirchner Peronist Francisco de Narvaez, and daughter of a general accused of torture during the dictatorship ('Por mano dura', 2009). The conclusions we are supposed to reach after reading these articles are that anti-insecurity demonstrations are the political expression of those sectors of society that oppose the government and supported military dictatorship in the past. This is so also because of the ways that anti-insecurity demonstrations cite previous calls for law and order in the context of violent guerrilla warfare in the early 1970s: contemporary calls for the 'mano dura' and curtailment of human rights for criminals echo earlier narratives of the war against subversives.[15] Yet, curiously, in late 2012 the denunciation of insecurity could also sit alongside accusations of Cristina's tendency towards dictatorial politics.

The common element was of course opposition to the government, but it might be granting official opposition figures too much agency to suggest that they were able to organize or even channel outrage against insecurity into street protests. They could just as easily have been jumping on the bandwagon in an attempt to co-opt that outrage for their own political project. It would be impossible to know which is true. For now, I want instead to highlight three linked points: 1) these mass mobilizations are open to multiple contested readings (pro-dictatorship or anti? Anti-corruption or anti-K? Anti-police or anti-criminal?), but 2) those readings depend to a large extent on just how spontaneous a demonstration is perceived to be. Finally, they express a moral politics of outrage and indignation, one increasingly characteristic of contemporary politics in Argentina and elsewhere.

Protest Moralities of Denunciation and Demand-Making

This is not to say that organized workers do not produce moral politics in their demonstrations. Quite the contrary: placards are full of statements that are both moral and material such as *'la crisis no la pagamos los trabajadores'* (we the workers will not pay for the [economic] crisis), or in 2008–9 when campaigning for child benefit, *'ni un pibe con hambre'* (not one kid hungry). Speeches at the rallying points at ends of marches clearly express moralities of outrage at government actions, including accusing politicians of dictatorial tendencies and connections. For example, in mid 2009, ATE/CTA were very concerned at the proposed lowering of the age of penal responsibility to fourteen, and the closing of a children's cultural activity centre in the city, called the Puerto Pibes, in order to house a new academy for the city police force. In the press and their pamphlets, they accused the proposed governor of the city's police force of links to the dictatorship. Nor is it to say that the poor do not suffer from or get outraged at problems of insecurity or capital controls: urban violence is concentrated in poor areas, and perpetrated there by both the police and residents (Auyero, Burbano de Lara and Fernanda Berti 2014); as Sarah Muir (n.d.) points out, lack of currency in circulation is a severe problem for the cash-based informal economy, as is rapid inflation. Friends of mine who are Bolivian migrants working in the informal garment industry are certainly indignant at the fact that they contracted informal debt in dollars and must pay much more to repay the money; a problem made even more acute by the fact that their savings were stolen from their house at gunpoint a few years ago.

Yet, it is possible to posit a distinction between the two kinds of mobilization ('spontaneous' and organized) and their moral politics. They even differ physically, as organized demonstrations tend to take the form of a march that flows through from one agreed meeting point on the Avenue 9 de Julio (usually) towards a rally at the Plaza de Mayo or Plaza del Congreso, with groups who have been convened usually by SMS, and identify themselves by banners and flags; while the 'middle-class' mobilizations are more amorphous massings at key sites, which people join individually and in groups, prompted by a call on social media that is then publicized in the mainstream media. In November 2012, organizers (if there were any) deliberately did not schedule a rally or speeches; at some point the crowd decided to make its way to the Plaza de Mayo, but it was pretty aimless once people had heeded the call on social media and convened at the obelisk, raising the question of the need for some form of 'post-spontaneous' organization (Dalakoglou 2012). Another difference is the emphasis on spontaneity versus leadership, each aspect being morally valued according to one's political positioning. Finally, the organized demonstrations make considerable effort to formulate specific demands, while the others express a much more diffuse and inchoate set of sentiments, which range from dissatisfaction with the state of the country to anger and disgust at the president.

Is the difference between the two sets of protest technologies and moral politics related to the class position of the protestors? Tania Ahmad (2014) is clear that during urban unrest in Karachi in 2007, the 'sociality of indignation' that she identified as an important political stance was associated with the middle classes. They retreated to their homes, and considered active participation in (street) politics to be very much for the lower classes. In contrast, the Argentine middle classes do take to the streets, if not as frequently as the organized workers do. We might want to draw a closer regional comparison with the mid 2015 and early 2016 protests in Brazil, where the 'middle classes' took to the streets to demand the impeachment of President Dilma Rousseff on charges of corruption (see the chapter by Mao Mollona). We should be wary, as Salvador Schavelzon (2015) warns, of falling for the PT line that all of those who protest against Dilma are 'neoliberals'; but it does seem to be the case that since 2013 the anti-Dilma protests have become more concentrated in middle-class areas, with whiter-skinned protesters and even pro-dictatorship slogans on display at times. As Gutierrez (2015) suggests, the right appear to have taken over the language of outrage against corruption that was previously heavily associated with the left (see also the chapters by Jansen and Steur; and Kalb 2009).

Returning to Argentina, we can see similar processes there. As this chapter has shown, on the eve of the 2015 elections, three themes dominated political discourse on the streets and in the media – namely, economic policy, insecurity and politicians' corruption. But when it came to how they played out in mass mobilizations, they constituted multiple threads all tangled together. The easy story of anti-neoliberal popular classes protesting against elite neoliberal governments, which captivated many of us in the early 2000s, no longer applies. By 2015, the regime was much more hybrid than that of the 1990s: social spending had increased but relied upon revenues from agribusiness and extractivism; the state expanded, granting more people more secure jobs; however, the police continued to be criminal and repression of popular demonstrations stepped up a gear over the course of the year. And so on. Even prior to Macri's electoral victory, some commentators were suggesting that the region had reached what Schavelzon (2015) calls 'el fin del relato progresista' (the end of the progressive story) as Argentina – along with other celebrated leftist regimes in the region such as in Brazil, Bolivia and Ecuador – turned even more towards developmentalist policies based on extractivism, even in the face of protest by indigenous communities and environmentalists (Svampa 2015). The probability of strain became much more acute with the slowdown in the Chinese economy, and the fluctuation of the commodity 'super-cycle'.

So, government opponents might have been people who objected to this rightwards trajectory or those who thought that it had not gone far enough. On the issue of insecurity, the former thought that it could be ascribed to social deprivation and police corruption, which should be addressed by reforms to the security forces, while the latter thought that policing was too weak, and 'mano dura' policies the only answer. Opponents might also be people who desired what they considered to be a well-functioning state on Anglo-Saxon lines; with sensible monetary policies that protected national budgets from the strains of over-reliance on one set of commodity exports, and uncontrolled expansion of state expenditure in the form of generous public sector wage settlements. In their view, such policies might eventually control the inflation that eroded the value of their wage packet almost weekly, and might allow an Argentine government that is perceived to be more responsible to borrow on the international capital markets.

Or, they might simply have wanted a change from a regime that they saw as completely corrupt and undemocratic, without necessarily wanting neoliberal economic policies. While it was clear that Macri would likely continue with the kinds of right-wing approaches he employed when he ran the City of Buenos Aires, and while his economic advisers came from an obviously orthodox background, his actual election campaign was rather more ambiguous. He campaigned simply on the grounds of 'change' in government regime; for 'happiness' *(alegría)*, and for working together as a team, clearly picking up on the common criticism of Cristina for being dictatorial. He created a technocratic option that appealed to those who had been left outside the previous government's deals with organized social forces. While the Kirchnerista candidate, Daniel Scioli, negotiated with many of the collectively organized groups, from cooperatives to unions, Macri bypassed them completely, setting up his own 'movement' of people whom he called 'volunteers' – making a clear contrast with the 'militantes' (best translated as activists) of the unions, pro-K youth groups and cooperatives (see Fidanza, A.

and G. Vommaro, n.d. and Lazar 2013). It was a very post-political campaign, in classically Mouffian terms (Mouffe 2005), but with the addition of a morality of disgust in much of the anti-Kirchner discourse. Many people thought the regime was hideous, corrupt, involved in drug trafficking and money laundering, and with a dictatorial harridan at the helm. And in response, government supporters could be hugely passionate in their love and reverence for Cristina; and loathing of those who insulted her, considering them to be apologists for the military, or media stooges for Clarín.

Meanwhile, organized social groups such as trade unions and neighbourhood assemblies conducted their moral politics of opposition in the form of social and economic projects that could be articulated through a set of specific demands. These varied but might include demands for wage increases, increases in the personal tax allowance, child benefit, adequate pension provision, or protest against reductions in the age of criminal responsibility, or the closure of a particular cultural centre, firing of a particular group of workers, and so on. Such a politics expresses outrage and uses moral language but tends very consciously to propose (or oppose) specific material measures. And from the earliest days of Macri's government, they had much to oppose, as tens of thousands of public sector workers were fired, and the regime removed currency controls (allowing the peso to float freely against the dollar and prices to rise accordingly), removed the contentious taxes on agricultural exports that had so incensed the rural oligarchy in 2008, cut subsidies on utilities, and agreed to pay off the holdout debtors through a massive issuance of bonds.[16] In response, especially to the firings, there has been a renewed wave of protest from some unions and other collective organizations such as popular cooperatives. In a worrying development in recent months, those protests have increasingly been subject to violent state repression, which is also condemned in moral language.

Conclusion: A Moral Politics of Outrage?

All the different attitudes to the government outlined above were present in everyday conversation, as well as in the politics of demand-making by organized sectors of civil society. However, at times of mass protest in the 'middle-class' mode they are distilled into a moral politics that is expressed predominantly as outrage directed at the established political class or the figure of the president. This is not peculiar to Argentina, or even to Latin America, having been a feature of significant mass mobilization in recent years in Southern Europe in particular; and even of (less powerful) political movements in Northern Europe. To some extent it could be seen as an expression of the 'moralization of politics' that Chantal Mouffe (2005) identifies as a consequence of the 'post-political' moves towards consensus-based politics in the 1990s and early 2000s (in Europe and the United States in particular). She argues that this means 'not that politics has become more moral but that nowadays political antagonisms are being formulated in terms of moral categories. We are still faced with political friend/enemy discriminations but they are now expressed using the vocabulary of morality' (2005: 75).[17] In this, she sees the degeneration of politics from a more preferable agonistic mode to one that is antagonistic.

In contemporary Argentina, the antagonism that characterizes everyday political culture is particularly overt during the protests I have discussed here; and has become, I think, more explicit and acute over the time that I have been conducting field research in Argentina (since 2009). When Mauricio Macri became president, the poles shifted, but the antagonism did not: the antagonistic nature of public debate could, for example, be seen in the reaction to the naming of Macri in the Panama Papers leak in April 2016. Kirchner supporters were horrified and called for his resignation on grounds of corruption; one began a court case against him. Macristas – including some in the mainstream media – tended to pay attention more to other corruption scandals, such as those associated with the Kirchners, as with the example of the naming of her associate Lázaro Báez in the same leak, or the subpoena of Cristina for her role in selling options on future dollar-peso currency exchanges, a case originally brought by Macri's supporters late 2015. In turn, Kirchner supporters denounced the partiality of the media, and turned out en masse to support Cristina when she attended the court on 13 April 2016. The polarization of politics evident in these events and in the discussion of them provides good evidence for a version of Schmitt's proposal that 'the specific political distinction to which political actions and motives can be reduced is that between friend and enemy' (Schmitt 1996: 26), so perceptively discussed by Mouffe.

Thus, a complex moral politics of outrage characterizes contemporary middle-class politics in Latin America and Europe just as much as (if not more so than) the moral sentiments of compassion identified by Didier Fassin as key to politics today. Fassin emphasized the 'humanitarian government' of 'precarious lives' (Fassin 2012, 2015);

especially through institutions and practices of the state and parastatal agencies such as NGOs. However, if we turn our analytical lens towards the claims-making and protest politics of people who are not engaged in government as part of the social state, then we see a different picture, and there is good evidence to suggest that outrage might be a more prevalent moral quality of politics. This is a point made by Theodossopoulos (2014) for Greece in recent years; and Tania Ahmad's work on Pakistan shows a similar sense of widespread indignation at the acts of the political classes (Ahmad 2014). Outrage at political corruption (at least at the highest levels of politics) is a consistent trope across the world, from Latin America to Africa (Roitman 2005), Europe (Theodossopoulos 2014) and South Asia (Gupta 1995; Ahmad 2014) at least. If apathy or disenchantment can count as moral – perhaps in the sense that they are moral evaluations when directed at mainstream politics – then we might wish to add them to the mix, especially as we pay attention also to those who do not take to the streets (Winegar 2012; Ahmad 2014).

What does this mean for how we understand the protest politics of recent years in Argentina? As the sketches above show, although antagonism is a striking feature of the political culture, a neat thesis of left-right polarization is inadequate to describe the contemporary situation. It may well be true that, as Loperfido argues in the following chapter, 'moral classification of the adversary' has become so important in part because progressives have renounced class-based distinctions as the explicit basis for political action. Yet, in Argentina, moral classifications, including those organized around class lines, have been a part of politics at the very least since the early twentieth century, and probably well before then.

The 'middle class' mobilizations described in this chapter demanded different things than did the organized workers (who may well be quite middle class themselves, in practice). The first group wanted policies like an end to currency controls and tougher penalties for criminals, while the second put forward a much more anti-neoliberal set of demands, and since Macri's election, this latter group have had to become even more vocal. Both groups made their claims through a moral language of politics, decrying Cristina Fernández de Kirchner's corrupt and dictatorial tendencies (as well as her make-up and clothes) on the one side, and the dangers of child hunger or mass redundancies on the other. One is a moral language of disgust and indignation, the other moral language condemns the anti-social effects of government policies or, more recently, expresses outrage at state violence towards protesters.

While I have characterized these as distinct moral languages of politics, and would argue that they do cluster in the ways that I have outlined, it should be remembered that they are not in practice confined exclusively to one group or the other, and there are overlaps, not least in the condemnation of political corruption.

This shows that in thinking about the relation between moral politics and political economy, we should watch that we do not assume that one kind of political expression ('progressive') is more likely than another to be articulated through a moral language. This also means that we should be careful before saying simply that the right has appropriated the technologies (e.g. street mobilization) and language of the left. That said, we should also recognize that this does happen as well, as with the language of corruption – and even, perhaps, of indignation. In the case of Argentina, acknowledging this complexity for the recent mobilizations leads to an important reconsideration of the iconic 2001–2 crisis. Analyses of those protests equated the cacerolazos too closely with other initiatives, such as the roadblocks by unemployed workers, barter networks and factory occupations, in lumping them all together in one ecology of resistance to neoliberalism. Although seductive, the discussion that I have presented in this chapter suggests that it may not be the best analytical strategy for understanding that political moment. We might then want as scholars to question our own implicit moral politics of protest, specifically in the desire to see progressive politics where it might not always exist. We should be wary of how we implicitly constitute a friend/enemy distinction out of a situation that is in practice much more indeterminate.

One issue to consider especially carefully in this light is that of spontaneity. For my informants, spontaneity of mobilization demonstrates and creates authenticity of outrage; in the middle-class street mobilizations of my first list, the massing of people must be as self-convened as possible for it to be a genuine expression of their feelings. This means that each demonstration is a new beginning. The problem is that this position occludes the hard work that has gone before in order to foment and articulate outrage and create 'spontaneity', the historical experience of street protest as an action that can be effective, and the need for some kind of political organization during or after the event to make it meaningful in the longer term.

Sian Lazar is Professor of Social Anthropology at the University of Cambridge. She researches collective politics and social movements, with a special focus on labor and Latin America. She is the author of *El Alto, Rebel City* (2008), *The Social Life of Politics* (2017), and most recently, *How We Struggle. A Political Anthropology of Labour* (2023).

Notes

1. A series of street demonstrations and strikes in Cordoba against the military leadership of Onganía, and associated very strongly with oppositional unionist currents. See Brennan (1993).
2. Return to international capital markets was made costlier by the result of the legal cases brought in 2014 by creditors who refused to accept the government's renegotiation of the debt – as other creditors did in 2003 and 2005. Instead, these vulture funds demanded that the Argentine government honour the full face value of debt they bought in the immediate aftermath of the crisis for something like 20 per cent of that value. Their case was upheld in the US Supreme Court. In early 2016, the new president of Argentina, Mauricio Macri, agreed to pay the vulture funds, and in April issued an eye-watering amount of public debt to fund that. See Elliott (2014), Phillips and Johnston (2013) and Moore, Mander and Platt (2016).
3. Since 2007, ATE and others have argued that the national statistics office (INDEC) has been subject to government interference aimed at disguising the true rate of inflation.
4. These details come from the email list of the CTA-Autonoma, which is the 'Autonomous CTA', namely the faction of the CTA run by Pablo Micheli and dominated by ATE. In 2011 the CTA split into two factions, one led by Micheli and ATE, the other led by Hugo Yasky and the teachers' unions.
5. Political will is growing to set the minimum pension at 82 per cent of the official minimum wage, a provision established by law in 1958 but only met between 1958 and 1962. See 'La jubilación mínima está a sólo un punto del 82% móvil' (2015).
6. A number of the prominent events – such as the 2001 riots and the 1983 protests against the Malvinas war – were in fact multi-class; but a significant part of the visual language of protest in the Plaza de Mayo and Avenida 9 de Julio refers to mass mobilizations called by the unions in the mid twentieth century – especially 17 October 1945, but also key historical events such as when Eva Peron announced her resignation from the vice presidential candidacy in 1951.
7. Also associated with the middle class city (Muir n.d.).
8. Although it would be important not to read too much into this, as of course white tops are common dress, for those of all classes; and the point of the demonstrations is to mark the participants out as ordinary people. Nonetheless, a consistency between the demonstrations is developing over time.
9. The repeal of these measures was one of the first acts of Macri's government.
10. This was a theme of reporting on the Kirchners from at least 2008, as shown by The Economist's report from June of that year. See 'Cristina's Climbdown'.
11. UNODC data: Argentina homicide rate for 2010 was 5.5 per 100,000 population. The country with the highest homicide rate in the world in 2012 was Honduras, with 90.4/100,000; followed by Venezuela at 53.7/100,000. See http://www.unodc.org/gsh/. The Mexican NGO, Seguridad, Justicia y Paz, publishes a list of the fifty cities with the highest homicide rate in the world, using estimates based on data from the UN, WHO and national statistics offices. In 2014 that

list was topped by San Pedro Sula in Honduras, with an astonishing rate of 171.2; followed by Caracas at 115.98. Buenos Aires does not figure in the list at all. See http://www.seguridadjusticiaypaz.org.mx/biblioteca/prensa/send/6-prensa/198-las-50-ciudades-mas-violentas-del-mundo-2014.

12. See Bonner (2014) for a detailed discussion of the ways that crime and fear of crime have become discursively framed in these terms, and the implication for questions of human rights and transitional justice.
13. Gandsman notes that Blumberg had died in an area thought to be governed by criminals in collusion with the police; also that neighbours had witnessed him being beaten when he tried to escape and call the police, who did not come.
14. See Tomoyose (2009) for a somewhat incredulous discussion of the role of new technologies such as Twitter in convening the marches.
15. See, for example, Gandsman, who argues that the 'anti-crime rhetoric [of the Blumberg movement] is not a simple equivalent to the military dictatorship's anti-communist discourse. It is its contemporary post-political version' (Gandsman 2012: 90).
16. For more detail, see (Lazar 2016a).
17. See also Alan Bradshaw (2015), on the morality tales of European austerity politics.

References

Ahmad, T. 2014. 'Socialities of Indignation: Denouncing Party Politics in Karachi', *Cultural Anthropology* 29(2): 411–32.
Atzeni, M. and P. Ghigliani. 2007. 'Labour Process and Decision-making in Factories under Workers' Self-management: Empirical Evidence from Argentina', *Work, Employment & Society* 21(4): 653–71.
Auyero, J., A. Burbano de Lara and M. Fernanda Berti. 2014. 'Violence and the State at the Urban Margins', *Journal of Contemporary Ethnography* 43(1): 94–116.
Barros, R. 2013. 'We Were the Middle Class', in D.S. Parker and L.E. Walker (eds), *Latin America's Middle Class: Unsettled Debates and New Histories*. Lanham, MD: Lexington Books, pp. 197–213.
Blustein, P. 2005. *And the Money Kept Rolling in (and Out): The World Bank, Wall Street, the IMF and the Bankrupting of Argentina*. New York: Public Affairs.
Bonner, M.D. 2014. '"Never Again": Transitional Justice and Persistent Police Violence in Argentina', *International Journal of Transitional Justice* 8(2): 235–55.
Bradshaw, A. 2015. 'European Austerity and Collective Blame', *FocaalBlog*, 12 August 2015. Retrieved from http://www.focaalblog.com/2015/08/12/alan-bradshaw-european-austerity-and-collective-blame/.
Brennan, J. 1993. 'Working Class Protest, Popular Revolt, and Urban Insurrection in Argentina: The 1969 "Cordobazo"', *Journal of Social History* 27: 477–98.
'Cristina's Climbdown'. 2008, *The Economist*, 19 June 2008. Retrieved 4 December 2017 from http://www.economist.com/node/11586057.
Dalakoglou, D. 2012. 'Beyond Spontaneity', *City* 16(5): 535–45.
Dinerstein, A.C. 2007. 'Workers' Factory Takeovers and New State Policies in Argentina: Towards an 'institutionalisation' of Non-governmental Public Action?', *Policy and Politics* 35(3): 529–50.
———. 2003. '¡Que se Vayan Todos! Popular Insurrection and the Asambleas Barriales in Argentina', *Bulletin of Latin American Research* 22(2): 187–200.

Elliott, L. 2014. 'Argentina Debt Crisis Fears Grow after US Supreme Court Ruling', *The Guardian*, 16 June 2014. Retrieved 4 December 2017 from http://www.theguardian.com/world/2014/jun/16/argentina-debt-crisis-fears-us-supreme-court-ruling.

Fassin, D. 2012. *Humanitarian Reason: A Moral History of the Present Times*. Berkeley, CA and London: University of California Press.

———. 2015. *At the Heart of the State: The Moral World of Institutions*. London: Pluto Press.

Faulk, K. 2015. 'Truth and Meaning-Making in Liminal Politics: Unraveling the Death of Argentine Prosecutor Alberto Nisman', *American Anthropological Association 2015 Annual Meeting*. Denver, Colorado.

Fidanza, A. and G. Vommaro. n.d., 'La cara bonita de la nueva derecha', *Anfibia*. Retrieved from http://www.revistaanfibia.com/cronica/la-cara-bonita-de-la-nueva-derecha/.

Gandsman, A. 2012. '"The Axel Blumberg Crusade for The Lives of Our Children": The Cultural Politics of Fear and The Moral Authority of Grief in Argentina', *Canadian Journal of Latin American and Caribbean Studies / Revue canadienne des études latino-américaines et caraïbes* 37(73): 67–96.

Gotkine, E. 2004. 'Argentine Crime Sparks Protests', *BBC News*, 2 April 2004. Retrieved 4 December 2017 from http://news.bbc.co.uk/1/hi/world/americas/3592005.stm.

Grugel, J. and P. Riggirozzi. 2007. 'The Return of the State in Argentina', *International Affairs* 83(1): 87–107.

'Guillermo Moreno: "Que se metan las cacerolas en el orto"'. 2012, *Todo Noticias*, 27 September 2012. Retrieved 4 December 2017 from http://tn.com.ar/politica/guillermo-moreno-que-se-metan-la-cacerola-en-el-orto_273767.

Gupta, A. 1995. 'Blurred Boundaries: The Discourse of Corruption, the Culture of Politics, and the Imagined State', *American Ethnologist* 22(2): 375–402.

Gutierrez, G. B. 2015. 'Brasil: El relato del PT en el laberinto neoliberal', *democraciaAbierta*, 26 August 2015. Retrieved 4 December 2017 from https://www.opendemocracy.net/democraciaabierta/bernardo-guti%C3%A9rrez-gonz%C3%A1lez/brasil-el-relato-del-pt-en-el-laberinto-neoliberal.

Kalb, D. 2009. 'Conversations with a Polish Populist: Tracing Hidden Histories of Globalization, Class and Dispossession in Postsocialism (and Beyond)', *American Ethnologist* (36) 2: 207–23.

Kessler, G. 2011. 'La Extensiòn del sentimiento de inseguridad en amèrica latina: relatos, acciones y polìticas en el caso argentino', *Revista de Sociologia e Polìtica* 19(40): 83–97.

'La causa por la represión sigue sin definiciones'. 2007, *pagina12*, 13 March 2007. Retrieved from http://www.cepr.net/blogs/the-americas-blog/argentina-vs-the-vultures-what-you-need-to-know.

Laclau, E. 2005. *On Populist Reason*. London: Verso.

'La jubilación mínima está a sólo un punto del 82% móvil'. 2015, *Diario Registrado*, 31 January 2015. Retrieved from https://www.diarioregistrado.com/politica/la-jubilacion-minima-esta-a-solo-un-punto-del-82--movil_a56316a2142bd9ca81b19507a.

Lazar, S. 2013. 'Citizenship, Political Agency and Technologies of the Self in Argentine Trade Unions', *Critique of Anthropology* 33(1): 110–28.

———. 2015. '"This is Not a Parade, it's a Protest March": Intertextuality, Citation, and Political Action on the Streets of Bolivia and Argentina', *American Anthropologist* 117(2): 242–56.

———. 2016a. '"The Happiness Revolution": Argentina and the End of Post-Neoliberalism?', *FocaalBlog*. Retrieved from http://www.focaalblog.com/2016/03/17/sian-lazar-the-happiness-revolution-argentina-and-the-end-of-post-neoliberalism/.

———. 2016b. 'Notions of Work, Patrimony and Production in the Life of the Colón Opera House', *Journal of Latin American and Caribbean Anthropology* 21(2): 231–53.

'Los grupos detrás del cacerolazo del 8N'. 2012, *Realidad Regional*, 5 November 2012. Retrieved 4 December 2017 from http://www.realidadregional.com/quienes-son-los-grupos-detras-del-cacerolazo-del-8n/.

Moore, E., B. Mander and E. Platt. 2016. 'Argentina's Return to Markets Several times Subscribed', *Financial Times*, 18 April 2016. Retrieved 4 December 2017 from https://www.ft.com/content/10066178-0550-11e6-a70d-4e39ac32c284.

Mouffe, C. 2005. *On the Political*. London: Routledge.

Muir, S. n.d. 'The Durable Crowd: Solidarity, Legitimacy, and the Gift in Post-Crisis Argentina'.

Phillips, A. and J. Johnston. 2013. 'Argentina vs. the Vultures: What You Need to Know', *CEPR*. Retrieved from http://www.cepr.net/blogs/the-americas-blog/argentina-vs-the-vultures-what-you-need-to-know.

'Por mano dura'. 2009, *Pagina12*, 18 March 2009. Retrieved 4 December 2017 from http://www.pagina12.com.ar/diario/sociedad/3-121718-2009-03-18.html.

Robben, A. 2007. *Political Violence and Trauma in Argentina*. Philadelphia, PA: University of Pennsylvania Press.

Roitman, J.L. 2005. *Fiscal Disobedience: An Anthropology of Economic Regulation in Central Africa*. Princeton, NJ and Oxford: Princeton University Press.

Schaumberg, H. 2008. 'In Search of Alternatives: The Making of Grassroots Politics and Power in Argentina', *Bulletin of Latin American Research* 27(3): 368–87.

Schavelzon, S. 2015. 'El fin del relato progresista en América Latina', *La Razòn*, 21 June 2015. Retrieved 4 December 2017 from http://www.la-razon.com/index.php?_url=/suplementos/animal_politico/fin-relato-progresista-America-Latina_0_2292970735.html.

Schmitt, C. 1996 [1923]. *The Concept of the Political*. Chicago: University of Chicago Press.

Sitrín, M. (ed.). 2006. *Horizontalism: Voices of Popular Power in Argentina*. Oakland and Edinburgh: AK Press.

———. 2012. *Everyday Revolutions: Horizontalism and Autonomy in Argentina*. London: Zed Books.

Svampa, M. 2015. 'Termina la era de las promesas andinas', *Revista N*, 25 August 2015. Retrieved 4 December 2017 from https://www.clarin.com/rn/ideas/Termina-promesas-andinas_0_BJvEN4tv7e.html.

'The Kirchners v the Farmers', 2008, *The Economist*, 27 March 2008. Retrieved 4 December 2017 from http://www.economist.com/node/10925670.

Theodossopoulos, D. 2014. 'The Poetics of Indignation in Greece: Anti-austerity Protest and Accountability', in P. Werbner, M. Webb and K. Pellman-Poots (eds), *The Political Aesthetics of Global Protest: The Arab Spring and Beyond*. Edinburgh: Edinburgh University Press, pp. 368–88.

Tomoyose, G. 2009. 'La marcha de la inseguridad desde la Web', *La Nación*, 19 March 2009. Retrieved 4 December 2017 from http://www.lanacion.com.ar/1110183-la-marcha-de-la-inseguridad-desde-la-web.

Watts, J. 2013. 'Argentina's President and Grupo Clarìn go Head-to-Head over Media Law', *The Guardian*, 20 August 2013. Retrieved 19 September 2013 from https://www.theguardian.com/world/2013/aug/20/argentina-supreme-court-media-law.

Webb, M. 2014. 'Short Circuits: The Aesthetics of Protest, Media and Martyrdom in Indian Anti-Corruption Activism', in P. Werbner, M. Webb and K. Pellman-Poots (eds), *The Political Aesthetics of Global Protest: The Arab Spring and Beyond*. Edinburgh: Edinburgh University Press, pp. 193–221.

Winegar, J. 2012. 'The Privilege of Revolution: Gender, Class, Space, and Affect in Egypt', *American Ethnologist* 39(1): 67–70.

– Chapter 5 –

'NEITHER LEFT NOR RIGHT'

Crisis, Wane of Politics and Struggles for Sovereignty

Giacomo Loperfido

Introduction

When I arrived for fieldwork in Rome, in early 2008, I was seeking to track and interview the ex-militants of the fascism-inspired 'Spontaneista groups'. Active in the late 70s, these had been very violent and had claimed to be 'neither left nor right'. Their name made reference to the supposed 'spontaneity' of their constitution and action, announcing an ideological predilection of instincts and drives over reason and thought. All of these movements had a short life of four to six years between the late 70s and the early 80s. I was then very surprised when – on my arrival in Rome – I ran into a crowd of students, dressed in black and with shaved heads, rallying against the reform of lower education and crying in the streets the slogan: *'Non rossi, né neri, ma liberi pensieri'*.[1]

Proclaiming somewhat similar statements, the Italian Movimento 5 Stelle (5 Stars Movement), initiated by the public figure Beppe Grillo and the internet consultant Gianroberto Casaleggio, has collected an increasing amount of votes, up to the point it has recently become Italy's second largest party. Grillo, who previously had a successful career as a political satirist, was known for his polemics against the entire political establishment but – in a country in which any criticism of power has almost always come from the left – his critiques were also relegated to that side of the political spectrum. This perception changed when Grillo's Vaffanculo-Day, 8 September 2007,[2] collected around 1 million Italians protesting against corruption, moral decay, and tax evasions of Italian politicians from left and right. Grillo has recently been able to gain strong electoral momentum by pumping up the volume of his accusations and extending his attack to the European Union's politics and institutions, making statements against illegal immigrants and claiming that 'popular sovereignty' has been stolen from the people by the politicians.

Also recently, the so-called 'Rakes Movement' has raised claims even more angrily against – generally – any institutional target. Once again, the EU, the government and 'the politicians' from the left and the right were under attack. It started as a spontaneously gathered group of 'desperate farmers, petty entrepreneurs, artisans: an impoverished middle class, held together by the only common denominator of not being able to "take it [the crisis] any more"' (Marco Revelli, Il Manifesto, 12.12.13). One spokesman of this group claimed that '… the Agency of Revenue has to be closed, high finance forbidden, the Euro erased'. Moreover, they asked 'for the Government to fall, and [for] all of the public institutions to be disbanded: the Parliament, the President of the Republic, and every other institution all along' (cit. in Gigante, Il Giornale, 10.12.2013).

All of these recent spontaneous claims sound significantly similar to formulations I encountered while studying the Spontaneista groups of the 70s. Stretching analysis a bit further, the constitution of similar ideological forms seems to have appeared even before on the European public arena. This was at the dawn of the last century, with the ensemble of anti-materialist intellectuals that Sternhell has described as the 'generation of 1890' (1997: ix–lxxx): Gustave Le Bon, Pareto, Mosca and Sorel all participated in the constitution of an intellectual debate, a part of which eventually concretized politically in the Fascist regime.

A common feature of these historically diverse experiences is the recurrent anti-rationalist element of the discourse: a primacy of action and instinct that is constantly reasserted over reason and thought. The latter oppositional dichotomy is generally part of a larger critical discourse about the state, seen as a promoter of institutional rationality, which is considered to be bad. Specifically, the praise of unrational forces is used to sustain the idea that the political articulation of diverse social interests into left/right alignments is nothing but a spurious rationalistic mystification. In this view, institutional blocks identifying with left or right ideologies would only be superficial distinctions disguising the fact that there is only *one* interest: the concern of the political class (working together as a social class) for its self-preservation, and the conservation of its own privileges. Thus, one should reject all of the declinations of politics provided by instituted politicians and situate oneself 'beyond left and right'.[3]

Finally, and as a consequence of what is stated above, the practitioners of this 'post-ideological turn' often end up claiming to represent the voice of 'the people' against a corrupted and globalized political establishment that is not aware anymore of what happens underneath its cosmopolitan stratosphere (Friedman 2003; Mouffe 2005; Kalb 2011). What are, then, the social and political conditions in which these ideological formations tend to emerge, take direction and shape? Is there a specific set of structural variations that we can possibly identify across time, and relate to the emergence of these specific discourses? One common feature stands out quite clearly if we look at the historical circumstances in which those groups and discourses emerged: they all happened in a time of significant crisis and transformation of the established left.

If the beginning of last century was the period marked by the decline of the hopes Marxism had raised in the late nineteenth century, the late 70s are characterized in a similar way by the hopes the Italian Communist Party (PCI hereafter) had fomented. But when in 1976 the PCI eventually managed to accede to the governmental arena by supporting a Christian Democrat[4] Cabinet, the expectations of a positive transformation were left without answer. Less than one year after, it was the beginning of the so called 'movement of 1977', when spontaneously constituted groups and movements started a radical contestation of the whole political system, making little distinction between left and right. Even if we look at the emergence of more recently constituted political formations like Movimento 5 Stelle, or the Blocco Studentesco, we will notice how they all established themselves as relevant political phenomena between 2007 and 2008, just when the second left-wing government of the last forty years was turning out to be completely disappointing, once again, with regards to the expectations it had raised. It would thus appear that some kind of structural relation binds the crisis of the left to the emergence of political reactions that claim to be 'post-ideological'. But –we should ask – what are the underpinnings of this failure, and how does the latter come to transform the logics and mechanisms of ideological production within a given political arena?

The following chapter aims to focus on the historical experience of the 'Spontaneista' groups I studied in Rome, and attempts to isolate generalizable features that could help us understand the constitutive logics of movements that claim to be 'neither left nor right'. I will try to show how fundamental transformations in the composition of the labour force and class structure in Italy perversely interacted with changes in the instituted political sphere and in the mechanisms of political representation, in ways that dramatically changed the reproduction of ideologies within the social space. More specifically, I will show how the overgrowth of a post-industrial middle class corresponded to a process of alienation/marginalization of other subjects and groups in the public sphere.

Somehow similarly to what Lazar has indicated (this volume), I will use Chantal Mouffe's work to show how the removal of class from the political world operated by 'Third Way' postulations tends to be answered by grassroots feelings of outrage and indignation. It is perhaps not by chance that – in these two cases – these mobilizations are qualified as 'spontaneous'. The redrafting of social mobilizations as 'spontaneous' seems to rechannel frictions and tensions that emerged in the midst of conflicting class interests into a morally defined frame, and to 'naturalize' them. Here, nature is resurgent against culture and reason, since the crisis of class politics is also the crisis of the rationalities that animated its emergence, late in the nineteenth century.

Overall, I will try to show how the decline of the left and the rise of 'Third Way' politics tends to transform political idioms into moral ones, thereby eroding the egalitarian presuppositions of political representation, and reorganizing the ways in which difference is reproduced in the political arena.

'The Limits of Growth': Austerity, Clientelism and the Transfer of Economic Distress to the Political Realm

If the two years of 1968 and1969 had inaugurated – as it is known – one of the longest lasting and most violent and powerful mobilization cycles in the whole of the West, the oil crisis of 1973 would have hit even harder and imposed a structural, irreversible change to the functioning logics of the Italian political system as a whole. Only a few years before, in 1969, man had set foot on the moon, moulding an imagination of expansion of mankind into the universe, which seemed to have no limits. In 1973 the oil crisis would suddenly show a shockingly different reality. Italy's situation was, by the way, worse than anywhere else in Europe, since as other countries had already implemented restrictive economic policies, Italy was then trying to sustain production and growth with inflation and devaluation of its currency (Tarrow 1979; Crainz 2003: 438–39). In this situation, the combined impact of further inflation and general economic stagnation was meant to be devastating.

Austerity was only the immediate issue of this conjuncture. Class conflict was – quite obviously – another immediate one, although it unfolded in ways, as we shall see, that ended up eroding the 'class' part of it. A deeper and more structured way to look at it, however, is to pay attention to changes that were occurring in class structure. More precisely, with an observer of the day, I would point at the articulation between the transformations of the labour force in Italy and the paralysis of the political class as the epicentre of the Italian crisis (Foa 1976: 259–60).

As it is known, after the constitution of early industrial centres in the late nineteenth century, production in Italy nearly did not evolve until the aftermath of World War II. Then, the reopening of global markets, the demand of goods for the postwar reconstruction all over Europe and the European Recovery Plan sponsored by the United States ignited a vertiginous growth that transformed a substantially underdeveloped country into one of the industrial powers of the late twentieth century. This sudden expansion, however, did come at a price. Between the 1950s and the 1970s, a large majority of the labour force was transferred from agricultural to industrial production, undergoing a significant urban drift, and sustaining massive migration flows, both internal and external to the country. On one hand, these processes produced a massive reservoir of cheap labour, the winning factor of the industrial boom. On the other hand, this also created – through processes that seem similar to the Marxian primitive accumulation – pockets of uprooted and alienated populations, whose presence would help the capitalist classes to keep competition high and labour force costs low. The divisions between the established class of specialised workers and the new army of cheap, uprooted, unqualified workers produced the margination of the latter, especially in small-medium towns (Barbarano 1979: 188).

Simultaneously, the 60s and 70s saw the emersion and consolidation of a so-called 'middle class' (Sylos Labini 1974), based on the upward social mobility that 'the miracle' had sustained and on the progressive tertiarization of the economy. Part of this process was politically driven. As noted by Filippo Barbarano, municipal policies allowed the formation of a middle class of self-employed small retailers and shopkeepers, by the generous concession of licences, de-taxation and economic incentives. Abundant were – also at the municipal level – the policies successfully triggering petty real estate rent and the formation of rentier classes (Cervellati 1976).

Lastly, a number of observers have described the formation (and later overgrowth) of an unproductive middle class, whose employment in the public sector was generally driven by clientelistic logics of preservation of the block of power and of the social peace, rather than by actual administrative needs (Barbarano 1979: 190; Lanaro 1992: 340; Pizzorno 1997: 307). This was a politics that exploded throughout the 70s, partly as a means of the Christian Democratic Party to control social conflict and preserve its electoral basis. As noted by Donolo, 'the mediation within [different segments of] its own constituency became one of the main activities [of the Christian Democratic Party] and progressively sabotaged the capability of the whole political system to take governmental decisions' (1977: 11–12).

This overgrowing political/administrative personnel (Crainz 2003: 420) started to function as a social class in its own right, and reproduced itself thanks to the power to 'control the distribution of public funding, decide appointments, entrust enterprises with contracts, and strengthen clienteles' (Pizzorno 1997: 307). Especially this last segment of the emerging Italian middle class will play a major role materially, and most of all symbolically, in the fractures within which the conflicts, disputes and struggles that are the subject of this chapter eventually unfolded. The emersion of a class of privileged public servants, seen as the product of political clientelism and benefiting from the latter, could do nothing but raise anger during years in which economic certainties were disintegrating and a future of progress suddenly seemed to disappear to the many. In this context, the traditional sociological frame of working classes and bourgeoisie appeared to start giving way to new dichotomies. The expanding domain of the precarious workers, unemployed youth, dropouts and students, who could not see a professional future coming, was developing the feeling not to be represented any more by the political class, and they were harbouring their indignation at the margins of the political arena.

Parricide in the 'Old Left'

In 1977, turmoil in Italy was higher than ever because of a cycle of social mobilizations, which started in 1968 and would not stop (Tarrow 1989; Ferraresi 1996; Sommier 2008; Ventrone 2012). Particularly, as indicated before, tensions multiplied within the left as the Communist Party almost won the general elections of 1976, ending up with the endorsement of a Christian Democrat Government. PCI had never been even close to governmental power, and the actual need for its votes to support the DC cabinet was regarded as a great occasion for the left to eventually start wielding a positive influence over the administration of the country. The reformist attitude of the PCI had been raising hopes that – eventually – even the interests of the lower classes could be represented. Unfortunately, the government proved unable to create the radical inversion of a trend many had hoped for. On the contrary, it ended up 'burying the hopes of transformation, and making clear that the country could not go back from the ongoing process of degeneration and decline of public enterprise' (Crainz 2003: 545).

Within this context, a symbolic and devastating rupture within the left was produced by the events of La Sapienza – the main university of Rome – on 17 February 1977. There, the general secretary of Confederazione Generale Italiana del Lavoro (CGIL), the major general union, which was endorsed by the Communist Party, was chased away by leftist militants after a long scuffle with the security service of the union and PCI. As reported by one witness, a 'parricide was almost materially consumed when the general secretary of CGIL union Luciano Lama – one of the most powerful figures of the working-class movement – got expelled from the University of Rome. Just a few months before, this would have been an almost unimaginable act: something that was breaking into pieces all of the taboos and credos of working class mythology' (Annunziata 2007: 4).

The episode itself was bound to change the historicity of the Italian 70s: an 'event' – as defined by Alban Bensa and Eric Fassin (2002) – representing a 'rupture in intelligibility', changing the principles through which reality is interpreted and understood in the everyday. This foundational rupture was probably creating an irreversible split between the developmentalist and institutional left embodied by PCI – on the one side – and what started then to be known as 'the movements' (note the plural): grassroots, anti-institutional and often culturalist formations on the extreme left.[5]

The fragmented scene that emerged from the latter breakup was based on the original divide between those who thought they could sustain a project of social reformation, and those who had lost that belief and aimed at transformation by a radical rupture with the present. Within this context, the idea of an armed struggle, which would trigger a revolutionary process, gained legitimacy in the later part of the decade, and some of the militants of the aforementioned groups ended up joining armed organizations like the Brigate Rosse (Red Brigades) and – later on – Nuclei Armati Proletari (NAP – Proletarian Armed Squads) or Prima Linea (Front Line).

While it is clear that the 'Lama episode' was the historical epicentre that changed the historicity and the logics of political reproduction of the Italian left, it may be less obvious that the latter 'rupture' within the left was crucial also in generating powerful ideological transformations of the extreme right in the following years. It was after that 'event' that many political actors, historically rooted within either left or right social spheres, started questioning the 'left/right' horizontal configuration of the political spectrum. As an alternative, the political space was reconfigured through the vertical opposition between those who identified with the institutional order and those who did not.

It could also be argued that the emergence of the Italian 'New Right' has often been poorly understood because left-wing academics were reluctant, out of 'moral' prejudice, to connect it directly to the crisis of the old left. To our spatially organized minds, left and right are radically distant phenomena, and – in a very Douglasian way – we are not keen to accept any kind of mutual contamination (Loperfido 2013). Yet, there is abundant evidence. One of my former Spontaneista informants, Biagio Cacciolla, has been a central figure in the effort of younger generations of the right to claim a direct connection between the 'Lama episode' and the new course of their ideology. As a matter of fact, he has gotten as far as claiming to have been an active party in the confrontations between the leftist movements and the security service of the PCI/CGIL.

The presence of extreme right militants on 17 February 1977 was never confirmed, but what is interesting is the will of a young right-wing leader to identify with a major turnaround moment of the left, and – also – to rhetorically mark that moment as a point of genesis, the beginning of a new way of being a right-winger.

> In May 1977, I gave an interview to the newspaper L'Espresso, where I was alluding to the fact that I – all together with other people from the Fronte Universitario d'Azione Nazionale (FUAN) – had been taking part in the riots against Lama, at La Sapienza, Rome … In that interview, I was explaining how the ideology of the movement of 1977 was much more a product of our own [right wing] world view, than of the leftists'. The next day, our party branch had become a pole of attraction for right wing militants all over Rome and Italy. Now, one must acknowledge that we were dynamic and creative: we were curious about Pasolini, we were eating macrobiotic … we were looking with interest at the artistic underground currents …

and we were making ourselves known! ... As soon as I went to the central MSI[6] committee, people were mad at me: 'for Christ sake, Biagio, the press is talking more about you than about the party secretary!' (Biagio Cacciolla cited in Rao 2009: 138–39)

Several themes that were consolidating within the left movements in those years are prominent here as well: curiosity towards 'heretical figures' of the left, interest in countercultures, attention to nature and food cultures coming from the East and – most of all – a sort of antagonism between the actors of grassroots politics and correspondent established political actors.

Later on in 1977, some militants of FUAN also appropriated the 'foundational breakup' of the left and constituted an alternative genealogy in which the 'Lama episode' was inspired by an earlier one, which had happened about a decade before within the right-wing circle.

> One day, in Piazza del Popolo, somebody wrote a sentence on a wall, which became the symbol of that season of ours: Caradonna, 1968, Lama 1977. FUAN was the signature, followed by a Celtic cross. (Biagio Cacciolla cited in Rao, 2009: 139)

The name of Giulio Caradonna is known thanks to this episode. In 1968, some of the students from the extreme right had decided – against the advice of Movimento Sociale Italiano (MSI) – to take part in the universities' occupation all together with students of the left. On 16 March, Giulio Caradonna was the MP of MSI to lead hundreds of neo-fascist batterers in a gigantic brawl with students, which would force younger occupants from left and right to leave the premises of the university. For Cacciolla and his associates, this episode would constitute an antecedent to the 'Lama event'. Here – once again – the distinctions between left and right were obscured in favour of a stronger opposition between grassroots movements and instituted political powers.

Another informant explicitly told me about 'a generational accord for the struggle against the system', and then brought up their own little 'Lama episode':

> Many started accusing the MSI of being unable to handle [the situation] any longer ... I don't remember precisely ... it was after Acca Larentia,[7] or after another one of those violent deaths [of our militants]. We all went to the party [MSI] headquarters via Alessandria, and we basically smashed up ... we destroyed the party branch beating the crap out of people there, understand?! Because they clearly couldn't protect us any more ... I mean, I was troubled myself [by what we did], it felt unfair, but on the other hand ...

you had to unleash your anger against somebody, and – politically speaking – those people were our fathers, after all, they were responsible for us and to us ... so to whom are you going to turn to? ... I mean: our family was destroyed ... this is important: because our family, to us, were the [neo-fascist] comrades, the camaraderie ... (P., interview, 2010)

In all of those cases, disintegrating patterns of internal solidarity within established ideological universes seem to trigger a rather violent process of fragmentation of larger factions into smaller political segments, and to generate conflict among those. A general feature of this conflict was the breakdown of authority structures within political fields, and the subsequent transformation of internal logics of political opposition. Quite suddenly, ideological dispute ceased being monopolized by the conflict between traditional political opponents, which followed the horizontal scheme of confrontation 'left vs. right'. Instead, smaller and culturally defined units started to proclaim their autonomy from their established institutional representatives, on the basis of having a radically different relationship to 'lived reality'. To their minds, established political actors were living in a different world of privileges and were no longer able to protect or represent instances from lower social orders. Old friends became new adversaries, following a vertical axis of internal opposition between 'grassroots' and 'established' political actors of the same faction.

Spontaneismo and the Uncanny Effects of Fragmentation

This transition from horizontal to vertical oppositions points us to the right direction in understanding larger and more general transformations that were probably underlying the 'post-ideological' turn of grassroots radical movements. The breakdown of structures of authority within the left was directly connected to the crisis of its project: after a decade of economic regression and stagnation, 'progress' and 'developmentalism' had become increasingly difficult to sustain as the underpinnings of a political enterprise. With the growth of inequalities and social exclusion, 'social justice' was also on the wane, while the aftermath of elections in 1976 had made it clear to everyone that the participation of PCI in governmental action would wield no positive influence whatsoever. In other words, it appeared to many that the lobbies and established political elite were taking control and mitigating the influence of the left, rather than the reverse.

Just a few years earlier, Pasolini's metaphor of 'Il Palazzo' (the palace), describing the self-referentiality and inaccessibility of the corridors of power, had started to gain enormous success everywhere outside those corridors. But when the crisis of the left became evident, or – more precisely – when it became evident that the left was being integrated within the logics of vertical power, rather than the contrary, the arrogance of the political class was laid bare, and allowed to continue unchallenged. Grassroots militants from left and right began to feel betrayed by their institutional representatives – as we have seen – and engaged in internal conflict. The result was a widespread fragmentation of political organizations with the proliferation of grassroots movements, generally prone to violence, and opposed to both left and right established actors.

The constitution of Spontaneismo, and its 'neither left nor right' attitude, seems to be a sub-product of this process of rearticulation of the logics of political reproduction within the Italian system. The slow disintegration of ties of political solidarity within party organizations called for new formations, new alliances and new ideological postulations. The main groups within the Spontaneista galaxy were Costruiamo l'Azione (CLA),[8] founded in 1978, Nuclei Armati Rivoluzionari (NAR)[9], founded in 1979, and Terza Posizione (TP),[10] also founded in 1979. All three were animated in their political passions by a strong, unmediated refusal of the political system as a whole and, at the same time, by the desire for an alliance with the extreme left, in order to fight together the political elite. In 1978, for example, Costruiamo L'Azione group declared on its fanzine:

> We recognise our former mistakes and we are saying to leftists: wake up boys! Don't let them fuck you again, haven't you been the trained monkeys of the state for long enough? ... *Our enemies are the same and they all gang up against us, let's fight the filthy shit-hole together*! (Anonymous, Costruiamo l'Azione, April 1978, n. I, p. 1, my emphasis)

While offering alliances to the radicals, young Spontaneista militants appeared disappointed by the 'betrayal' of the institutional left:

> Only dull minded people would not realize, at this point, that the left-wing front ... is substantially siding with the [instituted party] system, since they have fully become a part of it. (Costruiamo L'Azione, April 1978, n. I, p. 3)

Third Position, on the other hand, indicated by its own name the will to overcome the distinctions between left and right, in favour of a total identification with 'the people', of which they claimed to be the only authentic representative.

Of all three groups, NAR was the more radical, and somehow a little different. It had consolidated as a group around the leadership of Valerio Fioravanti, who was considered the 'military leader' of the Spontaneista circle. They were all about violence and launched their 'political career' with the cold-blooded killing of a number of leftist militants, among other innocent people. Nevertheless, in a second strand of their campaign of terror, their targets seemed to change. Policemen and judges were killed, to demonstrate that the state was the enemy they were going for. Fioravanti himself started to preach for putting aside the struggle against leftists, who were fighting the same enemy, and thus had become potential allies.

Next to these more established groups, the neo-fascist circle, however small in numbers, exploded in the late 70s into a nebula of small organizations, micro communities and temporary cells. All of these were a real expression of the process of fragmentation by which non-established groups multiplied and engaged in an intense activity of boundary-making and endo-social practices. Especially the more violent groups renounced any kind of unnecessary relationship to the exterior, wanting to hang around only with the members of the in-group. But also more peaceful experiences like the Comunità Organiche di Popolo (People's Organic Communities), in which some Spontaneista got involved, were basically self-referential and represented a trend of disinvolvement from larger segments of social life.

This breakaway from society and sociality seems to have represented for my informants – at least initially – a certain degree of satisfaction and security in a world in which difference was becoming threatening. In this sense, this general fragmentation of political identities implied also a fragmentation of space: the Spontaneista had a very clear map of the Roman neighbourhoods where they could circulate safely as opposed to those controlled by 'enemies' or members of rival groups, where right-wingers, or even just people who looked like them, would run a serious risk of being beaten or shot. This was, of course, also true in reverse: the Spontaneista killed several young militants of the left, just because they had been spotted circulating in a right-wing controlled neighbourhood.

Political struggle, at that stage, was no longer considered to be about enacting a left- or right-wing social project by taking control of administrative institutions. The declared goal was to fight the institutional order itself, or, at least, to escape its gravitational field: its norms, rules and impositions.

From 'Class for Itself' to 'Class in Itself': Vertical Reproduction of Power, and the Rise of Violence

All of these groups were – in fact – denouncing a general verticalization of the ways in which power was practised and exercised in the society of their day. But, curiously, their refusal to identify with traditional ideological distinctions such as 'left and right' appeared to reflect trends of political convergence among instituted parties. Parties engaged in numerous trans-ideological alliances even though they did not always explicitly seek to overcome existing differences between left and right. The so called 'Governo di Unità Nazionale',[11] the 'Compromesso Storico'[12] between DC and PCI, the 'Arco Costituzionale' against extremism,[13] all represented – to the eyes of my informants – political embodiments of this trans-ideological tendency of the established elite. These were all publicly justified by the need to federate against violence, where 'violence' usually meant the Spontaneista people, or radical groups from the left. If it is true that these groups were often actually violent, one must also acknowledge that their criticism of political power struck sometimes quite close to the truth.

According to a plurality of accounts (Asor Rosa 1977; Lanaro 1992; Crainz 2003), the mechanisms of political representation were in fact substantially eroded already in late 70s Italy: the once different segments of political society had been assimilated into one another and categories like left and right were becoming increasingly irrelevant. As two observers had already noted in 1974, it had become very difficult 'to distinguish a Social Democrat from a Christian Democrat, a Communist from a Socialist, and even certain given Liberals from certain weakened Marxists' (Scalfari and Turani 1974: 9).

Chantal Mouffe (2005) has analysed a similar kind of transition in relation to much more recent times. Mouffe indicates that a movement towards 'a post-adversarial' mode of politics has been supported not only by the political convergence (and sometimes alliance) of the institutional left and right, but also by academic banner-men of the 'Third Way' like Anthony Giddens and Ulrich Beck. The result is the 'incapacity of traditional parties to provide distinctive forms of identification around possible alternatives' (Mouffe: 2005: 55, but see also Žižek 2000).

The convergence of the political antagonisms towards an undifferentiated centre had an unforeseen consequence – that is, the progressive exclusion (and successive alienation) of those 'marginals' of the political system that were once included in a much more far-reaching mechanism of political representation. This was actually deliberate in the Italian 70s, where this kind of rearrangement even had a name. 'Opposti Estremismi' (opposed extremisms) was known as the logic according to which the more violent and radical the extreme, non-institutionalized wings of the political arena, the more likely the forces occupying the institutional centre would be to keep their electoral basis and to consolidate their interests and privileges by reassuring a frightened middle class.[14]

This seems to be the context in which 'neither left nor right' ideas and ideologies find meaningfulness and political momentum. They, in fact, bypass the trap of opposed extremisms by declaring the dichotomy 'right/left' obsolete and channelling the emotionality of their critique against the political establishment as a whole. They establish themselves in the political arena – quite paradoxically, one could say – as responses to the uniformization of political and social differences between the established left and right. Their aim is to collect the support of those left out by the shrinking mechanism of representation. These groups claim to represent a 'post-ideological' form of politics that is curiously similar to the political convergence of the parties they contest. Nevertheless, if the former promote a 'post adversarial' ideal, the latter rearticulate conflict and heated forms of political opposition as their basic operational modes.

As Italy shows, this particular realignment of power is not new in itself and tends to appear in socially and historically situated circumstances. Looking at these would allow us to make the connection with particular social and economic transformations that might be involved in the formation to these political epiphenomena. In this regard, what Mouffe fails to grasp – while focusing only on the political level – is that there are social processes of class transformation underlying the political transition to the 'post-ideological mode'; I believe the early case of Italy helps us make these processes more visible.

Again in one of the 'Costruiamo l'Azione' mimeographs, we can read: 'The masters Agnelli and Berlinguer, along with their servants, are plotting together to criminalize every substantial opposition' (Anonymous, Costruiamo l'Azione, April 1978, n. I, p. 1). Identified with 'the masters' here, are Berlinguer, the general secretary of the PCI, and Agnelli, the owner of Fiat (the biggest industry in the country), and later president of the Confederation of Industrialists. It is important to note that the quote is not simply a denunciation of the connivance between people that are meant to represent left and the right. In that case, Andreotti (then the Christian Democrat Prime Minister backed by the Communist Party), and not Agnelli, would be standing together with Berlinguer. The condemnation of an alliance between the major industrialist of the country and the secretary of the major 'working class party' decries, in fact, a relevant transformation of class interests. These are articulated through political positionalities that were once (but are clearly not any longer) considered to be the expression of solidarities internal to, and consistent with, class structure. But to denounce the betrayal of these internal solidarities is also to renounce them. The latter mechanism seems, thus, to implicate the dis-integration and dis-articulation of the internal sodalities of class, at least at the representational level. It is a process that opens up symbolic room and opportunities for the formation of inter-class and intra-class alliances at the political level, ending up with the quite likely formation of class, subclass and intra-class new clusterings.

In relation to the Italian case, Scalfari and Turani have noted how – in those years – a commonality of interests between the ruling elite and the liberal bourgeoisie had created a 'new class' that they termed 'state bourgeoisie'. Massimo Paci gave a sociologically detailed description of these new social formations:

> The industrial bourgeoisie has attended the emergence of a new 'financial bourgeoisie', with which it has only partially integrated. On the other hand, the latter has engaged in a rather tight partnership – in terms of speculative business – with the governmental political class, this one itself appearing to have recently become a social class on its own terms. (Paci 1996: 701)

The obvious outcome of these processes of change is what Strathern has described as a disintegration of the class paradigm, understood here as the framework of social meaning upon which our socially situated 'point of view' rests (Strathern 1992: 142). Wolf has shown – in a powerful exploration of the relationships between power and meaning – how a new social axiom (or 'framework of meaning', in Strathern's terms) enters into conflict with an old one and thereby it also challenges 'the fundamental categories that empower its dynamics' (Wolf 1990: 593). In this sense, a 'logico-aesthetic [dis]-integration' of the categorical order is likely to mirror the disintegration of class sodalities, and change the nature and subject of more general discourses that animate social life.

In Italy, for example, reference to the 'working class', common during the 70s, seems to have progressively disappeared, not only from the discourse of its traditional adversaries, but also – Guido

Crainz notes (2003: 563) – from the narratives of the political left itself. More radical groups, especially the ones derived from the experience of Operaismo (workerism, see above), had somehow tried to resist this tendency. They were, in fact, attempting to formulate a more inclusive idea of 'working class', where unemployed people, students, housewives and off the books labour were also seen as its constitutive elements. However, the breakdown of authority structures within the internal cosmos of the left (with the explosion of competition between different segments of the latter and, more generally, the opposition between instituted and grassroots formations) appeared to impede the transmission of instances that had emerged 'below' to the upper – instituted – block. At the same time, even within the extreme left, competition was high, and political positioning very diverse. Fringes of the radical groups decided on armed struggle, whereas other fringes, like the aforementioned 'creative wing',[15] were rechannelling the expression of their dissent into artistic performances and lifestyles. In this confused situation, when the radical left tried to federate and challenge PCI hegemony at the institutional level by taking part in the 1976 elections as a political party, it was faced with disastrous electoral results. Despite the enduring success of the theoretical tools that the workerist experience had produced, what was left of it as its offspring of political formations came, there, at an end (Filippini 2011). Class struggle seemed about to be won, but not by those who had initiated it in their attempt to establish welfare rights and social justice for 'the people'.

The category of 'the people' was largely present in public discourses of the 70s, but nowadays is nowhere to be found, claims the French journalist Eric Conan. Not only in politics, but also when it comes to art, literature and cinema, the 'working class', once almost over-represented as a subject, has today basically disappeared (Conan 2004). Others have noted how 'the cultural and political removal of working classes [from public debates] has permitted to establish the image of a pacified society, hegemonized by the middle class and fully consensual. The invisibility of the working class evacuates the very idea of conflict' (Guilluy 2010: 9).

'Conflict' is then brought back into the public sphere by the fury of 'neither left nor right' ideologists, with an animosity that one of the editors of this collection has previously labelled – quoting Slavoj Žižek – as 'the return of the repressed'. 'Class' is, of course, the repressed:

> The workings, effects, exploitations and humiliations of class are the repressed and denied but never forgotten trauma that expresses itself in neo-nationalist populism, as the wider public culture of neoliberal growth, gentrification, and cosmopolitan class formation denies its denizens the availability of the language of class. (Kalb 2011: 14)

The latter process is also evident in the ethnographic record I was able to collect in the field. 'C.' – for example – was one of the more active Spontaneistas in the late 70s, one of those who drove the whole scene into a spiral of violence. In the effort of spelling out his life history, he shows how the transformations of a world that is no longer organized around a class-based paradigm triggered a significant rearticulation of the principles through which a life is planned, thought of and lived through. This seems to be true even for somebody like him, who clearly did not sit on the left side of the political arena at that time.

> the divide started between those who still believed in 'the future of labour', and those who had begun to refuse this view. Among people of my age there was a kind of opposition: ... some believed that our society would have been functioning well in any case, and thus they aimed at finding a girl, getting married as soon as they could, and creating a family. Some others believed they could look at things in a different way ... On the one side, people felt free to do whatever they liked, or at least they knew they had just to follow their own interests; whereas, on the other side, people were still expecting things to always follow the same scheme, because 'it is like that, it's always been, and so it will be forever'. (C., interview)

The inability to identify with a future based on the expansion of labour seems to be pushing life structures into new shapes and organizational principles. C.'s description of a dichotomized social life, based on generational difference, only confirms the fact that these variations are the expression of a change in the logics of social and political reproduction of the system. The class paradigm not only disappears from the discourse of the younger ones, but is basically rejected by them, despite the fact that they appear as the very victims of its dissolution. The predicament of the younger generations becomes 'to follow one's own interests'– that is, to engage in a process of individualization of interests, which they refuse to frame in a class paradigm.

In this sense, the violence produced by Spontaneista groups (as well as radicals on the left) can be understood as the 'class conflict' minus the class paradigm: an aggressiveness, in Freudian terms, which could no longer be expressed in an organized manner.

Conclusions

The overgrowth of a post-industrial middle class coupled with the progressive dis-integration of the remnants of the industrial working class seems to have encouraged a process of dichotomization of social/political identifications. Here the principal distinction is no longer related to one's position within the worlds of labour, but simply to having or not a stable occupation, and thus 'before being above or below in the social hierarchy, one is included or excluded' (Sue 1994: 219).

The political rearticulation of these processes of social transformation is one that claims to be not only a-political, but anti-political. Spontaneista movements claimed to represent the end of ideologies and to have buried politics. As our informant once mentioned to me, 'the goal [of political conflict] is no longer to get a higher salary, or to be integrated into a higher system of privileges, but is an affirmation of identity, ... while at the same time representing a rupture with the social structure in its totality' (C. interview, 15).

Identity, and the expression of the self, often interpreted as the enactment of a lifestyle, a form of behaviour, a praxis, seem to overrule class as a social paradigm. As Holmes (2000) has shown, style can become an aestheticized basis of solidarity in the wake of the dis-integration of larger axioms of social behaviour. In this sense, I hope I was able to show how the proliferation of 'styles' as markers of difference is directly related to the verticalization of power and its logics of reproduction. They are, of course, expressions of 'a fierce antagonism toward the respectable "settled" society amid which [their practitioners] live as persecuted aliens' (Herbert 1991: 249), but are also a source of satisfaction produced by the reintegration of impaired and alienated subjects into larger fields of belonging.

The sociologist Marco Revelli also seems to see the verticalization of politics as the origin of the 'neither left nor right' politics of the 'Rakes Movement':

> politics are banned from the order of the discourse. Too deep is the abyss that has representatives and represented, between the language spoken 'above' and the vernacular spoken 'below'. Too vulgar has been the exodus of the left, of the entire left, from the spaces of life. (Marco Revelli, Il Manifesto, 12.12.2013)

In a political universe in which lower segments of society do not feel represented anywhere by those who are in power, class does not fit any longer as the social-organizational paradigm through which sovereignty can be practised and articulated into politics. One could note – en passant – how the slow disappearance of class as a relevant political category has weirdly corresponded to the progressive expansion of a discourse on 'civility'. Since the 80s, the growing categorical hegemony of notions like 'the civil society', 'civil' or 'human' rights seems to include implicit references to what is considered 'not' to be so. Once again, similar processes were happening during the Italian 70s as well: the established society defined itself more and more in opposition to an expanding domain of alienated outsiders. Even one of the leaders of the Italian Communist Party (PCI), for example, stated in 1974 that 'out of the party system, within the actual social reality of our country, there's nothing but authoritarianism and dictatorship' (Cossutta 1974: 107).

Asor Rosa (1977) foresaw the descent of these processes into essentialized political categories, thereby establishing the representation of politically situated alternatives as the expression of voices of 'two different societies'. In this view, the 'two societies' look at each other as alien entities, each threatening to disintegrate the other, in order to satisfy its own needs. On the one hand, the established society of warranted people recategorizes its own drop-outs and outsiders as dangerous criminals, uncivil or undemocratic. On the other hand, the outsiders tend to federate while reappropriating the category of 'the people' as a unifying symbol capable of overcoming the old distinctions between left and right. As in the opposite case, this also happens via a moral essentialization of the 'other' against which the unwarranted society defines itself: the established society (Asor Rosa 1977: 63–68).

In this frame, the progressive renunciation of the possibility of playing an adversarial conception of politics organized around class lines seems to force changing structures of sociality into a polarized mode of behaviour where social conflict and negotiation among peers are repressed by means of moral classification of the adversary. This leads to a paralysis of the 'adversarial model of politics' through which sovereignty is usually negotiated and expressed in democratic systems (Mouffe 2005).

While generally subscribing to Mouffe's analysis, I have tried to make an argument against an understanding of these changes as simply political. The Italian case shows how processes of social verticalization are not separable from these political transformations. What we saw in Italy in the 70s (and I believe we increasingly see in the present day) is a process of disintegration of life structures in which impaired subjects search for security while trying to integrate themselves into collectivities that, not relying on class any longer, can only define themselves in aesthetic/cultural terms.

To sum up, the crisis of the left in the Italian 70s triggered a process of redefinition of the mechanisms of social reproduction in the entire political system. Specifically, the left's failure to represent instances from lower segments of the social ladder opened up space for a verticalization of society in which instituted powers found themselves no longer in need of legitimation from below. This created in turn the decline of class as the paradigm organizing political confrontations, on the one hand, while it fostered – on the other – angers that could no longer be expressed through class politics. The result, yesterday as today, appears to be an exclusive logic of political participation whose fundamental divide is between (those who see themselves as) 'established' and 'outsiders' of the political system. Here, the very logic of confrontation changes: it is not any longer about seeing one's argument prevail over the other's, but about disqualifying the moral legitimacy of the other as an interlocutor.

Within this context, both the established and outsiders tend to develop logico-aesthetic apparatuses asserting the increasing irrelevance of left and right categories, while producing 'neither left nor right' ideological patterns and formations ('Third Position', 'The Third Way', the 'Neue Mitte', etc.). As we have seen, 'neither left nor right' politics succeed in erasing the class paradigm (and, progressively, class consciousness) from public debates, but also seem to enhance processes of fragmentation of the social/political world, where emotionally charged systems of incommensurable values divide rich and poor, rooted and uprooted (Holmes 2000: 112).

There – to my mind – lies the problem with these ideologies, be they grassroots or instituted: the incommensurability of diversity they end up postulating makes mutual recognition impossible and political negotiation vain, leaving violence (be it symbolic, physical, or even just ideological) as a dangerous option looming in the background.

Giacomo Loperfido is a member of GER (Group d'Estudis de Reciprocitat), Spain, and affiliated to the SarchI Chair for Social Change at Fort Hare University, South Africa. He is the editor of *Extremism, Society, and the State* (2022) and co-editor of *Populism and Conspiracy Theory. Case studies and Theoretical Perspectives* (2025). His monograph, *Power, the People, and the Stories about Them. Populism and*

Conspiracy Theory within the Italian 5 Star Movement is forthcoming in this series with Berghahn Books.

Notes

1. 'Neither left nor right: we're only free minds'.
2. 'Fuck-off Day'.
3. For a bright example of these postulations see one of the foundational texts of the Italian new right: Tarchi, Solinas and Veneziani (1982). In relation to the constitution of fascist ideology, Sternhell has analysed the 'post-ideological' dimension of political discourses in Sternhell (1987 [1983]) and Sternhell, Sznajder and Asheri (1989).
4. Democrazia Cristiana (DC).
5. These had already had a long history of militancy within the area of the left. Since the mid 50s, in fact, after the disclosure of Stalinist crimes by the secretary Khrushchev and the violent repression of Hungarian revolt had exposed the authoritarian shadows of Sovietic communism, non-aligned political and intellectual formations had started to emerge within the Italian left. Central among these had been the journal 'Quaderni Rossi' (Red Notebooks, first published in 1961) and the group of militant intellectuals that animated it, a current of thought that subsequently became known as Operaismo (Workerism). A second journal – named 'Classe Operaia' (Working Class) – had originated from the former in 1963. This journal, and the people who gravitated around it, was the basis for what then became one of the prominent leftist organizations of the Italian early 70s: Potere Operaio (Workers' Power). After the historical experience of Potere Operaio ended, in 1973, a new formation was constituted from the ashes of the former: 'Autonomia Operaia' (Workers Autonomy), which was active mostly in the later part of the decade and was led by people who had been active in Potere Operaio (Oreste Scalzone, Franco Piperno) or both Potere Operaio and – before that – Quaderni Rossi (Toni Negri). Autonomia was actually a crucial segment of the organized protest that had chased the CGIL secretary Lama away from La Sapienza, in February 1977. 'La cacciata di Lama' (The Lama Chase-away) – as it subsequently became known – triggered also a process of internal fragmentation within Autonomia Operaia, making what was known as 'ala creativa' (the creative wing) more marginal, whereas more radicalized elements clamoured for the need to raise the level of conflicts (by which many meant a call to armed struggle). The seminal experience of the 'Red Notebooks' generated another organization, 'Potere Operaio Toscano' (Tuscany's Workers' Power), which was created in 1966 around the charismatic figure of Adriano Sofri. This was later to become the funding group of Lotta Continua (Continuous Struggle), which would be – throughout all of the Italian 70s – the largest and most important formation of the radical left.
6. Movimento Sociale Italiano was the extreme right party in Italy, founded in 1946; many of its active members had previous connections to Mussolini's fascist party. For an articulate history, see Ignazi (1998).
7. Acca Larentia was a foundational event in the history of Spontaneismo. On 7 January 1978, two young MSI militants were ambushed and killed by a supposedly

left-wing commando while getting out of a MSI party branch, in via Acca Larentia. Hours later, after the whole roman right- wing circle had gathered on the spot, riots arose in the neighbourhood, and a third militant was shot and killed by the police. The event collapsed old enemies and old friends into a single threat, and young neo-fascists reacted violently, committing a series of murders that targeted both the state and the left.
8. Let's Build the Action.
9. Armed Revolutionary Squads.
10. Third Position.
11. 'Government of national unity' was the government of 1976, when the PCI eventually supported a Christian Democrat cabinet hoping that majority and opposition would federate against the terrorist violence that was proliferating wildly throughout the country.
12. 'Historical Compromise' was the offer of a political collaboration that the Communist Party made in 1973 to the long standing adversaries of DC. The idea of a less confrontational attitude between the two major Italian parties was guided by communist fears of an authoritarian turn in the country (as it had been the case in Chile that very year, and would be one year later in Greece). The Compromesso eventually concretized in the 1976 government of national unity, and – before that – brought the two parties to less hostile political positions for half a decade.
13. 'Gathering of constitutional parties': it referred to the block of forces who had participated to the redaction of the Constitution. These were – of course – all the established parties of the time (with the exception of the neo-fascist MSI), and thus the expression implicitly excluded the grassroots movements that had emerged during the late 60s and 70s. Mention of the Arco Costituzionale generally implied a negative reference to the forces this expression excluded, which implicitly stood out as less civilized or democratic.
14. There were, of course, enormous differences in political behaviour between the parties at stake, and especially – I must specify – between the PCI and the rest. PCI remained, in many ways, the institutionalized political force representing the working class, and – somehow – its morality trumped that of the other established formations of the political spectrum. Nevertheless, a tendency of PCI to lose contact with its electoral basis was present in the minds of many. It seems quite intuitive that the rupture between the PCI and leftist movements subsequently pushed the former to increasingly give up dialogue with non-instituted realities.
15. This included small formations like 'Indiani Metropolitani' (the Metropolitan Indians), similar to the German contemporary phenomenon of Stadtindianer, or the visionary 'Gli Uccelli' (The Birds). These groups were often composed of people disguising themselves by using symbols of nature, thereby trying to translate their criticism of the political system as a whole into an 'expressionist' politics of life (in ways that are not dissimilar to Isaiah Berlin's use of this term 1976: 153). Politics were here translated into an act of art – of rebellion; they were aestheticized into the theatrical representation of one's own alterity to 'the system'.

References

Annunziata, L. 2007. *1977. L'ultima foto di famiglia*. Turin: Einaudi.
Asor Rosa, A. 1977. *Le due società: Ipotesi sulla crisi Italiana*. Turin: Einaudi.
Barbarano, F. 1979. 'Struttura di Classe e Crisi', in L. Graziano and S. Tarrow (eds), *La crisi italiana*. Turin: Einaudi, pp. 179–231.

Bensa, A. and E. Fassin. 2002. 'Qu'est-ce qu'un événement?', *Terrain* 38. Paris: Editions de la Maison des Sciences de l'Homme, pp. 5–20.
Berlin, I. 1976. *Vico and Herder: Two Studies in the History of Ideas*. London: Chatto & Windus.
Conan, E. 2004. *La gauche sans le peuple*. Paris: Fayard.
Cossutta, A. 1974. *Il finanziamento pubblico dei partiti*. Rome: Editori Riuniti.
Cervellati, P.L. 1976. 'Rendita Urbana e Territorio', in V. Castronovo, *L'Italia Contemporanea, 1945-1975*. Turin: Einaudi, pp. 337–78.
Donolo, C. 1977. *Mutamento o transizione? Politica e società nella crisi italiana*. Bologna: Il Mulino.
Ferraresi, F. 1996. *Threats to Democracy: The Radical Right in Italy after the War*. Princeton, NJ: Princeton University Press.
Filippini, M. 2011. 'Mario Tronti e l'Operaismo Politico degli Anni Sessanta', *Cahiers du GERM* 2: 1–51.
Foa, V. 1976. 'Sindacati e Classe Operaia', in V. Castronovo, *L'Italia Contemporanea, 1945-1975*. Turin: Einaudi, pp. 253–76.
Friedman, J. 2003. 'Globalisation, Dis-integration, Re-organisation', in J. Friedman (ed.), *Globalization, the State, and Violence*. Lanham, MD and Oxford: Altamira, pp. 1–34.
Guilluy, C. 2010. *Fractures Françaises*. Paris: Flammarion.
Herbert, C. 1991. *Culture and Anomie: Ethnographic Imagination in the Nineteenth Century*. Chicago, IL: University of Chicago Press.
Holmes, D. 2000. *Integral Europe: Fast-Capitalism, Multiculturalism, Neofascism*. Princeton, NJ: Princeton University Press.
Ignazi, P. 1998. *Il Polo Escluso: Profilo Storico del Movimento Sociale Italiano*. Bologne: Il Mulino.
Kalb, D. 2011. 'Introduction', in D. Kalb and G. Halmai (eds), *Headlines of Nation, Subtexts of Class: Working-class Populism and The Return of the Repressed in Neo-liberal Europe*. New York and Oxford: Berghahn Books, pp. 1–36.
Lanaro, S. 1992. *Storia dell'Italia Repubblicana*. Venise: Marsilio.
Loperfido, G. 2013. 'Du point de vue de l'ennemi: Négociation de l'accès au terrain dans un milieu néofasciste', in A. Benveniste (ed.), *Se faire violence: Analyses anthropologiques des coulisses de la recherche*. Paris: Téraèdre, pp. 79–117.
Mouffe, C. 2005. 'The End of Politics and the Challenge of Right-Wing Populism', in F. Panizza (ed.), *Populism and the Mirrors of Democracy*. London: Verso, pp. 50–71.
Paci, M. 1996. 'I Mutamenti della Stratificazione Sociale', in F. Barbagallo (ed.) *Storia dell'Italia Repubblicana: III. L'Italia nella crisi mondiale. L'ultimo ventennio: 2. Istituzioni, politiche, culture*. Torino: Giulio Einaudi Editore, pp. 699–773.
Pizzorno, A. 1997. 'Le trasformazioni del sistema politico italiano, 1976–92', in F. Barbagallo (ed.), *Storia dell'Italia Repubblicana: III. L'Italia nella crisi mondiale. L'ultimo ventennio: 2. Istituzioni, politiche, culture*. Torino: Giulio Einaudi Editore, pp. 301–44.
Rao, N. 2009. *Il piombo e la celtica*. Milan: Sperling & Kupfer.
Scalfari, E. and G. Turani. 1974. *Razza Padrona, storia della borghesia di Stato*. Milan: Feltrinelli.
Sommier, I. 2008. *La violence politique et son deuil*. Rennes: Publications Universitaires de Rennes.
Sternhell, Z., 1997 (1978). *La Droite Révolutionnaire, 1885–1914*. Paris: Gallimard.
Sternhell, Z., M. Sznajder and M. Asheri. 1989. *Naissance de l'idéologie fasciste*. Paris: Gallimard.
Strathern, M. 1992. *After Nature: English Kinship in the Late Twentieth Century*. Cambridge: The Cambridge University Press.
Sue, R. 1994. *Temps et Ordre Social: Sociologie des Temps Sociaux*. Paris: Presses Universitaires de France.
Sylos Labini, P. 1974. *Saggio sulle classi sociali*. Bari: Laterza.

Tarchi, M., S. Solinas and M. Veneziani (eds). 1982. *Al di là della Destra e della Sinistra*. Rome: LEDE.
Tarrow, S. 1979. 'Aspetti della crisi italiana: Note introduttive', in L. Graziano and S. Tarrow (eds), *La crisi italiana*. Turin: Einaudi, pp. 3–40.
———. 1989. *Democracy and Disorder: Protest and Politics in Italy 1965-1975*. Oxford: Oxford University Press.
Ventrone, A. 2012. *Vogliamo Tutto: Perché Due Generazioni di Giovani Hanno Creduto nella Rivoluzione 1960-1988*. Bari: Laterza.
Wolf, E. 1990. 'Facing Power', *American Anthropologist* 92: 586–96.
Žižek, S. 2000. 'Why We All Love to Hate Haider'. *New Left Review* 2: 37–45.

– Chapter 6 –

Rebels and Revolutionaries
Urban Mobilizations of the Kamaiya Movement in Post-conflict Western Nepal

Michael Peter Hoffmann

Introduction

The study of urban activist practices has recently gained currency within anthropology (see Smith 1999; Nash 2005; Lazar 2008; Harvey 2012; Graeber 2013; Karakatsanis 2013). In line with this trend, the anthropological interest in urban activism has increased also in South Asia (Baviskar 1998; Aiyer 2007; Dorron 2008; Subramanian 2009). However, much of this new scholarship remains trapped in a 'methodological nationalism' that focuses explicitly on India. Gellner's (2010) volume on the varieties of activist experiences – which covers areas other than India, including Nepal, Bangladesh and Sri Lanka – remains a notable exception, though still remains within a 'culture area' paradigm of regionalism. Yet, for urban small towns in Nepal there still remains a dearth of published scholarship, despite a vibrant urban activist scene.[1]

This chapter is based on eighteen months of fieldwork between January 2008 and July 2009 in the urban small town Tikapur in Kailali district in the western Tarai region of Nepal. It focuses on a large landless movement in the western lowlands of Nepal[2] – a movement of ex-bonded labourers (Kamaiya), who served as debt-bonded labourers until the Nepali government put an end to the practice of bonded labour in 2000. The decision to abolish this system came after a decade of agitation by a host of non-governmental organizations that together constituted the Kamaiya liberation movement.

After the government resolved to end bonded labour in the western Tarai region and threatened to fine landlords who retained such workers, many of the latter became free men and women overnight. They came to form a landless proletariat, a section of which would go on to organize a Kamaiya-led movement, the Mukta Kamaiya Samaj (Freed Bonded Labourers Society). Throughout the second half of the people's war between Maoists and the state in the period from 1996 until 2005, this movement captured public land in urban areas and rural community forests in the western Tarai region. In Tikapur, a local airport, parts of the University Campus and a high school compound were occupied and six settlements for ex-Kamaiyas, known locally as *bastis* (slums), were established.

Hence, long before the occupy movement began to capture urban space in the Western hemisphere, the Kamaiya Movement occupied and squatted en masse public terrain in urban centres of the western lowland of Nepal in the shadow of the Maoist Revolution. This chapter examines the history and activist practices of this Kamaiya Movement, paying close attention to the larger political context. In another publication (Hoffmann 2015) I have documented that the larger Maoist policy allowed this movement to emerge after the abolition of bonded labour in 2000. A section of formerly bonded labourers united and began to mobilize and organize formerly bonded labourers against the state. Thereby the Maoist Movement tolerated the emergence of this movement, as it viewed it as a 'friendly association'. Yet, the fact that the Maoist Movement changed its policy to the NGO-driven Kamaiya liberation movement led by BASE (Backward Society Education) and began to physically attack both its infrastructure and the movement's leaders helped the Freed Kamaiya Movement to emerge (see Hoffmann 2015). As a result, the Freed Kamaiya Movement (FKS) grew into a powerful grassroots movement amongst ex-debt bonded labourers. This chapter focuses on the FKS's organizational structure and practices, and offers a detailed ethnographic description of two urban mass protests undertaken by the FKS in 2009. I argue that such urban mass protests represent rituals of confrontation with the state that are intended to make the local government more responsive to the demands of the FKS. As I further explain, they are also emblematic of a struggle for visibility. I finally suggest that while the FKS confrontation with local state bodies resonates with the broader U-CPN Maoist aim of reforming the local state and there is thus an overlap of interests, the struggles discussed here are operating separately.

Stepping back from the specific ethnographic context, this chapter makes two broader analytical points: firstly, it introduces the analytical concept of 'rituals of confrontation' to better understand urban movements. By doing so, I want to highlight that public and highly ritualistic confrontations with the state can remain a legitimate and effective strategy for urban movements to gain and keep the state's attention. In the case described, the protests were more than just purely symbolic acts of resistance, as the Freed Kamaiya Society managed to effectively fight for compensation and resettlement schemes. This lesson might be important to remember against the background that in societies with a well-developed media ecology, activists tend to think of street protests as somewhat archaic and instead develop multiple channels to confront and gain attention from the state (Tufekci 2013). Secondly, this chapter also follows the analytical proposition suggested in the introduction (Mollona and Kalb, this volume): as I have outlined elsewhere already (Hoffmann 2015) the tactics of the Freed Kamaiya Movement were informed by the broader political context. For example, the movement of formerly bonded labourers shied away from forming an alliance with the local Tharuhat movement in the region – who advocated for a separate autonomous Tharuhat state – as some of the members of the latter had been the former landlords of the Kamaiya activists. Only through a 'realist' or political economy perspective on urban activism do such non-formed alliances between a working-class and a middle-class movement become more obvious and plausible.

Organizational Structure and Practices

Today, the Freed Kamaiya Society (FKS) is the largest organization of its kind in terms of membership. FKS chairman Pashubathi Chaudhary estimated that the total general membership of the Society was 'approximately 300,000', most of whom are illiterate and live in Kamaiya camps in the western Tarai region. While this figure seems exaggerated, the exact number of general members across different districts is unknown. Moreover, Pashubathi estimated that there were between 300 and 400 active representatives, with Kailali considered a stronghold of the FKS.

The FKS has a strong hierarchical organizational structure that is widely known among its members. Directives usually flow from the FKS central level down through district, regional and basti (neighbourhood) levels. In 2006 the FKS central committee established a women's wing, the Mahila Kamaiya Samaj (Women Kamaiya Society) and a youth wing, the Yuva Kamaiya Samaj (Youth Kamaiya Society) with the same hierarchical structure. These two organizations are supposed to communicate 'women's' and 'youths" problems to the FKS (though both were largely inactive during the period of my fieldwork). In this respect, the FKS organizational structure mirrors that of the U-CPN Maoist Party, which also founded a women's wing (All Nepal Women's Association Revolutionary) and a youth wing (Young Communist League). However, when asked, the chairman of the FKS insisted that this organizational form was a product of his own creativity rather than an imitation of existing political structures. To maintain its wide organizational structure, the FKS undertakes various practices that are intended to foster solidarity between its members and cohesion of the movement as a whole. The most central features included (1) a strongly centralized leadership, (2) frequent meetings and institutionalized 'awareness classes', and (3) the nurturing of contacts with NGOs and human rights groups and participation in external events to represent the movement to non-movement activists.

The five activists who founded the FKS in 2002 still serve today as leaders of the organization. As mentioned previously, Mr Pashubathi Chaudhary has acted as *adheje* (chairman) of the FKS since its formation. During this period, he has won two general assembly elections, the first being held in the general assembly near Tarathal in Gularia in 2005, and the other near Lumky, Kailali in May 2009. Similarly, Ms Moti Devi Chaudhary, being part of the FKS since its inception, has been committed to addressing issues of former Kamaiya and holds the post as vice chairman. Similarly, the co-founder Nathu Ram Kathariya is a central committee member of the FKS and chairperson of the district-level committee of Kailali district.

As a result of this continuous leadership by its founding members, the decision-making process within the FKS has become strongly centralized. Whenever the central committee members of the FKS call for a district-wide or western Tarai-wide rally, the regional- and basti- level leaders follow, and local leaders discuss important decisions such as the organization of a rally with the chairman of the FKS, an issue to which I will return in due course. More generally, the leaders enjoy respect within the freed Kamaiya community, at least from the worm's eye view of those living in the freed Kamaiya neighbourhoods of Tikapur. The latter trust that their leaders will make the right decisions for the Kamaiya Movement to develop. However, the chairman of the FKS is also aware that he needs to visit many freed Kamaiya neighbourhoods and discuss local issues with regional- and basti-level leaders in order to maintain the trust of the freed Kamaiya community as a whole. Pashubathi Chaudhary came often to visit the freed Kamaiya leaders in Tikapur, as the town was an important strategic enclave for the Freed Kamaiya Society to win. Here, freed Kamaiya had captured many places in the urban terrain and their fight was particularly symbolic (Hoffmann 2015).

The FKS leadership used frequent meetings and 'awareness classes' as tools in their attempts to create cohesion and solidarity among different members. From the early days of the movement, FKS leaders organized meetings with freed Kamaiya and advised new members to meet regularly and discuss local issues. In Dhangadhi (Kailali's administrative centre), the central- and Kailali district-level committee meets at the FKS office, which has been financed through Action Aid for the last three years. Regional and village committees meet within freed Kamaiya bastis. Their discussions reflect local conflicts, and often focus on how to secure access to potential 'donor' organizations or state funds for the rehabilitation[3] of ex-Kamaiya.

In 2008 the FKS also organized awareness classes (again sponsored by Action Aid) within freed Kamaiya bastis. A limited number of FKS leaders were told by the central committee to visit other bastis and give these classes to local inhabitants, with the aim of raising the latter's awareness of 'problems' within their community. For example, the leader of one such neighbourhood in Tikapur, Jagdhish, was told to pay frequent visits to the bastis near Vashini in order to give lessons on the nature of their poverty, gendered violence and how to pressurize the local government to provide scholarships by conducting a rally. However, these meetings were attended by only a small number of inhabitants (around twenty), which reflects the general view that awareness classes were only of limited use to produce solidarity among members.

The FKS relies on financial support from external donor organizations for both its practices and the organization of a variety of forms of collective action. There has therefore been a great need to cultivate relations with other groups and donors since the organization's inception. It was not until 2005 that Action Aid representatives began funding the FKS.[4] Moreover at the basti level, leaders seek material support by local donor organizations. But seeking support does not only mean developing financial links; it also implies that leaders should represent the movement to local institutions. Jagdhish Prasad Dhangaura took this policy seriously, representing the FKS in meetings at the Tikapur Intellectual Society, a local civil society organization that aimed to enhance dialogue between different groups in the town, and he distributed an Action Aid-sponsored leaflet of the movement to the local police station, the Area Development Officer and staff members of the municipality. This policy is intended to present the FKS as a homogenous whole to the outside world, thereby strengthening the organization's internal cohesion.

Staging Rituals of Confrontation with the State

Throughout its six-year-long struggle, the FKS leadership has resorted to a variety of forms of public protest in order to make their demands heard by the Nepalese state: these have included *chakka jams* (highway blockages), lockouts of state government buildings,[5] rallies through urban centres and public meetings. Of these various kinds of collective struggle, the ethnographic examples described in this section include a protest summit in Dhangadhi and a militant protest in Tikapur. These were some of the most dramatic and spectacular forms of FKS protest that I witnessed during my fieldwork. Others included assembly programmes in public and in the bastis (neighbourhoods), which, in contrast, caused little disturbance to the everyday routines in town. I show how the FKS used symbolic rituals of confrontation with the state in order to broadcast their demands to state officials.

Importantly the FKS mobilizes large numbers of participants from different freed Kamaiya neighbourhoods, as in order to demonstrate *ekta* (unity) and *shakti* (power) the numbers of participants is crucial. While numbers undoubtedly matter in many protest movements across different cultural contexts (for Japan, see Turner 1995:42; for Bolivia, see Lazar 2008), here the need for numbers is a result of conflicting narratives regarding how many freed Kamaiya currently live in the western Tarai. Although FKS leader Pashubathi Chaudhary estimates that around 300,000 freed Kamaiya are living in the western Tarai, the government holds that the number is in fact much lower (around 30,000);[6] there is therefore a need for large-scale participation in FKS demonstrations. In what follows, I begin with an ethnographic description of one such demonstration – namely, the protest summit in Dhangadhi.

The Protest Summit in Dhangadhi

In mid September 2008, the newly elected President of Nepal, Pushba Kamal Dahal (aka Prachanda) of the Maoist Party announced publicly that he would solve the 'Kamaiya issue' by rehabilitating all former bonded labourers within the space of two weeks. By November 2008, however, according to FKS President Pashubathi Chaudhary, the government had only rehabilitated 14,500 out of approximately 32,000 free Kamaiyas (families) in Dang, Banke, Bardiya, Kailali and Kanchanpur.

In October 2008, in reaction to this perceived failure, activists of the FKS hammered out a strategic plan of protest action in order to force the Maoist-led government to fulfil its promises. Rather than capturing further public property, as they had done in the past, they decided to organize a five-day protest programme, which took place in November 2008. This decision was made with the backing of all members of the FKS central committee. As usual, the FKS leadership expected its lower ranks and commoners within the Freed Kamaiya Society to follow their decision. The plan involved the organization of several protest rallies in villages and semi-urban centres in Kailali, where freed Kamaiya camps were established for a period of four days. On the fifth day of action, protests culminated in a large protest demonstration in Dhangadhi, Kailali's capital.

My experience of this five-day long protest week began at a rally in Vashini, where I met up with Daniram Chaudhary and Bishnu Chaudhary, two FKS leaders from Tikapur. A few hundred freed Kamaiya, mostly women, joined the FKS rally, chanting slogans for the rehabilitation of their people. After the demonstration in the centre of Vashini we returned to the basti, where the two leaders met up with Sunnita, a very tall female FKS leader discussing the rally with other freed Kamaiyas in the basti. The next morning, Daniram and Bishnu travelled by bicycle from Vashini to Hazimpur in order to help local leaders prepare for the next rally, a task that was repeated on each of the following three days. Then, on the fourth day, we all headed to Dhangadhi to make arrangements for the final large protest.

Arriving in Dhangadhi at night-time, we went to an abandoned building in town that used to belong to the Nepali Congress Party. The building was a hive of activity, with scores of freed Kamaiya arriving from bastis all over Kailali. Some people were brought in by tractors, a few took buses and the rest cycled or even walked to get to the rally. Women prepared food in the evening for all participants, and many slept in the abandoned building at night. Some used their free time to cross over the open border and buy cheap rice in a neighbouring Indian town. But as there was no need to get to know the protest terrain, most of those taking part spent the night sleeping in the abandoned building.

The following morning, after a *nasta* (breakfast) that consisted largely of cheap 'beaten rice', several thousand men, women and children from the FKS began to gather at a chowk (roundabout) in the centre of Dhangadhi. Here they began their descent along the main street towards the building of the CDO (Chief District Officer), where a large meeting with local politicians was being held. When the rally began, we walked in two lines through the centre of the town. Local FKS leaders were shouting slogans from a rickshaw fitted with a PA system, which the crowd repeated together. Significantly, there was no police presence, the constabulary being seen as impotent in the face of such a large gathering.

After marching for thirty minutes through the town centre, the crowd finally arrived in front of the CDO's building. Here participants left their organized ranks and began mingling and sitting down in front of the office. There was a podium from which the leader of the FKS, Pashubathi Chaudhary, and chairperson of Dhangadhi Town Development Committee, Tika Ram Sapkota (a Maoist Party district committee member), were to address those gathered. Pashubathi began his speech by outlining the grievances of the FKS. He warned the CDO that a new wave of protests and agitation would occur if the local government bodies failed to effectively rehabilitate freed Kamaiya. Furthermore, he accused the local government of failing to compensate freed Kamaiya to date due to 'conspiracy, fraudulent tendency and pretension'. He added that Nepal could not be described as a republic as long as Kamaiya had not been compensated. Sapkota welcomed Pashubathi's speech, agreeing that the lands of the 'bourgeoisie' should be distributed to landless people. He added that the land occupied by the airport in Dhangadhi should be given to freed Kamaiya, but accused Nepali Congress and UML representatives of blocking the land redistribution process. Because of rivalry between different political parties, the government had compensated just 14,500 of the 32,000 freed Kamaiya in the western Tarai districts of Dang, Banke, Bardiya, Kailali and Kanchanpur.

But despite Pashubathi's threats and Tika Ram Sapkota's promises, most of the participants at the rally did not seem particularly emotionally involved, in contrast to what one would expect for such a scenario. Instead, many of the ordinary participants listened calmly and remained seated during both speeches. Some moaned about the government's promises, which had so far gone largely unfulfilled, while others speculated that the slowness of the rehabilitation process was intended to disrupt their movement: by distributing land only gradually, the government was attempting to take the force out of their movement.

The leaders continued their speeches for another hour before the protest was drawn to a close. By this point most of the participants were tired, and many decided to go back home. Many had a long journey ahead of them. Strolling back through town, I met three freed Kamaiya from Tikapur. They had been to the rally in Dhangadhi by bicycle. It had taken about seven hours, as they had gathered firewood along the way. For those who had walked from Tikapur, they explained, the journey home would take some twelve hours.

Militant Protest in Tikapur

One evening in June 2009, I was returning to Ramnagar neighbourhood in Tikapur having spent the day at a nearby brick factory. Kaluram, the owner of a chai shop located on one of the two roads cutting through the area, told me that the neighbourhood committee had met and announced a demonstration for the following day, which all households in the basti were requested to join. Unlike for previous demonstrations, however, the committee had demanded that people prepare homemade *lathis* (wooden batons) and bring these to the rally. Kaluram told me that inhabitants of all other freed Kamaiya bastis in the town were also asked to take part in the rally, and he assumed that the following day all would join the rally. Kaluram's neighbour Tullu Chaudhary, the owner of a local rickshaw repair shop, who had joined us at the chai shop, added that the mood around the upcoming demonstration was serious; some of the basti inhabitants were afraid, while others, particularly the young, were eager to take part in order to demonstrate their strength to the leaders of local political parties. He warned me that I risked injury if I planned to join their rally. After more than one year participating in their struggle, many considered me a part of their struggle and were similarly worried about my safety.

The demonstration began the following morning at around 10 AM, with inhabitants of Ramnagar basti gathering near the burned-out control tower in the centre of their neighbourhood. There were an unusual number of people present, indicating that each household had contributed more than one person on average to the rally. At around 11:30 AM the first contingent of about forty people arrived from neighbouring Ganeshnagar; they were followed by many more from the town's other bastis. The square next to the control tower slowly filled up. Most men and women had heard about the rally through their neighbourhood *chaukidar* (neighbourhood watchman) who had announced it while walking through the area the previous day. Many had brought homemade lathis (wooden batons) to defend themselves in case of a clash with police. As usual, nobody seemed particularly concerned about the possibility of violence. Various individuals approached me to explain what they planned to do during the next few hours and what they hoped to achieve from the day's action.

Tulsi Chaudhary, an older resident and one of several *guruwars* (Tharu priests) living in the basti, explained the plan. Today was the annual public discussion of the municipality's financial budget, which took place in front of the municipality building; by demonstrating their shakti to the general public, the freed Kamaiya hoped to force local politicians to provide more financial resources for the development of their bastis. Accordingly, in the previous year the Kamaiya were represented by Bishnu Chaudhary, the leader of nearby Bishenagar basti. Despite his lobbying work for the freed Kamaiya community at last year's event, he managed to obtain a budget of 1.4 lakh for the development of six different Kamaiya bastis in the town. This, according to Tulsi, was generally considered insufficient, and the community as a whole demanded 10 lakh for the development of all bastis.

Others talked about the importance of having a large number of participants at this event. They expected several hundred freed Kamaiya at the rally, a demonstration of unity that would convince the Tikapur Town Development Committee and local political parties of their urgent need for basic infrastructure. Dipendra, one of the rickshaw drivers from Shaktinagar whom I knew, came with a lantern in order to 'give light to the politicians'. Two other young men approached me to show off their homemade weapon: a wooden rod with metal spikes. They wanted to be prepared in case the Kamaiya decided to 'lathi charge' the politicians. This kind of talk characterized the morning's discussions, and continued as the protestors began marching through town towards the municipality building at around 1 PM.

I later learnt that at about the same time as the Kamaiya rally got underway, a contingent of Maoist cadres and supporters had begun a separate protest at the inauguration ceremony of the municipality. The group gathered in front of a colourful tent where local politicians and municipality staff members were supposed to present the yearly budget to the public. Separated from the politicians by a chain of armed police, the Maoists were waving black flags at the chief guest at the programme, the State Minister of Power, Mr Chandra Singh Bhattarai. As Bhattarai was alongside people from the Nepali Congress Party, the local Maoist cadres and supporters felt cheated. According to them, one of the Maoist Constitutional Assembly Members should have been invited instead. Thus, every five minutes the Maoists tried to interrupt the programme by shouting a variety of slogans and waving their black flags in protest. Among the most common chants were 'down with the liar government' and 'the government is a puppet government', which implied that the current UML-led government had been installed by the imperialist powers of India and the United States. A potent mix of tensions filled the air, and many of the civil society spectators expected something to happen.

When the Maoists began throwing pieces of gravel and even their shoes over the armed police line towards the chief guest, the organizers interrupted the programme. At this point, the Maoists collapsed the tent where the event was taking place. Instead of attempting to defuse the situation, the Chief of the Armed Police began to charge the Maoists, and clashes soon ensued. At the same time, however, the 400 freed Kamaiya protesters arrived outside the municipality gates. On seeing this, as the area administration officer later explained to me, the local chief of the armed police panicked and fired two tear gas canisters towards the Kamaiya community.

As a result of police actions, a fierce street battle broke out between the AP and freed Kamaiya, lasting for some thirty minutes. The former attempted to protect the politicians and the chief guest inside the compound of the municipality by forming a police chain, while a group of a few hundred members of the FKS attacked the armed police furiously by throwing stones and bricks that they found on the street. The armed police contingent, being outnumbered but well protected with helmets and shields, tossed the stones back at the protesters. When a group of young men and women pried open the gate of the compound with an iron rod, a mass of FKS activists swarmed in. Brandishing stones from a nearby construction site together with their homemade weapons, the FKS members began to form a line to confront the police. Worried that my FKS friends would be hurt, I ran inside the municipality compound, positioning myself between the armed police and the FKS members. I had the idea to protect my Kamaiya friends by filming the clash. However, less than a minute later the police began hitting the FKS members and beating them with their lathis. At this moment I escaped, though I was nearly hit by a hail of bricks tossed from outside the municipality compound towards the armed police. Unscathed, I ran back out of the compound.

Following the clash, the freed Kamaiya regrouped in a field near the bazaar, where everyone was busy trying to make sense of what had just happened. Journalists soon appeared and began interviewing some of the freed Kamaiya leaders, who explained that several of us had been seriously injured in the clash. Together with some of the FKS activists, I rushed to the local hospital in order to find out who had been brought there. We found Kalu, a carpenter from Ramnagar, who was one of seven freed Kamaiya who had been severely beaten up. I also met Netra Adhikari, a Maoist friend, whose head was bandaged following a violent police beating. When I turned back to the city centre, many of the freed Kamaiya had begun to move back towards the municipality compound, where a two-day lockout of the main building was about to start. Local politicians had apologized to Maoist leaders and the FKS activists for attacking some of their members and agreed to begin negotiations with both parties. Tired and shocked, I decided to return to my house to take a rest.

In the course of the next two days Maoists and FKS members would organize additional actions. The UCPN (Maoist) announced a one-day-long district-wide *bandh* (closing down of markets, all businesses, schools and state institutions) to protest against police violence. To enforce this, Maoist cadres drove around the centre of town in a rickshaw double-checking that businessmen, schools and state institutions had followed their command. Only a few shopkeepers dared to disobey them, leaving their shutters half open to continue their business. The FKS leaders from the basti, however, were unhappy with the violence at the Maoist programme of the previous day. As one FKS leader told me the next morning, 'It was wrong to hold our andolan when the Maoists had their andolan at the same time. We still have to learn a lot.' Others were less upset about the timing of their programme and more upset about the attack of the armed police. After a meeting between leaders and active members in Bhulai Chaudhary's chai shop, the FKS decided to continue their andolan by holding a second rally. Again, members from all bastis gathered in Ramnagar before marching through town, wielding their homemade lathis. They followed the same route through town until they arrived inside the municipality compound. The demonstrators came by the hundreds, and several leaders gave speeches in small circles. The activities in the afternoon followed the same pattern. In the evening, a small contingent of FKS activists stayed at the municipality compound, while the rest returned home. The following day they returned to find FKS leaders negotiating with the local area development commissioner. The FKS had decided to propose a four-point programme. They demanded not only a higher financial assistance to the basti but also compensation of land, access to free health care and free access for freed Kamaiya children to higher education. However, after a heated discussion in the morning with local politicians and the local area development commissioner, they decided to cancel the programme. The local state officials claimed that their rehabilitation was a national issue and that there was little that they could do for them. The meeting ended around midday, at which point the leaders returned to the municipality building to announce the results of the andolan. None of their demands had been fulfilled, they had admitted, but the politicians had promised to settle the issue of their rehabilitation in the near future.

Struggle for Visibility

Given that the protests described above was staged in front of state officials in urban centres, media images of thousands of freed Kamaiya marching through these towns are crucial for negotiations with state officials at both the local and central levels. As a complete analysis of the local and national press coverage of both events – and of the FKS struggle more generally – is beyond the scope of this chapter, suffice it to say that descriptions of mass protests by freed Kamaiya rarely make it beyond the local print media. The struggle of the FKS remains largely localized, having been neglected by the major media houses in Kathmandu. Without question, this is related to the dominant media discourses in Nepal, which tend to portray the Tarai as dangerous and a hotbed for criminal groups.[7] As a result, both the peaceful mass protest in Dhangadhi and the militant protest in Tikapur received little attention, with the news spotlight instead falling on the emergence of criminal outfits in the region. In the remainder of this section I give a short description of my own experiences in order to illustrate how the Maoists attempted to support the freed Kamaiya in their struggle for visibility.

At around 8 PM of the first day of militant protest in Tikapur, I received a phone call from Saikdheja Chaudhary, the Constitutional Assembly Member for the UCPN Maoist. She asked me to come over to the Maoist office in town and bring along the video I shot of the pitched street battle between armed police and freed Kamaiya. Curious about her intentions, I immediately set off on my motorbike through the empty streets towards the UCPN Maoist Party office. Upon arrival, I spotted five Maoists waiting for me outside the office. There was the YCL district leader in charge, Akanda, Gorav Lohani, Saikdheja, and a further Maoist member whom I could not identify. When they spotted me they joked about my unexpected popularity – 'Comrade Michael, you were brave today in joining the battle with the police; now everyone knows on which side you stand' – before changing to a more serious subject. 'Can you show us the video of the struggle between police and freed Kamaiya?' Lohani asked. I took out the small silver video camera and we all began watching the tape. When he saw the scene of the armed police beating the Kamaiya, Lohani asked me to stop the tape. 'Here,' he said, 'could you please get a screenshot and send it to us? We want to publish it in our national newspaper to show the people of Nepal how the armed police in Tikapur beat up civilians.' I nodded my head: 'Of course, I can.' I then left the group and drove back home. Together with a friend I spent almost two hours trying to get a screenshot from the video. Since my computer did not have an appropriate programme I was unsuccessfull, and finally had to concede, somewhat embarrassed, that I would be unable to send the photo to the national Maoist newspaper as requested. I phoned Saikdheja and asked if any of the other Maoists had a computer programme that would allow me to get the screenshot. She told me no, thanked me for my support and hung up.

This ethnographic vignette illustrates that the absence of freed Kamaiya in newspapers and journals was related not only to assumed hegemonic media production, but also to a basic lack of appropriate technology with which to produce these reports in a short time span. In this context, the tactic of organizing mass protests in urban centres became all the more meaningful, as it is through such endeavours – as opposed to, say, sophisticated media production – that the Kamaiya struggle was made visible to state officials.

Making Sense of their Andolan

> During the first Kamaiya movement it was the NGOs who took the initiatives and mobilized the Kamaiyas for the movement. But this time the ex-Kamaiyas have involved themselves. Now they have become empowered and know that they can fight for their right. The government ought to solve the Kamaiya rehabilitation problem also to avoid that they only in frustration choose sides in the conflict and join the Maoists. Most of the former Kamaiyas feel that they have nothing to lose, and they are well aware of their rights not being fulfilled, so that might very well be a reaction. The government has to understand this aspect.
> —Yagya Raj Chaudhary, quoted in Action Aid (2006)

This quote is from the Dhangadhi-based Kamaiya activist Yagya Raj Chaudhary, who works mainly for BASE. The ethnographic descriptions of mass protests in Dhangadhi and Tikapur presented previously illustrate his core argument: former bonded labourers expressed their discontent about the state's attitude towards them through a range of forms of collective action. They denounced the passivity of the local state towards their situation, while at the same time their urban protests undermine the symbolic order from which the legitimacy of the authority of the local state was derived. Therefore, it is important to highlight how in Dhangadhi the FKS sought to achieve its aim by organizing non-violent mass protests, while in Tikapur the same association chose to engage in what the anthropologist Jeffrey Juris calls 'performative violence' (Juris 2005) in order to achieve similar ends. But unlike in Juris' description of militant black block activists at the anti-G8 summit in Genoa in 2001, FKS activists used this tactic not to 'capture media attention' (2005: 414), but rather to force local state institutions to be more responsive to their demands. It was clear to the leaders that Kamaiya obtained their rights at the national level through the Kamaiya Abolition Act of 2001, but the local state has been slow to acknowledge this. As FKS leader Pashubathi Chaudhary explained to me, 'the state here in Kailali is blind in front of us, so we need to force them through action.'

But why had the state been so slow to implement the rehabilitation and resettling of freed Kamaiya? Let us consider some of the common explanations given by the FKS leaders. First, it was clear to many that part of the problem was that the local government continued to be dominated by Brahmin and Chhetri bureaucrats whose families originated from the hilly areas of Nepal. As Tharus, Kamaiyas, who are classified in Nepal as a *matwali* (liquor-drinking) category of mid-ranking caste, had a significantly lower caste ranking. Hence, caste discrimination was one reason given as to why the state remained 'blind' or apathetic with regards to the Kamaiya community. A second explanation concerned bureaucratic incompetency. During the insurgency period, as one leader told me, bureaucrats were reluctant to visit landlords' houses to register freed Kamaiya. They were fearful of being caught up in the conflict between Maoists and the state, and so for the most part failed to fulfil the government's plan to compensate freed Kamaiya. It was said that even when they came to the landlords' houses, bureaucrats often sided with the owners and cared little about conducting the proper registration process to identify how many freed Kamaiya lived on the land. Third, it was clear to the more active leaders that part of their problem had been the political rivalry between representatives of the District Land Reform Office (DLRO) and the District Forest Office (DFO). Both state institutions had a vested interest in accusing the other of non-cooperation in the process of finding suitable land for freed Kamaiya, as neither wished to distribute public land under their command.

The FKS struggle was thus a struggle over structural inequalities (e.g. caste discrimination, bureaucratic indifference, urban exclusion), but several questions remained: why did so many freed Kamaiya participate in these mass protests? Why continue if the struggle had been going on for over six years already? What motivated the former bonded labourers to fight for a common cause despite the risk to their safety, as illustrated in the case of the militant demonstrators in Tikapur? The answers were multiple and largely commonsensical. As mentioned previously, the general policy of the FKS was that each freed Kamaiya household had to provide at least one individual as 'manpower' for collective action. Although the extent to which FKS basti leaders implemented this rule remains unknown, it appears that many of the non-leaders had been coerced into participating in the FKS actions. However, my interviews with those who participated in these events suggested otherwise. In truth, many participated not only because of their unjust and unfair treatment by the local state agents but also because they were aware of their right to obtain a compensation package from the government and therefore felt cheated. Sometimes people talked about the 'blindness' of the government, and many indicated that this had been a critical stimulus for the struggle since the beginning. Some also claimed that the government was 'still treating us like bonded labourers', while talking about their commitment using idioms that reflected the Maoist discourse of the necessity of 'liberation' of poor people. For example, one young FKS activist told me that there was not a lot of choice: 'Either we win our andolan, or we will die a thousand times every day because of poverty.' As another woman explained, 'the Maoists showed us how to fight. Now we fight our own struggle.'

For the leaders of the FKS, the six-year-long struggle had helped them to become more assertive and articulate. As Daniram, a leader from Ramnagar, told me in an interview, 'before joining the FKS I was very shy. I didn't know how to speak in public. Now I talk in front of hundreds.' Forging new friendships beyond the boundary of one's own basti was thought to be another motivation for the continued struggle. Bishnu, a leader from Bishenagar basti, attested to this: 'Like Daniram, previously I didn't know about the rights of my community. Through the FKS I learned our rights and I made many friends.'

For many of the ordinary punters within the FKS, being part of a broader network of freed Kamaiya also provided an element of pride and excitement. Unlike the old days, when NGOs advocated on their behalf, they now had their own leaders. Many noted how the FKS provided 'shakti' to the freed Kamaiya community. Many hoped that through their Constituent Assembly member, Saikdheja Chaudhary, they would be able to gain better bargaining powers at higher political levels. But there were also doubts among members about the FKS. In the privacy of their homes in the bastis of Tikapur, some complained about the Society's leaders. As one middle-aged man told me, 'the FKS is a society of leaders and followers and its leaders are no different from other corrupt organizations.' Nevertheless, this kind of criticism was fairly rare.

However successful the FKS has been for its members, its representation to outsiders (including myself) as a movement for *all* ex-debt bonded labourers was clearly overstated. In reality, it advocated only for those living in freed Kamaiya bastis under their control. Those who lived outside of the Kamaiya camps, toiling in brick factories, for example, or dwelling on unregistered pieces of land, had benefited little from the FKS struggle.

Conclusion: Strong versus Weak Targets

This chapter has focused on history, organization and urban mobilization of the Freed Kamaiya Movement, a movement of formerly bonded labourers in western Nepal. Since its initiation in 2002, the Freed Kamaiya Society has prospered largely because the Maoist Movement – which led a guerrilla war against the Nepali state until 2006 – tolerated its activities during the period of the insurgency and later 'captured' the movement through the provision of strong political support following immediately after the comprehensive Peace Agreement. As a result, the contemporary Freed Kamaiya Society became the frontrunner within the broader Kamaiya Movement, emerging as a powerful organization that undertook repeated and concerted collective action. This chapter has given ethnographic descriptions of some of the most dramatic actions that were witnessed during my fieldwork between 2008 and 2009, which included a mass demonstration in the municipality in Dhangadhi and the violent militant protest against politicians at the local municipality building in Tikapur in 2009. They suggest that, notwithstanding the threat of police violence, the Freed Kamaiya Society was very active in pressing the state to adequately resettle its community and support their demands.

Ironically, however, this strong activism has declined in recent years for a variety of reasons. Firstly, the different occupations that form the basis of the movement have been partially resettled by the government. With different communities being resettled, the willingness to support further demonstrations, road blocks and government lock-outs largely declined among the broad base of the movement. Secondly, after the Maoist government came into power, its leadership negotiated with the central-level leaders of the FKS several deals in the period between 2009 and 2011, in which the Kamaiya leadership finally agreed to accept a sum of 1.5 lakh in cash instead of 5 khatta of land as compensation from the government. This led to a general mistrust of the broad base of the movement to its leadership, as the sum of 1.5 lakh was often too little to buy sufficient land in urban areas due to rapidly growing property prices. Finally, after the elections in 2013 – with the old ruling party of the Nepali Congress (NC) – taking over once again, the top leaders of the movement saw themselves forced to restrain from agitation due to fear of police violence. The NC was perceived as having a much tighter hand over protests, and the Kamaiya Movement, like other movements in Nepal, saw the 'andolan' period as over.

Nevertheless, the potential for revolt by the Freed Kamaiya Movement continues to exist. By engaging in various forms of collective action, the leaders have not only learnt how to protest against the state, but have also become more articulate in the formulation of their demands and more self-confident. While participation in FKS events remains a rarity for the majority of ordinary freed Kamaiya, such actions do provide a source of pride and dignity that enables people to cope with the uncertainties and insecurities of their everyday lives.

From a Marxist perspective, however, even a re-emergence of a strong activism by the FKS would remain limited to challenge the contradictions of contemporary capitalism. This is because FKS protests continue to target only state institutions, such as the local municipality building, the land reform office or the office of the CDO (Chief District Officer). At the risk of overgeneralizing, one could argue that the FKS deliberately selects weak targets and demands more land for more ex-debt bonded labourers. What it appears to ignore, however, are the strong targets, such as the lords of local capital. They also do not interfere in everyday labour relations in town.[8] In essence, the actions of the FKS mirror Maoist politics more generally. It embraces capitalism by neglecting labour issues, but aims to eradicate the old 'feudal' institutions by providing access to land, which is not only crucial for obtaining a livelihood, but also remains an important local cultural symbol of political mobilization that the movement has to acknowledge.

Michael Peter Hoffmann is a social anthropologist with a PhD from the London School of Economics, based on long-term ethnographic research in Nepal. He has held postdoctoral research positions, including at the Max Planck Institute for Social Anthropology, Humboldt University Berlin, the University of Cologne, and Martin Luther University Halle-Wittenberg. His last book: *The Partial Revolution: Labour, Social Movements and the Invisible Hand of Mao in Western Nepal* (2018). He also holds a degree in Computer Science and is currently working as a research scientist at the Leibniz Supercomputing Centre in Germany, developing a research agenda integrating anthropology and artificial intelligence.

Notes

I would first of all like to thank the Institute of Social and Cultural Anthropology at the University of Cologne as well as the Max Planck Institute for funding me during the period when I wrote this chapter. Furthermore, I would like to thank my PhD supervisors, Professor Jonathan Parry and Dr Laura Bear, for their guidance and reading of my work. I would also like to thank all the participants who heard me present an earlier version of this chapter at the EASA panel on urban mobilizations in Tallin in 2014. Finally, I am particularly thankful to my research assistants Mr Pushba Chaudhary

and Kucchat Chaudhary for their help and assistance throughout various periods of fieldwork in Nepal.
1. For an account of labour union activism in western Nepali towns see Hoffmann (2014a, forthcoming 2018).
2. I will comment on recent developments of the Kamaiya Movement in the final section of this chapter.
3. In the aftermath of the liberation, the Nepali government promised to compensate the Kamaiya community through a rehabilitation and resettlement scheme. Everyone who had previously worked as a Kamaiya was promised a small sum of money and a parcel of land in the Bonded Labour (Abolishment) Act of 2001. The main issue of contestation, however, has been that the government neither conducted a survey to count how many people worked as Kamaiya in the western Tarai region, nor took the rehabilitation and resettlement agenda particularly seriously. As a result many Kamaiya settled on unregistered pieces of land and soon began occupying parts of urban municipalities.
4. AAN supports the FKS without any interference in the political decision-making process of the organization.
5. For example, in Tikapur FKS activists locked out the local municipality building for a period of two days in May 2008 in order to press for the allocation of public land to their community. Though I followed this event closely, its analysis is beyond the scope of this article.
6. For a detailed discussion regarding conflicting estimates of the number of freed Kamaiya, see Fujikura (2007).
7. In the post-insurgency period several Maoist splinter groups were formed that claimed that ethnic demands put forward by the Maoists were mere discourse. New ethnic militant movements emerged, such as the Janatantrik Tarai Mukti Morcha (JTMM), an armed Madheshi group, which were united by the principal goal of achieving ethnic autonomous zones. These militant movements could only surface and emerge in the aftermath of the conflict, with public security remaining weak and local governance best described as 'patchy'. The frequently cited 'culture of impunity' enabled these groups to gain ground. Up until 2010, not a single prosecution had been made for war crimes, and such a climate facilitated the growth of militant movements.
8. For an account of the everyday lives of former bonded labourers in brick kilns in post-conflict western Nepal, see Hoffmann (2014b).

References

Action Aid. 2006. 'New Kamaiya Movement: Time to Solve Land Problem'. Retrieved 2 January 2017 from http://www.ms.dk/sw32784.asp.Aiyer, A. 2007. 'The Allure of the Transnational: Notes on Some Aspects of the Political Economy of Water in India', *Cultural Anthropology* 22: 640–58.

Baviskar, A. 1998. *In the Belly of the River: Tribal Conflicts over Development in the Narmada Valley*. New York: Oxford University Press.

Dorron, A. 2008. *Passages of Resistance: Caste, Occupation and Politics on the Ganga*. London: Ashgate.

Fujikura, T. 2007. 'The Bonded Agricultural Labourers' Freedom Movement in Western Nepal', in H. Ishii, D. Gellner and K. Nawa (eds), *Political and Social Transformations in North India and Nepal Volume 2*. New Delhi: Manohar Books, pp. 319–59.

Gellner, D. 2010. *Varieties of Activist Experience: Civil Society in South Asia*. London: Sage.

Graeber, D. 2013. *The Democracy Project: A History, A Crisis, A Movement*. New York: Spiegel & Grau.

Harvey, D. 2012. *Rebel Cities: From the Right to the City to the Urban Revolution*. London: Verso.

Hoffmann, M.P. 2014a. 'A Symbiotic Coexistence: Nepal's Maoist Movement and Labour Unions in an Urban Municipality in Post-conflict Far-Western Tarai', *Journal of South Asian Development December* 9: 213–34.

———. 2014b. 'Red Salute at Work: Brick Factory Work in Postconflict Kailali, Western Nepal', *Focaal* 70: 67–80.

———. 2015. 'In the Shadows of the Maoist Revolution: On the Role of the "People's War" in Facilitating the Occupation of Symbolic Space in Western Nepal', *Critique of Anthropology* 35: 4.

———. (Forthcoming 2018). 'From Casual to Permanent Work: Maoist Unionists and the Regularization of Contract Labour in Industries in Western Nepal', in C. Hann and J. Parry (eds), *Industrial Labor on the Margins of Capitalism: Precarity, Class and the Neoliberal Subject*. New York and Oxford: Berghahn Books.

Juris, J. 2005. 'Violence Performed and Imagined: Militant Action, the Black Bloc and the Mass Media in Genoa', *Critique of Anthropology* 25(4): 413–32.

Karakatsanis, L. 2013. 'Political Frontiers, Parallel Universes and the Challenges for the Gezi Park Movement', *Chronos* 3. Retrieved 5 December 2017 from http://www.chronosmag.eu/index.php/l-karakatsanis-political-frontiers-parallel-universes-and-the-challenges-for-the-gezi-park-movement.html.

Lazar, S. 2008. *El Alto, Rebel City: Self and Citizenship in Andean Bolivia*. London: Duke University Press.

Nash, J. 2005. *Social Movements: An Anthropological Reader*. New York: Blackwell.

Smith, D. 1999. *Confronting the Present: Towards a Politically Engaged Anthropology*. Oxford: Berg.

Subramanian, A. 2009. *Shorelines: Space and Rights in South India*. Stanford, CA: Stanford University Press.

Tufekci, Z. 2013. '"Not This One": Social Movements, the Attention Economy, and Microcelebrity Networked Activism', *American Behavioural Scientist* 57: 848–70.

Turner, C. 1995. *Japanese Workers in Protest: An Ethnography of Consciousness and Experience*. Los Angeles, CA: University of California Press.

– Chapter 7 –

THE BRAZILIAN 'JUNE' REVOLUTION
Urban Struggles, Composite Articulations and
New Class Analysis
Massimiliano Mollona

The June Revolution that shook Brazil in 2013 took everybody by surprise. It started in Sao Paulo as a small gathering protesting a looming rise in the cost of public transport, and in two weeks it spread across 400 cities and towns, bringing millions of people (6 per cent of the national population) into the streets and forcing President Dilma Rousseff to start a process of constitutional reform.

For some, June 2013 signalled a new phase of radicalization of the 'Pink Tide' – a wave of radical political mobilizations sweeping through Latin America, which brought left-wing parties into power in Brazil (2002), Argentina (2003), Uruguay (2004), Bolivia (2006), Chile (2006), Ecuador (2006), Paraguay (2008) and Peru (2011). The tide reflected the massive societal mobilization against the dislocation brought by dictatorships in the 1980s and the radical privatizations and austerity measures pushed through by neoliberal social democracies in the 1990s. The main characteristic of this new democratic phenomenon was the cross-sectional and horizontal alliance between anti-imperialist white middle classes, the traditional labour movement and indigenous, women and urban organizations and the cooperation between traditional labour forces and the grassroots social movements that emerged from the World Social Forum (WSF). For sociologist Göran Therborn (2012) the June Revolution reflected a new kind of socialism spreading in Latin America based on 'ideological bricolage' and 'movements of movements', rather than on clear-cut class distinctions and the assumption of the vanguard[1] of the industrial working class as per the Eurocentric model of socialism. But are these bricolaged working-class formations truly 'atypical' in relationship to the Western model? The very idea of a typical Western industrial working class is problematic, since, historically, this has been consistently fragmented in uneven patterns of labour relations, ranging from wages, slavery and informal labour, kinship and cooperativism (Van der Linden 2008). Besides, the re-emergent communism in Spain and Greece is based on similar cross-sectional alliances and ideological meshes, but these countries are hardly typical of how capitalism articulates itself in the centre.

In September 2016 President Rousseff was impeached, ending thirteen years of rule of the Workers' Party (Partido dos Trabalhadores, PT). The impeachment followed the public investigation Operação Lava Jato (Operation Car Wash) into the kickback schemes of Petrobras – Brazil's mighty state-run oil company, the largest oil producer in the world. It turned out that *all* political parties received kickbacks from Petrobras and were involved in briberies, money laundering, misinformation and illegal tendering. The top echelons of the PT, including the party treasury and the president of the lower house, were put under investigation. The ex-president Lula da Silva himself now faces investigation. Thirty-five of Petrobras' top managers, including the CEO, resigned, and the company faces a $98 million lawsuit from US shareholders. With the Congress paralysed in March 2015, half a million Brazilians took to the street in anti-corruption demonstrations. These were especially tense in Rio, where Petrobras has its headquarters and main facilities, and the company cut 40,000 jobs at the beginning of that year. Unlike in June 2013, the 2015 demonstrations were led by the two new movements Free Brazil (Movimento Brasil Livre – MBL) and Join the Street, associated with the mainstream PSDB and to the PMDB parties and the business elites. In addition, the demonstrations included several smaller right-wing and even fringe organizations,[2] some of which advocated a military coup and the return to a dictatorship.[3] In 2015 the general atmosphere was one of indignation and anger against the whole Brazilian political system and there was also a generalized attack on the left-wing regimes that came to dominate Latin America.[4] The MBL produced the Free Economy manifesto, which proposed in classic 'Friedman-economics' style extreme privatizations, tax cuts and reforms to the Labour Code. The MBL's references to Margaret Thatcher, Rand Paul and free market economy marked an unprecedented break with Brazil's long tradition of developmentalism and 'cepalism'.

The crisis of the PT coincided with the broader crisis of the Latin American Pink Tide. In summer 2015, US President Barack Obama met Cuban President Raul Castro at the United Nations in a historical reopening of diplomatic relations and lifting of the economic embargo on Cuba. Shortly after, in Colombia, Tirofijo's Marxist guerrillas and the rebels of the Revolutionary Armed Forces of Colombia (FARC) agreed to submit to a legal process from a state whose laws they had never recognized. In September, right-wing candidate Mauricio Macri became Argentina's president, having heavily defeated the Peronist candidate Daniel Scioli. In December, the centre-right opposition, the Democratic Unity Roundtable (MUD) coalition, swept to victory in elections for the National Assembly in Venezuela. On the 23 February 2016 in Bolivia the electoral authorities announced that voters in a referendum had rejected the constitutional amendment to let President Evo Morales run for a further term in 2019. According to *The Economist* (3 September 2016), the end of the Pink Tide coincides with a new pragmatic turn in Latin American politics, symbolized by the emphasis on restoring the economy in the electoral campaigns of Macri and ex-banker Pedro Pablo Kuczynski, Peru's new president. In fact, under the Pink Tide, left-wing governments across Latin America renationalized companies and set in motion massive programmes of poverty reduction and urban participation, which empowered women and indigenous and black minorities and brought together the middle class, the working class and informal and rural masses. In Brazil, Lula brought together governmental elites and the lumpen from the poor north-east, turning the PT's vision of class conflict into his personal struggle against the rich – a populist ideology that Andre Singer (2012) calls 'Lulismo'. The Lulista model combined programmes of poverty reduction addressed to the poor masses and a new form of financial capitalism led by the cadres of the Workers' Party.[5] But this populist model ultimately relied on extractivism (Zibechi 2015), which funded vast welfare programmes from commodities incomes and land grabbing, and, according to Raul Zibechi (2015), co-opted social movements within a 'compensatory state'. The end of the China commodity price boom and the global collapse of oil prices put an end to the extractivist model. The most dramatic instance is the bankrupt Venezuelan state, which now buys half of its oil consumption from the United States.[6] The 2013 demonstrations that I describe below were an expression of a new anti-hegemonic and composite working-class articulation against the PT in power, whose betrayal of its working-class base and marginal constituencies had become evident around the time of the preparation of the World Cup and the Olympic Games (Anderson, 2016). I also argue that the demonstrations in 2013 and those in 2015 were expressions of different class interests – of a new emergent working class and of the old conservative middle class respectively.[7]

The 'Event'

The June Revolution started when the Free Fare Movement (Movimento Passe Livre – MPL) led a demonstration against the impending rise in public transport fares. The MPL emerged as a movement of poor and lower middle-class students in the year 2000, when it organized a series of road blockades across the country to demand free bus fares for students. This small protest by a few thousand demonstrators quickly escalated due to violent repression by the military police. This led to a second phase of the struggle, which reached its apex between 17 and 20 June, when the movement numbered hundreds of thousands people. By now the demands had widened and included health and education, and opposition to the Constitutional Amendment Proposal (PEC) 37, which would restrict the attorney general's power to carry out independent investigations, de facto eliminating an important anti-corruption tool. The slogans focused on the corrupted practices of the PT in government, once the icon of utopianism and of working-class power. The recent conviction of several PT members (known as the mensalão scandal), including from the top echelons of the party from the previous administration, cast a heavy shadow over the Rousseff administration too. It was especially the government's unethical pro-business stance in dealing with the planned sports mega events – the World Cup in 2014 and the Olympics in 2016 – that generated greatest outrage. As for Argentina and Spain a few months earlier, the slogans did not touch specific issues or parties but rather the whole political system – 'all that exists' *(contra tudo que aí está).*

Symbolically, the movement unfolded in the same streets of the city centre – Candelaria, Avenida Rio Branco and Cinelândia – where the anti-dictatorship movement, led by the PT, marched in the 1980s. On 20 June, one million people marched in Avenida Vargas, the modernist avenue that Vargas built in the 1940s on the debris of Rio's imperial cityscape to celebrate his workerist state. As in other contemporary mobilizations, the Brazilian movement relied heavily on social media (Facebook and Twitter) to organize, in parallel with the mainstream demonstration, horizontal gatherings, flash mobs and direct action targeting corporate and state buildings across the city. In this initial phase, traditional labour movements such as the PT and the trade union confederation (CUT) were absent, whereas the more radical trade union confederation (CONLUTAS) – especially bus drivers, mass transit employees and auto- and metalworkers – supported them. In spite (or because) of their traditionally conservative stance, mainstream media and TV heavily covered and even explicitly supported the anti-government demonstrations. But, at the apex of its strength, when President Rousseff suspended the transport fare increase and promised a constituent assembly devoted to political reform – as well as more stringent punishments for corruption and investments in transport, health and education – the movement was furiously repressed. In the favela da Maré, ten people lost their lives in a confrontation between the police and local residents. More than one hundred activists were jailed. The violence unleashed by the police and the army on that night led the protest into a third phase. Demands became more dispersed and contradictory across a wide range of issues, including gay rights, the legalization of drugs, abortion and religious issues, inflation, public spending and privatization, traffic tolls, and the national contract of public sector lecturers and bankers. For Saad-Filho (2013), the movement was now 'out of control', fragmented and radicalized, and captured by a strong anti-left middle class.[8] In this phase, the traditional labour movement also joins the struggle. On 11 July, the National Day of Struggle, organized by the PT, CUT and eight trade-union confederations focused on traditional labour demands, such as the reduction of the working week from 44 to 40 hours, increase in pensions and opposition to Lei 4330, a radical programme of labour deregulation[9] proposed by the government. This radical about-turn of the CUT, which had so far supported Lei 4330 in Parliament, generated speculation that the federation was trying to co-opt the movement at a moment of internal fragmentation. A more optimistic view holds that this was a moment of convergence between the 'old' and 'new' left. The Rousseff government responded swiftly to the mounting criticism against the government. Already at the end of June, the president had proposed a national 'pact' to reduce corruption and to expand public services, to be funded in part by the sovereign oil fund. Later, Rousseff proposed to call a plebiscite to reform the electoral and party legislations and radically boost basic health services. At least on paper, the democratic revolution had succeeded.

Scales of Capitalist Dispossession in the City

But how did a brooding political discontent become a full-fledged urban revolution? Some structural urban factors, including the political economy of the city, need to be considered. Reflecting the dynamics of foreign capital accumulation and developmentalism, Brazil's shift from the coffee economy to industry was marked by a spatial reorganization from Rio de Janeiro to Sao Paulo (Mello 1982). As a result, Rio de Janeiro is now overdependent on real estate and tourism, sectors that are vulnerable to foreign speculative capital and inherently associated with high levels of informal and exploitative labour. Tourism, real estate and finance rely on armies of cleaners, gardeners, nannies, porters, receptionists, butlers, drivers, sex workers, waiters, shopkeepers, street vendors, builders and rubbish recyclers commuting daily to the wealthy suburbs in the south part of the city from favelas and poor neighbourhoods in the north. But most people are excluded from these sectors and survive on even more informal and illegal work. Perhaps more than any other Brazilian city, the 'wonderful city' is an explosive mix of extreme wealth and deprivation – of drug gangs and finance barons, favelas and luxurious real estates; ancient aristocracies and brutal police corruption; of pollution, infrastructural decay and stunning natural beauty. In the 2000s, thanks to the dealings of the powerful governor of Rio de Janeiro, Sergio Cabral, investments in urban infrastructures and real estate boomed in Rio, accompanied by processes of gentrification and forced relocations of poor neighbourhoods – often dressed up as measures of police pacification. In this already dystopic socioeconomic context, some disruptive global, national and regional processes converged in the city at the time of the protest, magnifying it and taking it well beyond the demonstrators' original intentions.

The Organization of Three Sports Mega Events

The protest was ignited by what was perceived as an unjust and racist planning of three major sports events – the Confederation Cup, the World Cup and the Olympic Games – to be held in Rio between 2012 and 2016. Discontent started to arise in 2012 when the newly formed Olympic Committee announced its plans for infrastructural investments in the city. Transport and housing improvements focused mainly on Barra da Tijuca, a high income area with a mix of multinational businesses and middle-class housing representing only 4.76 per cent of Rio de Janeiro residents, while bus and low-cost train networks for low-income families were to be radically scaled down. In 2012, there were several small protests against the bourgeoisification and 'whitening' of Brazilian football, connected to exclusive TV rights and increase in tickets prices. When the Fédération Internationale de Football Association (FIFA) set the price of football tickets above the financial possibility of even middle-class fans, discontent turned into anger, fuelled further by revelations of FIFA's corrupted deals. As the FIFA scandal spiralled out of control, uncovering global networks of bribery and corruption, it emerged that FIFA had been granted extra-juridical power to preventively arrest people suspected of violence. For the Carioca football fans, vastly black and poor, FIFA came to signify the arrogant and unaccountable power of international institutions controlled by rich nations.

Increased Military Repression

In order to enforce the plans of FIFA and the Olympic Committee, the municipality stepped up evictions and police occupations of favelas (see also Livingstone 2014), with Police Pacification Units (UPP). UPPs are officially aimed at reducing the drug factions' armed violence and community control. In practice, they empower corrupt state militias and clear the ground for private developments and gentrification of favelas in the rich southern part of the city. Poor favelas are not targeted for UPP, or they are targeted only when they offer some potential for market expansion (World Bank 2012). In 2012, a leaked report showed that the Olympic Committee had already completed hundreds of forced relocations in the area of the old port in order to develop transport and touristic infrastructures for the forthcoming events. Moreover, the municipality gained additional power of forced relocation after it gained UNESCO World Heritage status. Thousands of families, samba schools, quilombos communities, indigenous centres and squats located nearby the Maracanã Stadium were forcedly relocated by the police, following the example set by Olympic committees in other cities.[10] In addition, new policing bodies (the Security Force for Mega Events, Security for Tourism and the Special Force for Order) were created especially for the forthcoming sports events. These paramilitary bodies were given special powers, including that of holding guns, preventive detention and the destruction of identification documents to curb fans' violence. But in fact, they were mainly deployed to disperse homeless people from the city centre or join the UPP. The pacification of favelas and of the city slowly blurred. On 20 June, the 'lawless Friday', the armoured tank used by the special police unit to invade favelas was used to disperse the demonstration. Public teachers gathering outside the Parliament in protest against the proposed reduction of the national wage were cordoned off and violently dispersed. The municipal police, with the help of military personnel trained in urban warfare, attacked street vendors in the centre and around the Maracanã Stadium, as Law 11 had made street selling and advertising around stadiums illegal.[11] After an officer was shot dead during a protest in March, special forces stormed the Complexo da Maré, killing ten people, at least two of them bystanders. It also transpired that the navy had installed ballistic missiles on the rooftops by the Maracanã Stadium.

The National Commission of Truth (CNV)

Perhaps in normal circumstances the violence of the police would have passed unnoticed. But these heavy repressive measures coincided with public debates about the military regime and about Brazil's unfinished transition to democracy generated by the work of the National Commission of Truth (CNV). The CNV was established in 2011 to explore various aspects of repression and corruption during dictatorship, the epicentres of which were Sao Paulo and Rio de Janeiro. Especially during the 'leaden years' of the 1970s, the military's Department of Information (DOI) assaulted, tortured, killed and kidnapped thousands of militants in these cities. In June, when the military police moved its armoured tank from the favelas to the centre and beat up and jailed hundreds of demonstrators, anti-dictatorship slogans and photos emerged from everywhere. Connections between past and present forms of state repression were made. A graffiti 'no to dictatorship' was painted on the state security department's new image centre building. The Legislative Assembly was stormed. MPs inside the building were inundated by text messages reading 'Cabral dictator' or 'happy 1968'. Thousands of photos showing street fights in 1968 superimposed onto the present demonstration were distributed outside the building. But as well as mobilizing progressive forces, the ghost of dictatorship created a state of generalized fear and mounting speculation of an imminent military coup, especially after the police and the far right were revealed to have infiltrated the demonstration and were involved in violent actions. Saad-Filho (2014: 239) argues that the fear of an imminent collapse of democracy was magnified by the media, thus bringing to the fore the moderate anti-corruption and anti-government agenda of the middle class.

Regional Politics and the Infamous Story of Governor Cabral

The governor of Rio de Janeiro, Sergio Cabral, was a skilled politician who had built a powerful regional block against the federal government. Cabral reached the apex of his popularity in 2011, when, with a coalition of businesses, parties, municipalities, unions and NGOs, he organized 'the oil rebellion' against the federal government, forcing Dilma Rousseff to increase Rio's stakes in the oil royalties. When Cabral announced he would run for the presidency in 2014, he stood a very good chance of winning. But, at the time of the demonstration, Cabral's reputation was tainted by several accusations of bribery. Cabral's good friend, developer Norberto Odebrecht (who had donated R$200 million to Cabral's electoral campaign two years earlier), won several major bids for developing the Olympic Village. In addition, Cabral had taken big cuts on deals he brokered with global hoteliers and constructions groups – Hyatt, Hilton and Delta – and with national crony capitalists. It was also revealed that he owned seven helicopters, which he used to transport nannies and his children's friends and even to walk the dog. Suddenly, Cabral, Eduardo Paes (the mayor of Rio) and by extension their PMDB party became symbols of national corruption. During 'Occupy Cabral', hundreds of people camped outside the governor's mansion in the affluent Leblon area for several weeks, demanding Cabral's resignation and persecution for corruption and misuse of public funds. In a dramatic announcement on public television, looking weak and defeated, Cabral resigned, pleading with the occupants to leave him alone. But this moral campaign against the PMDB served the purposes of the right-wing coalition, who used it to bring down the PT/PMDB governmental coalition.

Forces of Labour

In a recent *Financial Times* interview (Leahy 2012), President Rousseff declared her intention to 'transform Brazil into a middle-class population'. If sociologist Saad-Filho[12] is right to claim that the June Revolution was essentially a middle-class phenomenon, then the president failed in her goal. Saad-Filho (2014) argues that the middle-class consistently opposed the PT government because of its policies of income redistribution, poverty reduction and expansion of citizenship, which radically reduced their privileges and economic power. Besides, Saad-Filho (2014: 229) argues that Lula's appointment of trade unionists, activists and NGO cadres to the federal government effectively changed the social composition of the state, pushing out the traditional elites and aligning it with the interests of the masses. In this optic, the revolutionary events of June reflect both the political isolation of the PT and the democratic accountability of its government vis-à-vis its base. Sociologist Ruy Braga (2014) gives a different reading of the June events. For Braga, they were not a middle-class phenomenon but rather a movement of the 'precariat' – made up mainly of those young unskilled and semi-skilled workers who gained formal employment when the PT was in power but who now suffered from low wage, high turnover and exploitative working conditions. In its first mandate, the PT government increased minimum wage and workers' welfare, and formalized the labour market, also thanks to the favourable economic context. During the second mandate, starting in 2008, Lula introduced labour market flexibility and cut welfare expenses. Of the employment created during the Lula and Rousseff administrations, 60 per cent was taken by workers between 18 and 24 years old, and 94 per cent of them are on an income of 1.5 times the minimum wage,[13] just above the poverty level.[14] Such pauperization of the working class was a sharp departure from the PT's early pro-labour policies, including a 70 per cent increase in the minimum wage.

For Braga (2014) the anger directed by the precariat against the PT – a workers' party that was betraying its base – was the culmination of a series of actions that public workers (lecturers, bankers) and service workers (teleworkers) had waged against the government since 2008. Besides, strong regional and municipal anti-systemic forces were at play, especially after the municipal elections in 2012, when almost all state capitals elected opposition mayors. These electoral upsets seemed to mirror the heavy slow-down of the economy in that year. The term 'precariat' captures well the contradictory articulations of a working class pulled in different directions, with casualized formal workers on the one hand, and upwardly mobile poor on the other. In addition to these traditional working-class constituencies the movement had the following internal articulations:

(1) Composed mainly of young activists ranging from fifteen to twenty-five years of age, the MPL has a strong anti-capitalist

agenda and a decentralized, horizontal and pluralistic structure. Since the early 2000s the MPL have organized free fares for students across the country. They have grown exponentially but have resisted incorporation into bigger left-wing fringe parties and the PT, thus remaining leaderless and consensus-based. Around 2007 and 2008, the MPL shifted its strategy from 'free fares for students' to 'free fares for all', recognizing transport as a basic right to the city on par with sanitation, medical care and public safety. Subsequently, the movement radicalized further, using a distinctive language of class and focusing on transport as a nodal capitalist infrastructure and 'a means of spatial, social, racial and gender segregation' (Legume and Toledo 2011). Rooting itself in poor neighbourhoods, the MPL broadened its constituency to include black, women, unemployed and informal workers and changed its form of activism – from the performative and situationist[15] direct action of the early days to the systematic creation of study groups and neighbourhood committees. It was through this systematic work in urban peripheries that the MPL entered into contact with political parties, NGOs and community associations that were resisting evictions caused by real estate speculation in relation to the World Cup in 2014, the most important of which was the Popular Committee on the World Cup. By the time of the demonstration of June 2013, the MPL had thousands of experienced activists who had organized hundreds of street actions, occupations of public buildings and bus terminal and road blockades.

(2) The Popular Committee on the World Cup was an umbrella of NGOs, neighbourhood associations and human rights organizations formed in 2008 by white middle-class academics and legal activists. It progressively widened its base to include black and poor families as it moved to the peripheries. The committee was supported by professional associations (particularly geographers), municipal council cadres, the MST (Movimento de Sem Terra), the association of Rio favelas and the powerful Order of Lawyers of Brazil (OAB). The Committee drew on the already existing Right to the City coalition and the rules of participatory planning contained in the 1988 constitution and the City Statute (2000) to expand its political actions in favelas and townships. Already during the Pan American Games in 2007 the committee struggled against the demolition of homes in favelas and organized high-profile debates and campaigns. Besides,

based on confidential data and information on forced relocation, municipal budgets and extraordinary legislation, the committee produced the damning report 'Mega Events and Human Right Violation in Brazil', which had a huge public impact. The report showed that in twenty-one townships and favelas in seven cities hosting the World Cup, the state was 'implementing strategies of war and persecution, including marking out houses with paint without explanation, the invasion of homes without court orders and misappropriation and disruption of property' (Comitê Popular Copa e Olimpiadas Rio, 'Megaeventos e Violações dos Direitos Humanos no Rio de Janeiro' 2011: 11). The report also showed that a small number of construction companies, close to Cabral and the PT, were adjudicating most of the public construction bids for the new infrastructures.

(3) An umbrella of left of centre parties and unions, such as the Socialist Party (PSOL), the Unified Socialist Workers' Party (PSTU) and the industrial confederation CONLUTAS, recently split from the mainstream industrial confederation CUT. CONLUTAS had the important role of bringing together the traditional working class (auto- and metalworkers) and civic organizations advocating for labour issues – mainly against the precarization of service work – and for identity and equality struggles. For instance, it supported the protests by LGBT organizations against the grotesque parliamentary proposal to give psychiatric assistance to gay people.

(4) Anarchist groups such as the Black Blocs, the Independent Popular Front of Rio de Janeiro (FIP) and the Popular Revolutionary Student Movement (MEPR) consisted mainly of 'precarious' university students. These anarchist and anti-parliamentary groups and the radical left parliamentary coalition clashed continuously and often violently.[16] Mainstream TV captured young anarchists and Black Bloc activists looting and destroying shops and violently attacking the police. Many of them ended up in jail. But their politics were not always 'spontaneous', as, for instance, they supported the strikes of primary teachers and university lecturers.

(5) Subaltern formation of street vendors: the Movement of Homeless Workers (MTST); the Landless Movement (Movimento de Sem Terra – MST) and the Earth, Labor and Freedom Movement (MTL). Street vendors had been resisting relocation from the

centre by the municipal police for some time. As in Egypt, Mexico and Bolivia, the street vendors in Rio mobilized a huge social network that blocked the action of the police and paramilitary in the centre. The MTST and MST consolidated their presence in rural favelas and urban farms in the north of the city, bringing to the fore the voices of indigenous and black communities against the gentrification and social exclusion generated by the sports events preparation.

(6) Precarious intellectual workers, mainly service workers and public university lecturers. Since 2000, teleworkers[17] had strongly opposed the government's proposal of labour deregulation contained in Lei 4330. The telemarketing industry incarnates Brazil's peculiar mixture of 'digital-molecular accumulation', dependent industrialization and informal and indentured labour, described by De Oliveira (2003) as 'The Duckbilled Platypus'. Most of its female, non-white, low-income labour force is from a very poor background.[18] Telework offers them some labour rights and the chance to study at night. But even so, telework is alienating and on average it lasts only one year. Brazilian teleworkers and other service workers are traditionally described as 'the neoliberal generation' – individualistic, apolitical and 'economically minded'.

In fact, since 2000, they have been very politically active and have developed a powerful social movement unionism, combining demands for higher wages and other social and civic struggles. In particular, they have campaigned against unequal treatment of women, racial discrimination against black people and homophobia regarding gay, lesbian, bisexual, transsexual and transgender communities. Moreover, service workers and teleworkers have been at the forefront of the recent struggles against labour deregulation. The current labour system forbids outsourcing 'core' productive activities. Under the terms of Lei 4330, recently passed in Parliament, the core productive process can be performed by outsourced workers. This will allow call centres to operate with full zero-hour workforces provided by contact centres, labour brokers and temporary hiring agencies and to move from higher skilled, trilingual and technical contract workers to low-skilled, low-wage employees. Lei 4330 was widely perceived as a deliberate response from the Rousseff administration to international call centres' ongoing demands for lower labour costs and increased outsourcing opportunities.

The campaign against precarization brought together the traditional labour movement, including precarious public lecturers (who in 2012 successfully campaigned to have their wages in line with those of private universities) and various grassroots and civic organizations, especially young women, black and LGBT communities, who share the precarious conditions of service workers.

(7) The traditional labour movement. In the early stages of the protest, the CUT and the PT remained absent. They entered the stage as late as July, when they organized, along with eight national trade union confederations and the MST, a 'day of action'. Part of the reason for this delay in demonstration is that the PT and CUT were marginalized and attacked by the main coalition early on because of their support for Lei 4330. CUT, its affiliated unions and the PT have been traditionally indifferent if not hostile towards non-industrial and informal workers, even if this category currently represents 40 per cent of the labour market. Only later with the mediation of CONLUTAS and the MPL did the traditional labour movement and the other factions enter into a stage of mutual recognition and cooperation.

Thus, the variety of working-class articulations brought together by the events of 2013 – old and new trade union confederations (CUT and CONLUTAS), subaltern organizations (MST and homeless) and the vertical and the horizontal left (MPL, PT and PSOL) – was impressive. Besides, Rousseff seemed to have taken seriously the protest and to be truly intentioned to radically change the electoral system and expand public services. On the whole, it seemed that the parliamentary left had survived the crisis and moreover that the possibility of a new articulation between the party in power and the movement had opened up. In fact, in spite of the damaging effect of the events in June 2013, Rousseff was re-elected a year later.

Middle Class, Poor or Precarious?

So what led to the sudden collapse of the PT? Was it because the 'movement of the movements' was indeed led by the middle classes? The answer is not straightforward, because the political and economic threshold between the precariat and the middle classes is fuzzy. For instance, they traditionally have similar views on inflation and corruption, although they are affected very differently by them. Inflation is especially explosive because of the enormous impact it has on consumption. The PT in government had made consumption the base of the social contract, with its working-class electorate as well as the engine of economic growth, and achieved this by raising minimum wages, credit and transfers to working-class families. But at the beginning of 2013, the 10 per cent increase in retail prices hit the working class hard. Most working-class families struggled to pay back mortgages and buy food and basic services. The middle class was hit even more violently by the raise in the costs of services. By the time of the demonstrations, a vociferous anti-inflation movement bringing together middle and working classes had emerged. As well as the price of basic food, people lamented the astronomical price of durables and high-tech goods, due to protective duties and high corporation taxes. That inflation hit differently the working class and the middle classes is seldom discussed. Instead, broad and cross-sectional anti-inflation coalitions tend to emerge. Anti-corruption movements are also typically cross-sectional. In May, just before the demonstrations, the trials against the PT politicians involved in the mensalão vote-buying scandal had just ended. The president's chief of staff, the president of the PT and several federal deputies were forced to resign. The PT went through a catastrophic loss of support. By trying to repel Constitutional Amendment Proposal (PEC) 37, the PT in power appeared to want to neutralize the power of the public ministry and refused to be held accountable by its citizens. Left-wing organizations led anti-corruption campaigns as struggles for democratization. Right-wing forces and the middle classes used the anti-corruption argument to topple the government, as in the case of Cabral, whose party PMDB was a central ally of the PT in government.

Moreover, the boundaries between the middle class and the precariat are economically fuzzy. The World Bank puts the middle class at an income between $2 and $13 per day – the first is the definition of absolute poverty and the second the poverty line in the United States (Ravallion 2010). Economists Banerjee and Duflo (2007) also emphasize the economic precarity of the middle classes, whose income they calculate between $2 and $10 per day, but the middle classes differ from the precariat because of their occupational stability. Besides, household debts make income inequality even more acute, as working-class families and marginal constituencies are hit by debt poverty through the expansion of social finance. Under the PT the Brazilian dream was to turn every worker into a 'class C' (middle-class) citizen. Marcio Pochmann's (2012) statistical analysis shows, in fact, how the middle classes exist on the verge of poverty. Set up in 2003 by the first Lula administration, the programme of poverty reduction, Bolsa Familia, today reaches 13 million families or a quarter of the national population. But on the backdrop of its massive social spending, which reached 23 per cent of the GDP in late 2000, the second Lula administration started a process of mass tertiarization across the economic board, which involved mainly older, female and black workers. Parallel to the precarization of formal sectors, there has been an increase in informal jobs (which today constitute 40 per cent of the economy) and low-income occupations such as domestic labour. The new middle classes, Pochmann argues, barely make it above the poverty threshold. Their occupations are as precarious as those of informal workers and of the poor who just entered the job market.

Besides, Singer's analysis (2014) of the socioeconomic profile of the June demonstrators confirms the porosity between the middle class and the precariat in Brazil. The majority of the demonstrators were very young, especially in Rio, where 41 per cent were under the age of 25 and 39 per cent under 34. That is to say, 80 per cent were under the age of 39. Moreover, participants overall had high levels of education. In most cities, no less than 43 per cent of demonstrators had a university degree (against a national average of 8 per cent). In Rio, this percentage was slightly lower at 34 per cent. But is high education enough to be middle class? In Rio, 34 per cent of the protesters had only one family minimum wage per month.[19] If we add those who earn between two and five minimum wages (still considered among the lowest income strata in Brazil), these groups accounted for 88 per cent of the demonstrators – against a national average of 50 per cent. Yet, according to economist Waldir Quadros,[20] this is exactly the profile associated with such low-income jobs as shop assistant, receptionist, domestic servant, maid, clerk, waiter, driver, nurse, primary school teacher, manicurist, hairdresser or telemarketer entering the job market today. This is not the middle class of the liberal professions – the lawyers, doctors and engineers who joined the anti-dictatorship movement in the 1980s. Yet research suggests that 30 per cent of the demonstrators defined themselves as being from the centre. Besides, adding those who classified themselves as centre-left and centre-right, the centre constituted 70 per cent of the demonstrators. Instead of co-optation by the middle classes, Singer (2014: 34) suggests that the June events show a 'much more subtle repositioning by a post-materialist center'. Inglehart's notion of 'post-materialism' – the idea that the relationship between income and well-being is relevant only at low levels of income and that for most people well-being is associated with such factors as self-expression and quality of life – continues to be a central term of reference in the debate about 'class C' in Brazil. Following Laclau (2005), we can argue that 'the centre' is an empty signifier that brings together two contradictory and convergent political and economic processes: the proletarianization of the 'middle class' (through casualization) and the bourgeoisification of the masses, through poverty relief, microfinance and incentives to consumption. But what are the implications of this blurring of middle-class and working-class struggles in Brazil and is Singer (2014) right? Is the working class endorsing non-materialist values?

Conclusion

How can the events of June 2013 be assessed in the light of contemporary developments? For one thing, the recent proliferation of free-market and authoritarian slogans does show that the heterodox economy of the PT represented an inclusive project although in line with Brazil's tradition of populism.[21] With the collapse of the economy, the populist consensus between big capital, middle classes, working classes and dispossessed masses broke down, and an expanding section of the working class (the so-called 'centre') was heavily undermined. Even if Brazil did not experience dictatorship in such radical forms as other Latin American countries, the ascent of extreme right-wing fringes in Brazil is worrying. If the PT failed to reconnect with the working-class and grassroots organizations that propelled it into power, the demonstrations of 2013 showed a remarkable rearticulation of the Brazilian left and the country's still strong tradition of grassroots activism, right to the city organizations, participatory democracy and working-class mobilization. The demonstrations of 2015 were an expression of a different class articulation and of the ascent of the old elites, who were dormant during the democratic opening but are now re-emerging in the space left open by the deep crisis of the Brazilian left.

How can the Brazilian situation be understood comparatively in relation to other instances of urban mobilization? Ethnographic comparisons of working-class struggles are difficult to draw. Elsewhere (Mollona 2014) I have stressed some differences in the way the industrial proletariat articulates its struggles in Brazil and the United Kingdom, based on the industrial fieldwork I conducted in steel towns in these two countries. In particular, the Brazilian experience of labour struggle was influenced by three factors: (1) a reduced public sphere, (2) a populist consensus that produced class emancipation without political emancipation and (3) the articulation of class struggle as anti-colonialist struggle. Particularly, the historical convergence of anti-colonialism and anti-capitalism led to cross-sectional collaborations between civic, rural and labour movements that toppled the military rule in the 1980s and later propelled the Workers' Party (PT) to power. As Aricò notes in *Marx and Latin America* (2013), these anti-colonialist cross-sectional alliances negated the classical Marxist[22] hypothesis of the vanguard of the industrial proletariat leading to that 'new social unionism' that has been broadly documented in subaltern labour studies.

In Brazil, it was the legacy of slavery that brought together anti-capitalist and anti-colonial struggles. Fighting for a freedom that encompassed both social demands and labour demands, slaves infused the labour movement of the early nineteenth century with powerful support structures, forms of struggles and civic consciousness. But boundaries between freedom and slavery continue to be fluid in Brazil. Outside the small and privileged enclave of formal workers, a vast universe of bonded and slave labour still exists. Besides, as in past forms of slavery, the civil liberties of the Brazilian poor are heavily restricted. As a result, economic and civic struggles – or, to paraphrase Nancy Frazer (2000), struggles for 'recognition' and struggles for 'redistribution' – go hand in hand so that woman, indigenous and black consciousness in Brazil are central elements of class struggle. Boaventura de Sousa Santos (2006) argues that southern socialist epistemologies combine cultural differences and economic equality. But as Eurocentric as the theory of convergence appears to be, there is widespread scepticism in the idea that the socialist regimes of Latin America are immune to the forces of neoliberalism. After all, did not the ex-metalworker-turned-president Lula da Silva subscribe to the neoliberal dogma of deindustrialization, financialization and tertiarization, in cahoots with the industrial working class and at the expense of precarious and informal workers and the rural poor?

In this chapter I have attempted to root these theoretical debates in the context of the struggles that took place in Rio de Janeiro in the summer of 2013 and in 2015, developing a new kind of class analysis located at the intersection of anthropology, radical geography and political economy. The deindustrialization, deregulation and financialization of the world economy have turned 'global cities' into invisible factories, where the dynamics of class are more complicated than in traditional, factory-based scenarios. Besides, capitalist relations attach themselves to places unevenly and invisibly, through the hidden folds of urban infrastructures and the complex politics of city planning. Take, for instance, the struggles of the dockworker unions, low-income communities and social movements against the development of the Olympic Village and the mega-tourist 'marvellous port' (Porto Maravilha) in Rio de Janeiro in 2013. Up until the end of the nineteenth century, the port of Rio was one of the epicentres of the Atlantic slave trade and a hotbed of radicalism and rebellion. Living in the same squats, cortiços and collective houses surrounding the port, slaves and dockworkers struggled together against the same masters. In 2012 the municipality bought from the federal government five million square metres of public land surrounding the port and sold it to private developers. A few months later, it evicted local residents and closed down primary schools, samba schools and community organizations to make space for the Olympic Village and the tourist port. Reacting to the eviction, civic movements, dockworkers and low-income residents joined forces to stop the development of the Porto Maravilha, although the gentrification of the area continues. This struggle may resemble similar anti-gentrification movements in global cities in Europe. In fact, Saskia Sassen's (2014) argument that old North-South and East-West divides have been replaced by a generalized logic of dispossession and urban segregation coalescing around 'global cities' applies well to the current processes of urban segregation taking place in Rio. Indeed, Rio de Janeiro is an interesting hybrid between the 'global cities' normally associated with the global north and the third-world 'mega-cities' that constitute the subject of much developmentalist scholarship.[23] In this sense, this chapter (and volume) is also intended to emphasize the complex, heterogeneous and multi-scalar geography of contemporary cities, as well as their entanglement with broader rural geographies and dynamics.

But as Mike Davis (2009) shows so well, the slummification of the South, of which Rio is such an iconic example, is based on an explosive mixture of industrialization and extreme urban segregation, unlike the processes of gentrification of global cities in the United States and Europe. The geography of the slum has produced a political landscape marked by three strong features. First, in urban peripheries the deterritorialization of capital has been so deep that the urban poor are going through the same experience already lived by the rural poor in the 1970s – occupying land and organizing close to the territory in small units and on a day-to-day basis. The convergence between urban and rural poor – for instance, the convergence between homeless and landless movements in Brazil – has created a new peasantry whose political force has to be reckoned with. Besides, political actions in urban peripheries take micro, dispersed and invisible forms. For instance, Bayat (2009) describes urban struggles in Cairo as an 'everyday encroachment of the ordinary'; Holston (2009) argues that the self-construction of houses in poor neighbourhoods is a form of civic struggle; and Zibechi (2010) emphasizes the subterranean and dispersed forms of resistance in the mobilizations in El Alto and Buenos Aires.

Second, urban peripheries have informal economies and family-based micro-entrepreneurship, which may empower marginal social constituencies. Urban-based forms of Petty Commodity Production (PCP) differ from those traditionally analysed in anthropology and development studies.[24] If the fusion of management and ownership in a rural context often leads to self-exploitation, in small-scale urban contexts it may empower ethnic communities, as in the cases of El Alto (Zibechi 2010), the worker-owned factories in Buenos Aires (Sitrin 2006) or the urban cooperatives in Sao Paulo (Singer 2006). On the other hand, it is disingenuous to cast the informal economy and PCP as forms of 'people's capitalism'[25] or to romanticize the economic mongrelization[26] of cities in the South – the other side of Bauman's dark vision of the Brazilianization of Europe. The emphasis here must be on the new forms of cooperativism that are emerging from the urban peripheries of the South.

Third, in the South, and especially in Latin America, the urban poor, peasants and precarious workers led powerful 'Right to the City Movements' fighting urban segregation and land grabs through commoning and grassroots participation, via the urban land committees in Caracas and Cochabamba or self-managed neighbourhoods in Argentina and Brazil. These movements, fighting for urban democracy, were originally independent from party politics[27] and were only later incorporated in the socialist governments of Morales, Chavez and Lula. Yet again, are these urban struggles for the commons not the same kind of working-class 'commoning' described by Susser (Susser and Tonnelat 2013) and Kalb (2014) for the United States and Europe? There has always been a great deal of overlap between the struggles of the urban poor, those of civic movements and those of the industrial or post-industrial proletariat. Perhaps the biggest challenge posed by contemporary urban movements worldwide is precisely the way in which they bring together all these different components into a composite class articulation, the understanding of which is fundamental for the future of class struggle.

Massimiliano Mollona is an anthropologist and filmmaker. He has conducted extensive fieldwork in Brazil and England around themes of class, work, racism and post-capitalism. He currently teaches at the Department of the Arts (DAR) at the University of Bologna. His most recent book is *Brazilian Steel Town: Machines, Land, Money and Commoning in the Making of the Working Class* (2020).

Notes

This chapter greatly benefited from a conversation that I had with my colleagues Marco Santana of Federal University of Rio de Janeiro (UFRJ) and Don Kalb (Bergen University).

1. Therborn describes them as 'drawing support from many layers of society – the urban poor, people of indigenous or African descent, the progressive element of the middle strata – and in which industrial workers are rarely in the vanguard' (2012: 16).
2. Such as Revoltados Online and SOS Forças Armada.
3. For instance, a banner reading 'Army, Navy and Air Force. Please save us once again from communism'.
4. Such as 'Brazil does not want and will not be a new Venezuela' or 'Nation + Liberty = PT [Workers' Party] Out!'.
5. See De Oliveira (2003), Singer (2012) and Mollona (forthcoming).
6. *New York Times*, 3 February 2016.
7. Although there are generational differences between the two, here old and new are intended as historical social formations.
8. Writing about Sao Paulo, he reports that 'in Paulista Avenue on Friday evening, three demonstrations took place with different demands, and in absence of any point of contact they did not engage with each other' (Saad-Filho 2013: 666).
9. The proposal would allow companies to outsource core workers and hence to operate with a workforce of zero full-time or permanent workers, relying instead on a reserve pool of workers provided by 'contact centres'– labour brokers and temporary hiring agencies.
10. In 2007, the UN-funded Centre for Housing Rights and Evictions (COHRE) concluded that over the past twenty years the Olympic Games have forced two million evictions. The Olympics were listed as one of the top causes of displacement and real estate inflation in the world.
11. Law 11 gave to FIFA exclusive selling, advertising and distribution rights over the World Cup.

12. He sees in the demonstrations 'evidence of the unremitting rejections of former President Lula, President Dilma Rousseff and the PT by large segment of the upper and middle classes and the mainstream media' (Saad Filho and Morais 2014: 241).
13. The minimum wage is R$700 per month.
14. Calculated at R$1,000.
15. One of the most successful of these involved a man dressed up in a Batman costume climbing on the roof of a building in central Rio with a placard reading, 'We want quality schools and hospitals – fuck the World Cup'.
16. In one instance, after the FIP and MEPR accused the PSTU of 'bourgeois pacifism' and reformism, some of its members physically assaulted an FIP group during a demonstration.
17. Ruy Braga (2014) has analysed teleworkers' conditions in depth.
18. They are mainly children of casual labourers, maids and cleaners – all jobs with earnings below the poverty line.
19. The dynamics of poverty and inequality in Rio are more extreme than in other cities, where on average only 15 per cent of demonstrators came from the lowest income level.
20. Waldir Quadros, 'Brasil: Um Pais de Classe media', *Le Monde Diplomatique Brasil*, 1 November 2012. Cited in Singer (2014).
21. For a discussion of Lula's populism, see Singer (2012).
22. In spite of these Marxists claims, Aricò (2013) argues, in his discussion of the Irish question, Marx did acknowledge the centrality of anti-colonial struggles in the peripheries for working-class struggles in the centres.
23. For a critical assessment of the dichotomy between 'global cities' and 'third-word cities' see Jennifer Robinson (2002).
24. These tend to be integrated in global commodity chains, located in a rural context and open to simple patterns of patriarchal proletarianization (Smart and Smart 2005; Kalb 2014).
25. See, for instance, the proposal of formalizing the informal economy of the South made by Robert Neuwirth (2013).
26. I am using the term of Merrifield (2013).
27. For an analysis of these contemporary urban movements in Brazil, see Santana and Mollona (2013).

References

Anderson, P. 2016. 'Crisis in Brazil'. *London Review of Books*, 21 April.
Aricò, J. 2013. *Marx and Latin America*. Leiden: Brill.
Banerjee, A. and E. Duflo. 2007. 'What is Middle Class about the Middle Classes around the world?', MIT Department of Economics Working Paper, no 7–29.
Bayat, A. 2009. *Life as Politics: How Ordinary People Change the Middle East*. Stanford, CA: Stanford University Press.
Braga, R. 2014. 'As jornadas de junho no Brasil: Crônica de um mês inesquecível'. Unpublished manuscript.
Davis, M. 2009. *Planets of Slums*. London: Verso.
De Oliveira, F. 2003. 'The Duckbilled Platypus', *New Left Review* 24: 40–57.
De Sousa Santos, B. 2006. *Another Production is Possible: Beyond the Capitalist Canon*. London: Verso.
Frazer, N. 2000. 'Rethinking Recognition', *New Left Review* 3: 107–20.

Holston, J. 2009. *Insurgent Citizenship: Disjunction of Democracy and Modernity*. Princeton, NJ: Princeton University Press.
Kalb, D. 2014. 'Class: The Urban Commons and the "Empty Sign" of "the Middle Class" in the 21st Century', in D. Nonini (ed.), *A Companion to Urban Anthropology*. Oxford: Blackwell, pp. 157–76.
Laclau, E. 2005. *On Populist Reason*. London: Verso.
Leahy, J. 2012. 'FT Interview: Dilma Rousseff', *Financial Times*, 3 October.
Legume, L. and M. Toledo. 2011. 'O Movimento Passe Livre Sao Paulo e a Tarifa Zero', 16 August. Retrieved from http://passapalavra.info.
Livingstone, C. 2014. 'Armed Peace: Militarization of Rio de Janeiro's Favelas for the World Cup', *Anthropology Today* 30: 4.
Mello, J. 1982. *O Capitalismo Tardio*. São Paulo: Brasiliense.
Merrifield, A. 2013. *The Politics of the Encounter: Urban Theory and Protest under Planetary Urbanization*. Athens, GA: University of Georgia Press.
Mollona, M. 2014. 'Anthropology and Class Analysis: Working-Class Politics in a Brazilian Steel Town', in J. Carrier and D. Kalb (eds), *Anthropologies of Class*. Cambridge: Cambridge University Press, pp. 149–63.
———. (Forthcoming). 'Labor and Land Struggles in a Brazilian Steel Town: The Reorganization of Capital under Neo-extractivism', in C. Kwan Lee and I. Breman (eds), *The Social Question*. Berkeley, CA: University of California Press:
Neuwirth, R. 2013. *Stealth of Nations: The Global Rise of the Informal Economy*. London: Anchor.
Picketty, T. 2014. *Capital in the Twenty-First Century*. Cambridge, MA: Harvard University Press.
Ponchmann, M. 2012. *Nova Classe Média?* Sao Paulo: Boitempo.
Ravallion, M. 2010. 'The Developing World's Bulging (but Vulnerable) Middle Class', *World Development* 38(4): 445–54.
Robinson, J. 2002. 'Global and World Cities: A View from off the Map', *International Journal of Urban and Regional Research* 26(3): 531–54.
Saad-Filho, A. 2013. 'Mass Protest under "Left Neoliberalism": Brazil, June–July 2013', *Critical Sociology* 39(5): 657–69.
Saad Filho, A. and L. Morais. 2014. 'Mass Protests: Brazilian Spring or Brazilian Malaise?', *Socialist Register* 50: 227–46.
Santana, M.A. and M. Mollona. 2013. 'Trabalho e ação coletiva: Memória, espaço e identidades sociais na cidade do aço', *Horizontes Antropologicos* 19(39): 125–48.
Sassen, S. 2014. *Expulsions: Brutality and Complexity in the Global Economy*. Cambridge, MA: Harvard University Press.
Singer, A. 2012. *Os Sentidos do Lulismo: Reforma Gradual e Pacto Conservador*. São Paulo: Companhia Das Letras.
———. 2014. 'Rebellion in Brazil: Social and Political Complexion of the June Events', *New Left Review* 85: 19–37.
Singer, P. 2006. 'The Recent Rebirth of the Solidarity Economy in Brazil', in B. de Sousa Santos (ed.), *Another Production is Possible: Beyond the Capitalist Canon*. London: Verso, pp. 3–42.
Sitrin, M. 2006. *Horizontalism: Voices of Popular Power in Argentina*. Oakland, CA: AK Press.
Smart, A. and J. Smart (eds). 2005. *Petty Capitalists and Globalization: Flexibility, Entrepreneurship and Economic Development*. Albany, NY: SUNY Press.
Susser, I. and S. Tonnelat. 2013. 'Transformative Cities: The Three Urban Commons', *Focaal – Journal of Global and Historical Anthropology* 66: 105.
Therborn, G. 2012. 'Class in the 21st Century', *New Left Review* 78: 5–29.
Van der Linden, M. 2008. *Workers of the World: Essays towards a Global Labor History*. Leiden: Brill.

World Bank. 2012. 'Bringing the State Back into the Favelas of Rio de Janeiro'. Washington, D.C.: The World Bank.
Zibechi, R. 2010. *Dispersing Powers: Social Movements as Anti-State Forces*. Oakland, CA: AK Press.
_____. 2015. 'Se acelera el fin del ciclo progresista sudaméricano', *La Jornada*, 30 October.

– Chapter 8 –

CONTRADICTIONS OF THE 'COMMON MAN'
A Realist Approach to India's Aam Aadmi Party
Luisa Steur

Reminiscing on the massive anti-corruption mobilization that had captured the political imagination of Delhi in the summer of 2012 and that had foreboded her joining the Aam Aadmi (Common Man) Party (AAP), Metha, a Hindi literature teacher at a Delhi college, told me:

> it was the first time since 'globalization' that we could see youth actually awake from their political lethargy, their fascination with consumerism, and find a greater purpose in life. All the poor and Dalit youth also were coming there. And as a woman, the possibility of being part of the crowd without being harassed. This was the moment when we knew we had to do something, to join.

I could recognize what she was saying – I had been to Ramlila Maidan[1] in 2012 too and had been impressed by the massive crowd and the horizontal mingling of people from very different walks of life, as well as the possibility for women to let their guard down (a bit at least) despite being in a crowd, the festive excitement in the air and the feeling that here was something building up that could have an actual political impact. On the other hand, I was also impressed by the overlay of spectacle on the Ramlila grounds. Queuing to pass the security check, being greeted by people handing out disposable Gandhi *topis* (caps) and seeing the broadcasting vans and their spotlights and the stage where the veteran Gandhian activist Anna Hazare was performing his hunger fast, admired by the thousands gathered around, it also felt like being at a professionally staged mega-festival in the heart of Delhi. The aesthetics of the movement revealed many such fascinating contradictions and would provide a rich source of theorizing for idealist approaches to the new popular uprisings (see e.g. Pinney 2014; Webb 2015). This chapter, however, takes a more 'realist-materialist' approach (see Kalb and Mollona, this volume) and seeks to understand these contradictions in the context of the heterogeneous class trajectories and experiences that constitute the AAP's rise in India's current political conjuncture.

We can start by noting that this conjuncture is characterized by a particular shift in the form of political engagement towards what Bornstein and Sharma (2016: 78) call 'technomoral politics': a form of political engagement that is not necessarily 'anti-political' but does tend to substitute the earlier ideological struggle between right and left by 'a moral struggle between right and wrong'. To come back to Metha, I could recognize why she experienced the mobilization as 'politicization', but it was not the kind of politicization of naming and confronting sociopolitical contradictions – on the contrary, it was a festive politicization, preparing to transcend contradictions in celebration of a common moral cause. Well suited to such a transcendent politics was the discourse against 'corruption', which could indicate anything from frustration with the lawlessness of Indian paupers or the 'third class' state of urban infrastructure to anger at the multibillion scams that had come to light that year and the increasing precariousness of working-class lives in the city. The fight against corruption, moreover, was especially apt at tying one's own moral strength – to resist being 'corrupted' – to larger social transformation, placing a heavy responsibility on the individual to live according to his ideals rather than the conditions he happened to be surrounded with. In that sense, the anti-corruption momentum in Delhi was reminiscent of the populist and 'prefigurative' response to capitalist contradictions that we saw in many cities in 2011 and 2012.

As this chapter will demonstrate, the political party that emerged in this particular conjuncture, the AAP, has an impressive ability to internalize rather than highlight contradiction. This party of the 'common man' – a more individualized version of the classic populist trope of 'the people' – holds together IT professionals and slum dwellers, veers ideologically from right to left and back again, while striving simultaneously for deep democratic 'self-rule' (*swaraj*) and success in the grand game of Indian elections. The AAP's founder and leader, Arvind Kejriwal, is a perfect embodiment of such ambiguity, both in habitus and speech. On the one hand, he carries the confidence of a former civil servant, born into a middle-class family, and has not shied away from asserting himself as a 'baniya' (a higher-ranking caste of moneylenders and traders) who 'understands business' (*Indian Express*, 29 December 2014) – on the other hand, the media have regularly printed images of this now Chief Minister of Delhi staging protests by sleeping on the pavement as a homeless person would, with no more than his muffler to shield against the cold of winter Delhi.

It is no wonder, then, to see opinions on the AAP among critical scholars of India vary greatly. Views are split between those who insist on the need to think with the AAP as an emerging popular-leftist or subaltern breakthrough into the status quo of Indian politics (e.g. Menon and Nigam 2011; Nigam 2014; Singh 2014; Visvanathan 2014; Zabiliute 2014a –hesitantly, also Chakrabarti and Dhar 2014) and those who criticize the party for being implicitly right wing and heavily dominated by elite urban 'middle-class', as well as upper-caste and male, concerns (see Chatterjee 2011; Sharma 2012; Illaiah 2014; Patnaik 2014; Roy 2014; Sonpimple 2014). These views do not necessarily overlap with idealist vs realist-materialist approaches: some who clearly follow the realist-materialist approach actually come to see the AAP's intervention as potentially very positive (e.g. Giri 2014), while some of those who focus more on the aesthetics and ethics of the movement reach rather damning conclusions on the nature of the AAP (e.g. Baxi 2014). This chapter does not draw any conclusions on the AAP's merits as such but does seek to offer a realistic-materialist understanding of three key contradictions within the AAP – of ideological tropes, of processes of cross-class alliance formation and of class experience – in order to shine a critical light on the state of counter-politics in the present conjuncture of Indian capitalism.

The first part of the chapter discusses the contradiction between the deeply spiritual idea of swaraj ('self-rule'), which requires the slow and conscious seeding of a different political culture, and the AAP's embracing of electoral politics, which tends to undermine the culture of swaraj. Secondly, the chapter moves to the contradiction of the social movement histories that converge in the AAP from opposite sides of the political spectrum: the one epitomized by the India Against Corruption campaign, galvanized by the anger of the urban 'middle class'; the other, the National Alliance of People's Movements, which grew out of rural struggles against dispossession. The final contradiction the chapter discusses, then, concerns the class background of AAP volunteers, who include both young 'middle-class' urban professionals and precarious and informalized lower-caste slum dwellers, each with rather different interpretations of and relations to the party. These three contradictions – all of which are also gendered – are not exhaustive of the tensions within the AAP but do give a good sense of the ambiguity of this now dominant political current in the governance of India's capital city. In concluding this chapter, I argue that the contradictions reveal a complicity with the larger political conjuncture that the AAP seeks to resist. This complicity fuels the success and overall coherence of the party, despite its contradictions, but at the same time limits its counter-political potential.

Swaraj and the Election Rush

Beyond the slogans of the 'common man' and the fight against 'corruption', a deeper philosophical commitment underlying the AAP is the idea of *swaraj* (self-rule) – also the title of the 2012 manifesto-like booklet published by Kejriwal. The concept of swaraj anchors the AAP in a longer populist tradition in Indian history. For Gandhi, swaraj was a way of achieving not just political freedom from colonial rule but the restoration of the civilizational strength of India that lay in its 'self-sufficient village republics' (Jodkha 2002). At a more interpersonal level, swaraj moreover is 'the capacity for dispassionate self-assessment, ceaseless self-purification and growing self-reliance' (Gandhi, *Young India*, 28 June 1928: 772). Voluntary work organizations were a key component of Gandhi's vision of swaraj and form a key component of the AAP's party-building as well. Kejriwal's booklet *Swaraj*, however, takes a mostly practical approach to swaraj. *Swaraj* draws on the experience Kejriwal gained through Parivartan (Change), the organization he founded in 2000 with a group of retired professionals and civil servants and that helped organize local assemblies and participatory budgeting in certain slums of East Delhi. The booklet offers a range of short, practical suggestions on how citizens and policymakers can go about decentralizing decision-making to the *gram sabhas* and *mohalla sabhas* (village and neighbourhood-level councils).

Already during the 2011–2012 Anna Hazare campaign, which directly preceded the founding of AAP, there was a certain division of labour regarding the spiritual and practical dimensions of *swaraj*. Front stage, Anna Hazare was performing his hunger fast – a ritualized, ennobling 'sacrifice' by someone who embodies upper-caste purity (Hansen 2014) – to 'persuade' the government to adopt an anti-corruption 'Ombudsman bill' and was carefully maintaining his integrity as a veteran Gandhian activist. Backstage, Kejriwal was the key organizer of 'Team Anna', the well-oiled and well-funded campaign that brought the crowds to Ramlila Maidan. The message of the Hazare campaign was that all politics were dirty and that only a parallel legal structure could restore India's ethical reputation. By the end of it, Anna Hazare himself remained absolutely opposed to the idea of entering electoral politics, as it was irreconcilable with his spiritual path to change. Kejriwal, however, had become convinced it was necessary to change the system 'from within' and, without opposing Hazare, claimed a practical solution: AAP would be the anti-system party; it would 'look like a political party but not behave like a political party'.

This, of course, did not make the underlying contradiction go away, and three elections onwards, in 2015, many analysts agreed that the AAP had converted into a 'mainstream hierarchical party, bringing an end to the ambitious project of nurturing an alternative politics, rather than simply offering an electoral alternative' (Palshikar 2016: 127). This degeneration of the party could easily also be analysed, however, through the philosophical perspective of *swaraj* itself, which is what I learned from Pankaj Pushkar, who I met in July 2015. Pushkar had entered the 2015 elections as an AAP candidate and had thus become an elected Member of the Legislative Assembly (MLA) for a North Delhi constituency. He had come to the AAP from the Bharat Jan Andolan (Indian People's Movement) – the movement for adivasi ('indigenous') self-rule led by Dr B.D Sharma and for a good part responsible for the passing of the PESA (Panchayat Extension to Scheduled Areas) Act of 1996, granting village councils control over natural resources in their area. Coming from an academic-cum-activist background, Pushkar had become frustrated with Kejriwal's 'utilitarian' appropriation of the idea of village self-rule as it had developed in the Bharat Jan Andolan. According to Pushkar, the AAP had become a reality due to the people's movements it grew from, but could not stay true to those movements in its rush to win elections: 'fine, now we have a not-so-corrupt Chief Minister but it's a far cry from the dream we had.'

By the time I met Pushkar, he had come to see the AAP more as 'a failed experiment in transformation'. He saw the problem not with the lack of ideology: this should not have been a disadvantage but an advantage, as it forced people to open their minds, to leave 'puritan' positions and, through dialogue, find sharper analysis and more political vibrancy. The problem was rather that the

AAP got saddled with the disadvantages of not having an ideology, while the advantages did not pan out. A true personality cult had arisen around Kejriwal, who, according to Pushkar, had come to 'lack the ability to deal with diversity, to digest something beyond his own mind … all have become a slave of that mind which itself has become a slave'. 'It's why we believe politics and spirituality go together,' Pushkar's wife explained to me, 'we cannot change anything without also changing the person.' With a stronger person, she argued, things could have turned out better. Indeed, the idea of *swaraj* opposes the obsession with personalities but the spiritual strength of a leader is, in fact, crucial.

The biggest problem in AAP now was, according to Pushkar, that genuine dialogue and the hard work of delivering a different political culture at the 'grassroots' had given way to a hasty desire to transform governance from above. The urge to win had taken over from an 'authentic people's politics' that on the contrary involved 'the capacity to be dissolved, as in love and friendship, a willingness to lose yourself, to not always win'. Things seemed to have almost come full circle: rallying against opportunism and corruption, the AAP had started giving out election tickets to candidates without consideration of their political commitment; after criticizing dirty politics, the AAP itself was now engaging in the actual sabotaging and intimidation of those critical of the party; and after the many sit-ins Kejriwal held to raise issues with the government, he was now refusing to spare some time to listen to those protesting in the same place where he himself used to stand.

A glimpse of just how hard it is to do politics differently could be seen, however, from Pushkar's own struggles to reconcile his work as an MLA with the ideal of promoting *swaraj*. There are structural incentives for corruption everywhere, as it is extremely difficult (and for those without personal savings impossible) to get things done on the official budget. Pushkar had to rely on wealthy members of his constituency to make available part of their homes to provide his staff and volunteers an office. And he had to rely on the idealism of volunteers who were attracted by his integrity rather than the prospect of getting paid for their work, as was the case now in most other AAP constituencies according to Pushkar.

Just how complex it is to realize *swaraj* while having become the official democratic authority is also well exemplified in the 'Khirki Extension incident' involving Somnath Bharti, Law Minister during AAP's first stint in power. In January 2014, complaints reached him from the local Resident Welfare Association about a 'drug and prostitution racket' run by Africans living in the neighbourhood and ignored by the police despite numerous petitions. Resident Welfare Associations (RWAs) are a pillar of the AAP's vision of decentralized urban decision-making – indeed, Kejriwal had been active in pushing the Local Government Bill that formalized RWAs to oversee civic amenities. It was thus frustrating to an AAP Law Minister to see the police's apparent reluctance to follow the RWA and enforce the law in his own constituency and he decided to go to the area himself, accompanied by Delhi police officers and AAP activists. There they barged into one of the African women's houses and allegedly forced those inside to give urine samples to check for drugs. Considering how Bharti's actions could easily be interpreted as racist (and sexist) vigilantism, the event evoked a storm of critique amongst AAP sympathizers. The AAP leadership, however, defended Bharti, and indeed some celebrated him as 'the symbol for a new kind of politics – the politics of agitation, which party members subscribed to as activists, outside the system, and later tried incorporating into a governance model, one that's now gaining traction' (Chikermane 2014: 24). Ironically, by September 2015, Bharti's behaviour had, however, gotten so out of hand that even Kejriwal was tweeting for him to 'surrender' to the police.

India Against Corruption and the National Alliance of People's Movements

A second contradiction in the AAP concerns the social movements that have come together in it from opposite poles of the political spectrum and distinct geographical and class trajectories. The main protagonists of the Anna Hazare/India Against Corruption (IAC) campaign from which the AAP grew were clearly on the right – Kiran Bedi, the famous now-retired female Indian Police Service officer who was a key leader of the IAC campaign, was even nominated as the BJP's chief ministerial candidate in the February 2015 Delhi assembly elections. Though the AAP attracted a rather diverse following according to the political flexibility of the notion of 'corruption' (see also the chapters by Lazar, Mollona and Jansen), initially the IAC protests were marked by so-called 'middle-class' – that is, upper-caste – anxieties. This urban, upper caste middle class, to which the grand majority of politicians belonged in the post-Independence period, had been bolstered by sustained government investment in higher education and had been overwhelmingly represented in civil service employment, where earlier the most sought-after jobs were. However, as lower castes gradually attained an ever-stronger presence in the political field, the 'middle class' started to consider politics a plebeian field of unprincipled pragmatism, corruption and greed (Jaffrelot 2003). Many members of the middle class started migrating to the United Kingdom and the United States, and with the liberalization policies of the early 1990s they became further pitted *against* the Indian state, which they now considered an obstacle towards high-end private sector employment (Khandekar and Reddy 2015: 225). Anti-corruption thus interpreted is about discrediting the political class and the poor and further dismantling regulation intended to reign in capital (Jenkins 2014).

In the past two decades, middle-class youth, moreover, have started to rally in particular around the notion of 'merit'– something the private sector supposedly rewards but the government undermines (Chatterjee 2011). This reached fever pitch in the 2006 protests by the largely upper caste Youth for Equality, a group to which Arvind Kejriwal was closely associated, and which in the name of meritocracy and anti-corruption, and with grand displays of upper-caste self-pity, agitated against lower-caste reservations for positions in higher education and civil service. It was immediately noticed, when the Anna Hazare movement arose in the course of 2011, that it was constituted by many of the same actors who had earlier led the anti-reservation protests. Many on the left considered Hazare's hunger strike for the setting up of a kind of parallel government structure to combat corruption, an attempt to hold Indian democracy hostage and undermine a Constitution that institutionalized some of the most important historical struggles of lower castes (Megwanshi 2011; Chatterke 2012). No less reassuring was the Bharat Mata (Mother India) symbolism that marked the early protests at Ramlila Maidan, generally associated with right-wing Hindu majoritarian and upper-caste politics (that of the BJP). Some of the people whom Kejriwal invited into the AAP embodied neoliberal middle-class politics quite perfectly – for instance Prithvi Reddy, an industrialist turned 'social entrepreneur' and co-founder of SmartVote. Or Pankaj Gupta, who was in senior positions at Tata Consultancy Services in the United States and KMG Infotech in Gurgaon before deciding to dedicate his fundraising capacities, technological prowess and experience in corporate social responsibility to the AAP, in fact becoming its general secretary.

With the BJP ascending and absorbing the more right-wing tendencies of the anti-corruption momentum, the AAP, however, took a rather different turn that was more in line with Kejriwal's practically oriented habitus, shaped by his experience as a social activist. The AAP reached out to the left, realizing that for the many lower-caste and slum-dwelling youth that had also come to the Anna Hazare protests, issues like the price of water and electricity were of much larger concern than the passing of an Ombudsman bill. In its political affairs committee, it included activists like Prashant Bhushan, a lawyer-activist well known for his legal battles against some of India's richest tycoons (especially the Ambanis), and Yogendra Yadav, a prominent political scientist actively engaged in reviving Indian socialism. And the latter in particular encouraged many other left-leaning activists and intellectuals to join the AAP, thus connecting the party to a very different, less urban and more left-wing people's movement trajectory, exemplified by the National Alliance of People's Movements (NAPM).

The movements connected to the NAPM gained their momentum from the many conflicts around 'primitive accumulation', especially against the land-grabbing for mining and other private industrial purposes that have characterized the post-Nehruvian (post-60s) era of Indian development where 'growth', at whatever social cost, has come to substitute national development as the hegemonic political imperative (Chatterjee 2008). Leading activists who joined the AAP from these struggles include Medha Patkar, leader of Narmada Dam struggle, and Christina Swamy, leader of the struggle against the sand-mining mafia in Tamil Nadu. Other related struggles have been resisting the informalization of labour and new forms of bonded labour in a period marked by jobless growth and forced circular migration (Breman 2008). A well-known activist fighting for the rights of such workers – and against bonded labour – is law professor Babu Mathew, who in 2014 also joined the AAP.

Rather than wanting to dismantle government intervention, as right-wing anti-corruption demonstrations sought to, these left-wing people's movements were pushing for the opposite – for the state to step in to protect labour and extend its welfare schemes to counter the effects of its narrowly growth-oriented development agenda. Indeed, since the 1980s, class struggle has largely shifted away from confronting capital in the workplace (e.g. through strikes), towards instead claiming and accessing basic welfare services from the state (see Pattenden 2016). For the movements leading this struggle, fighting against corruption was not to condemn the government in general but to call upon it to prevent the large-scale corporate land-grab that characterizes twenty-first century capitalism in India and to ensure that the poor would get access to newly introduced welfare schemes like the National Rural Employment Guarantee Act (NREGA).

But there were also emerging convergences between the left-leaning and right-leaning people's movements in the new millennium. Both started insisting on their distinction from (formally registered) NGOs, allied to donors and the state, as a marker of moral integrity (Bornstein and Sharma 2016: 82).[2] Both right- and left-wing people's movements, moreover, were undergoing a process of juridification, increasingly concentrating their energy on fighting court battles. In this, one piece of legislation became particularly crucial: the Right to Information Act (RTI), which is India's version of a sunshine law, aimed at empowering citizens and making governance participatory and transparent. The National Campaign for People's Right to Information, rooted in Aruna Roy's left-leaning Association for the Empowerment of Workers and Peasants (MKSS), had been the primary force behind the passing of the act in 2005. Arvind Kejriwal had been close to Aruna Roy and received his Ramon Magsaysay Award for the work that his Parivartan had done to promote the RTI. Perhaps unsurprisingly, considering both personal ambitions and ideological differences, Aruna Roy and Arvind Kejriwal, however, had a major disagreement at the time of AAP's founding and Aruna Roy never joined the AAP.

Many activists in the NAPM nevertheless had started reconsidering their earlier opposition to entering politics and had already made a first move towards engaging more closely with politics in 2004 with the creation of the People's Political Front (PPF). At the time, Medha Patkar, leader of the NAPM, legitimized the move in terms of the pervasiveness of corruption and the corporate sponsorship of electoral politics and the aim to 'challenge the changed culture of politics that ... brings not just religion but caste as a force, to carry on the game of numbers' (Patkar 2004). Against such opportunistic manipulation, Patkar advocated the 'values, sincerity, and commitment' of the people's movements, just as today the AAP juxtaposes its ethical commitment to the corrupt 'vote-banking' by existing political parties. When in 2014, the AAP leadership, mainly through Yadav, invited the NAPM to ally itself to the AAP, there was a round of tough negotiations, but the mood was optimistic. As Swamy described it, NAPM activists challenged Kejriwal on the extent to which his priorities lay with 'the poor', and not just with fighting corruption, but were satisfied when the AAP leadership agreed to their terms. They thus hoped that joining their strengths – the visibility and urban appeal of India Against Corruption leaders with the experience and rural grounding of the NAPM leaders – would allow for an effective change of the political system in favour of India's poor.

The contradictions between left and right within the AAP did, however, erupt in March 2015, a month after the sweeping election victory of the AAP. What seems to have happened is that the leftist opposition with the AAP, led by Bhushan and Yadav, had started becoming ever more vocal to the media – who were largely hostile to the AAP (Naqvi 2015) – about the way they disagreed on policy issues and the selection of election candidates. In the aftermath of this, Kejriwal demanded the resignation of Bhushan and Yadav from the party, rather cunningly orchestrating this internal power play (see details in, for example, Naqvi 2015). As the news came out it confirmed the worries of more left-leaning activists in the AAP about the party's right-leaning tendencies and the lack of internal democracy, and thus many of them, including Swamy and Patkar, also decided to leave the AAP.

Others did stay, among them Babu Mathew as well as Atishi Marlena, one of the few prominent female activists left in the AAP. With the expulsion of Bhushan and Yadav, who had been her former mentors, she too lost her position as spokesperson for the party. I met her in July 2015 in her office in the Delhi Secretariat, where she was now advisor to Deputy Chief Minister Manish Sisodia, a long-term associate of Arvind Kejriwal. Though unhappy about Bhushan and Yadav's expulsion, she explained she had decided to stay because ultimately what counted more for her than 'internal party issues' was how she could contribute to a public policy that was much more responsive to marginalized populations. She described the intense stand-off the AAP government was having with the electricity companies in its effort to prevent price hikes as evidence of the AAP indeed standing up for those 'otherwise unrepresented' and of its independence from corporate funding. In the hostility of the corporate-owned media to AAP she saw another sign of how the AAP was 'combating the combined forces of corruption and capitalism rolled into one'. Asking her about the quote that was one of the sole posters in her office at the Delhi Secretariat – 'Never doubt that a small group of thoughtful, committed citizens can change the world – indeed, it's the only thing that ever has – Margaret Mead' – she confirmed this had become her logo, for 'you have to believe that you are making a difference, that things are moving, are changing ...'

IT Professionals and Slum Dwellers

Since the Congress party has historically relied on an alliance of the elite with the downtrodden of India, bypassing the middle-ranking castes, it is perhaps no surprise to see the AAP, which has come up in the vacuum left by an imploding Congress, come to rely on a similar voter base: after attracting upper-caste outrage at 'corruption', gaining a foothold in the urban slums of Old Delhi, New Delhi and Greater Kailash had been crucial for the AAP's electoral success (Ramani 2013). The AAP, moreover, seems to return to a way of political mobilizing that avoids explicit reference to caste, regional or religious identity, something that goes against the trend of the proliferation of such political identities since the 1990s (Palshikar 2016: 128). Considering the AAP's strong reliance on volunteers, what is particularly interesting is that people from opposite sides of the class and caste spectrum indeed start interacting and being part of the same local party structures. Thus those positioned to draw huge incomes from the new opportunities of neoliberal capitalism in India come into direct contact with those who may have gained access to a few consumer goods but whose lives in general have become only more precarious and indebted in the past decade. This class contradiction finds its way into policy, as the ten points proudly proposed by the new AAP government in Delhi include a doubling of the budget for education and a substantial subsidy on electricity and water – both policies of great concern to the urban poor – together with more postmodern-bourgeois concerns such as the provisioning of free public Wi-Fi all over Delhi and the installation of CCTV cameras in all public buses and classrooms.

In Srirupa Roy's ethnographic work (2014) amongst AAP volunteers, we get a good sense of the kind of political culture that manages to cater to fundamentally divergent class trajectories. According to Roy, the success of the AAP in its initial stage relied on 'offering tens of thousands of individuals with spaces and opportunities to establish their uniqueness or distinction as effective, and new, political subjects' (2014: 50). The AAP offered urban youth a platform to practise their imagined managerial/CEO selves, to engage in the language of Harvard Business School filtered through the popular economics bestsellers that one can find for sale on the pavements of central Delhi. Roy moreover encounters a 'deeply engrained practicality' – of the kind that also keeps left and right together – translated into direct 'problem solving' through educating people on their legal rights or reviving defunct democratic mechanisms so that 'simple solutions' can be found to complex problems (2014: 48ff). AAP candidates are likely to engage in what Roy calls 'performances of political reluctance and renunciation' – the continued ethical and principled distancing from 'dirty politics' (2014: 50). That there is a 'middle-class' aura around this is obvious, as the poor in India are generally considered more 'opportunistic': AAP volunteers, Roy describes, will point at the wealthy background of AAP candidates as proof of their 'principled' character. As we will see, there is also, however, a related discourse of 'sacrifice' available to those AAP volunteers who cannot boast of having foregone huge corporate incomes to work for the AAP.

Indeed, in one Delhi constituency where I followed the work of AAP volunteers in the summer of 2015, it was particularly a slum-dwelling Valmiki (Dalit) woman who was being celebrated for the sacrifices she made for the AAP. As the real 'heroine' of the AAP, she was said to have the generosity of heart to work for others despite the difficult economic situation her family was in. One of the AAP volunteers who was particularly insistent that I should meet Anick, the AAP heroine in question, was Kunwar, a young wealthy stock manager in whose grand extended-family mansion there was enough space to dedicate a side room as a meeting space where AAP volunteers could discuss plans under the watchful eyes of his high-caste ancestors looking down from the framed sepia pictures on the wall. It was Kunwar who drove me in his car to the informal slum several kilometres away in the same constituency, where we indeed met Anick.

Finding our way through the narrow lanes of the slum, we find Anick's small but *pukka* (cemented) one-room home, and soon enough Anick, alerted to our arrival, comes running to let us in. Anick's one-room home swiftly becomes heavily air-conditioned and is packed with an impressive collection of new white goods, among them even a washing machine. As we start talking, Anick initially introduces herself as having worked for a 'call centre' and having given up her job when Kejriwal called on people to leave whatever it was they were doing and join the movement. Being a bit surprised to find a call centre employee living in a slum, the story soon enough takes what to me seems a more realistic turn as I learn the 'call centre' that Anick had wanted me to think she worked in was in fact a small phone shop where she would sell SIM cards. The owner was not paying her salary, she adds, which obviously added to her decision to leave the job.

On asking about the impressive collection of white goods around us, Anick shares with me that these days she is terribly stressed because all of those – and the room itself – were bought on credit. It is only her husband, a rickshaw driver, who earns for the family now, but that is a struggle too, since even his rickshaw was bought on credit. Anick meanwhile is so caught up in volunteer work for AAP that she does not have time for work at all, she says.[3] There are a lot of issues that neighbours have started asking her assistance with, from negotiating with the teacher at the nearby school to make him actually turn up for work, to what is perhaps the most urgent of people's problems these days: the issue of electricity bills. Anick explains that earlier, when Congress was in power, local politicians would posture as 'protectors of the poor', telling the slum dwellers privately that they need not pay their electricity bills. Meanwhile, however, the bills were not erased but simply kept on their account at the electricity board. Now that the AAP has come to power in Delhi the problem has surfaced, since it is in fact Modi's men (BJP sympathizers) who are running the electricity boards in Delhi, and to make things difficult for the AAP they have started demanding people pay their huge pending bills – bills of sometimes over 50,000 rupees. Kejriwal made it all much worse, Anick says, fanning the flames by publicly telling the poor 'I don't pay the bills, you don't pay the bills – burn the bills!'. Now men are coming here every day from the electricity board, threatening to cut people's electricity – 'And without electricity, our children cannot even study at night!'. Hence as an AAP volunteer, Anick is busy all the time uniting people to oppose those who come to cut their electricity while at the same time brokering between the slum dwellers and the company so that the bills can be lowered and a payment schedule can be agreed on. People are rather desperate and end up selling their family jewellery or even 'mortgaging' their (unregistered) house to pay the bills.

As we walk back from the slum, Kunwar points out the not so obvious to me: there is a 'silver lining' to all of this. 'With the AAP, for the first time slum dwellers have started becoming more responsible, spending less on alcohol and instead starting to pay their bills …' Indeed, Kunwar seems content that the AAP is leading to a more orderly rule of law-based economic functioning in Delhi – exactly the main concern of a newspaper like the *Financial Times* when it favours Kejriwal over Modi. Anick, for her part, seems attracted to the AAP at least partly for how it allows her, through association to someone like Kunwar, to indulge a certain fantasy of being on her way to 'middle-class' status, which she seems to try and confirm by surrounding herself with material objects befitting that status. Indeed, talking to Anick, I was reminded of Emilya Zabiliute's (2014b) description of youth in the Delhi slum where she did research, who could be seen gravitating towards the new extravagant shopping malls to indulge in fantasies that they could not in the least believe in. Where Kunwar, the stockbroker, was content to see an increasing 'financial responsibility' amongst slum dwellers, I was, however, struck by something quite different, namely the increasing precariousness of the material underpinnings of people's lives in this slum, as most of their income went straight to paying off interest while the threat of dispossession – and even suicide – was ever-present.

Though Kunwar and Anick may have shared a similar ideal of orderly middle-class living, their actual experience of this could not be more divergent. Strikingly different, moreover, is the relational logic that ties Anick and Kunwar to the party. In the case of Kunwar, since he is from such an influential and wealthy family, and since the space his family home provides is so useful to the activities of the AAP, the local MLP and other party workers make a daily effort of honouring him and maintaining links to him. The AAP member whom I first visited Kunwar with was made to wait a long time for Kunwar to turn up and she spent most of that time announcing how generous and brilliant Kunwar was. It was clear that even if Kunwar was starting to have moral doubts about the AAP as a political party – and was thinking of following his father, who had always been a fervent RSS (Hindu nationalist, paramilitary) volunteer but would have nothing to do with party politics (the BJP) – AAP workers would do everything to convince him to maintain his patronage.

Things were quite different with Anick: a few times during our talk, she expressed her sorrow at the fact that while she was doing so much for the AAP in this neighbourhood – she had become someone almost everyone in the slum came to with their problems and she was a key broker in negotiating these problems with the authorities – she had not been given a paid position by the AAP because of a 'corrupt' local slumlord who was spreading malicious rumours about her. One day she hoped to see a reward for the sacrifice she made while organizing people in the slum around the party. Anick emphasized that the reward was certainly not the reason she joined the AAP, but she felt terribly stressed about having to face another barely attainable debt payment deadline every week. While party workers visibly pay their respects and air their admiration for Kunwar, Anick, while put on a pedestal as a Dalit 'heroine' of the party, in everyday interaction was the one paying her respects to party workers rather than vice versa. Kancha Illaiah (2014) captures the ironies of caste and gender at play well, when in reference to the AAP's election symbol of the broom he remarks that 'it is nice to see men who would normally not like to be seen wielding *jhadoos* [brooms] at home brandishing brooms in public like trophies. The *aam aurats* [common women] of India must be feeling good that, at least, some middle class *aadmis* [men] have snatched their *jhadoos*, if not to sweep their homes then at least to sweep away old, foggy parties and politicians'.

The Invisible Hand that Wields the Broom

At this point the obvious question is: what, despite these tensions and contradictions, holds the AAP together? Firstly, there are certain internal dynamics that contribute to this. Regarding the spiritual idea of *swaraj*, which is so extremely difficult to combine with the logic of sudden 'revolution', political leadership, winning elections and actual democratic governing, it should be noted that the philosophy of *swaraj* at the same time allows for such stark contradictions to exist without the party entirely exploding. For *swaraj* also entails always remaining open to others' interpretations and their demonstration of having acted out of sincerity. The outcomes of intentions, as they interact with structures, may be a total disaster but, as Kejriwal keeps emphasizing, what matters is that his intentions are pure. In fact, the contradictions that are produced by the clash of *swaraj* with reality are sometimes even *embraced*, as they provide constant opportunities to test one's spiritual strength. *Swaraj*, moreover, sits well with the general emphasis on action – more so than ideology within the AAP – which also helps mediate the second contradiction I discussed, between left-wing and right-wing political processes of class alliance within the AAP. Despite the rightwards swing that followed a period in which more left-wing activists had joined the party, some of the latter could continue within the AAP precisely by falling back on the 'technomoral' focus on concrete impacts and results that also characterizes the realm of social activism (Bornstein and Sharma 2016). Having stepped into politics with the conviction that concrete social activism alone was not enough and that politics could and should be done differently, they ended up following the logic of prioritizing small concrete impacts on reality – particularly on the quality of the services delivered by government – over longer-term political implications or ideological concerns about left and right.

In its more extreme version, this focus on action over and above ideology is characteristic also of the culture of moral purity, managerial problem-definition and technological problem-solving that Srirupa Roy (2014) so poignantly captures in her work on AAP volunteers. However, for AAP volunteers there is more that binds them to the party than this action-oriented logic and the common aspirational culture. Especially beyond the 'party-building' stage that Roy describes, a more practical and relational logic comes into play to bind AAP volunteers from very different backgrounds. Whereas the party becomes dependent on – and makes claims on – volunteers from wealthy, professional backgrounds, slum-dwelling, working-class volunteers in contrast become dependent on – and make claims on – the party. Thus it is in fact the continuity of social hierarchies that assures that diverging class trajectories of those linked to the party do not make the party fall apart.

Still, despite these ways in which internal contradictions also lead to a certain coherence of the party, the AAP does seem to move 'from crisis to crisis', as an AAP member commented to me. Indeed, the forces keeping the party together ultimately come more from outside than inside: AAP's place in the wider political process certainly contributes to its survival as a party. For in the larger contemporary political conjuncture, the AAP has come to stand for the only possible political force for progressive change and the defence of secularism. Many still consider the Indian left – the communist parties – as much too closed and co-opted by capitalism to still be considered progressive. Kemal Chenoy, who joined the AAP from the Communist Party of India (CPI) but soon found himself drastically sidelined in the AAP, told me he would nevertheless stay with the AAP, because despite all efforts at de-Stalinization, the communist parties were all beyond reform and incapable of the kind of renovation necessary to connect to 'people' and speak their language. Atishi Marlena likewise told me that all other parties, including the Communist Party of India (Marxist)[4] and the other leftist parties, were completely corporately controlled. As she said, 'The Aam Aadmi Party is frankly the only vehicle for transformative politics in this country'. In the absence of other parties to which leftist political activists can turn for a credible alternative, the AAP has become the crucial secularist bulwark against the communal (religious) and casteist violence that has been on the increase since the election of Narendra Modi as Prime Minister.

Except in neighbourhoods with a history of strong leftist mobilization and education, this crucial distinction that many left-liberal activists see between the BJP and the AAP may, however, be seen as no more than hair-splitting. Indeed, any taxi driver or auto *walla* I spoke to in Delhi told me the opposite: that indeed the biggest problem in India today was 'corruption' and that they had voted for Modi in the national elections for this reason – and for Kejriwal in the state elections for the same reason and 'because it is good to not give too much power to one party'. The AAP, perhaps indeed in touch with the 'common man', had even made this logic into its election credo in November 2014, as it proclaimed 'Modi for PM [Prime Minister], Arvind [Kejriwal] for CM [Chief Minister of Delhi]', before hurriedly taking down these banners again because of the outrage they provoked amongst the liberal-leftist activists that had allied themselves to the AAP. When I tried to push 'common men', for instance taxi drivers I spoke to, on the difference between Modi and Kejriwal, they would sometimes clarify to me they were from different parties but then make the point that they were indeed the same. And this brings me back to what is perhaps the biggest irony of the broom-wielding AAP men that Kancha Illaiah described: the fact that half a year later, an even more unlikely explicit claimant to the title of the 'common man' could be seen wielding a broom in public, namely no other than Narendra Modi, new Prime Minister of India, enthusiastically embarking on a 'Clean India' campaign to celebrate the 150th birth anniversary of 'Bapu' (Mahatma Gandhi). One might be tempted to read into it a co-optation attempt by Modi, except that as the Prime Minister of India, only recently elected and with a clear majority, it seems doubtful Modi would need to care enough about competition from Kejriwal or the AAP – which hardly has a presence beyond Delhi – to organize such a campaign. What is more likely is that this was merely one of many ways in which the AAP and the BJP, despite their electoral rivalry, draw on the same conservative-moralist Hindu repertoire. In this respect, it is also striking how much the almost exclusively male leadership of both parties are paternalistically preoccupied with 'women's safety': Kejriwal is constantly battling to make Delhi 'safe for women' while Modi announced there would be 'no more attacks on women under Modi *sarkar* (government)'. As the BJP, to become mainstream, was moving slightly away from what are called the party's 'extreme fringes' of Hindu extremism,[5] and after a short period of more leftist involvement the AAP again moved rightward, the two parties indeed became difficult to distinguish.

This is no less the case, moreover, when we look beyond the shared Hindu repertoire bolstering these equally charismatic, 'morally impeccable'[6], 'non-elite'[7] leaders and look at the approach to Indian capitalism that they promote. Of course, there are what leftist and liberal activists consider to be crucial differences between the BJP and the AAP, notably the fact that the BJP tried to push through the most blatantly pro-corporate land acquisition bill in the history of India, whereas the AAP consistently declares its opposition to forced dispossession. The 'common man' in Delhi cannot, however, be blamed for overseeing such differences within the overall cosmology, which both leaders promote, of jubilant expectations around the wonders that real, unfettered capitalism will bring once it is liberated from the 'corruption' that is holding it down. Indeed, Kejriwal has been explicit on the topic: he is not against capitalism, only against 'crony capitalism'; he does not want 'first class citizens' to be saddled with 'third class government'; he wants to get rid of 'interference' by the government in industry; and he looks forward to the economic reforms of the previous governments, designed by 'excellent Harvard-trained Indian economists', becoming actually implemented under his 'corruption-free governance', turning Delhi into a 'global city'. Though there are substantial differences in the way the AAP envisions translating its visions into policy, at the level of language and political style it is very difficult to distinguish it from Modi's 'good governance', 'rapid economic growth', 'smart cities' and 'MyGov' platform for 'crowdsourced' governance ideas.

Thus, it may well be that this is an exciting moment in Indian history – one of those moments where 'the people' break through and upset the existing political establishment. The platforms through which the people – as the 'common man' – make this breakthrough, however, have set rather narrow limits to the extent to which relations of power and inequality will actually become transformed. Despite the flickering presence of universalist counter-politics, the 'quasi-counter-politics' of the right (Kalb and Mollona, this volume) has become hegemonic in 'emerging India'.

Luisa Steur is Associate Professor at the Department of Anthropology of the University of Amsterdam, and Lead Editor of *Focaal-Journal of Global and Historical Anthropology*. Her research is on capitalist restructuring of everyday life and the changing relationship of Communist politics to the struggles of racially oppressed people in Kerala and Cuba. She published *Indigenist mobilization: Confronting electoral Communism and precarious livelihoods in post-reform Kerala* (2017; and, most recently, "Sanitation workers and 'structural racialisation' in a globalising Centro Havana" (in the journal *Race and Class*).

Notes

1. Ramlila Maidan is a large ground located in New Delhi, traditionally used for staging the annual Ramlila celebrations, where the life of the Hindu deity Rama is re-enacted.
2. This vilification by both the left and the right of NGOs was interpreted by many Dalit NGO activists (who depended more fully on foreign support to be able to organize) as a marker of caste privilege (see Mosse 2011).
3. One might wonder though to what extent Anick's 'volunteer work' is not also compelled by the social relations of her indebtedness.
4. The CPI(M) is the largest communist party in India.
5. This trend towards moderation ended with the appointment of the fanatically anti-Muslim, radical Hindu cleric Yogi Adityanath as Chief Minister of India's most populous state – Uttar Pradesh – in March 2017.
6. An image that is a truly perverse irony in the case of Modi, who has benefited from anti-Muslim pogroms ('riots') at every major step of his political career.
7. Modi and Kejriwal are not Brahmins, and they are not from wealthy families.

References

Baxi, P. 2014. 'The Politics of Raid Governance – Aam Aurat v. Khas Aurat', *Kafila* [blog], 25 January.
Bornstein, E. and A. Sharma. 2016. 'The Righteous and the Rightful: The Technomoral Politics of NGOs, Social Movements, and the State in India', *American Ethnologist* 43: 76–90.
Breman, J. 2008. *Footloose Labour: Working in India's Informal Economy*. Cambridge: Cambridge University Press.
Chakrabarti, A. and A. Dhar. 2014. 'India and the Politics of "Corruption"', *Philosophers for Change*, 4 February.
Chatterjee, P. 2008. 'Democracy and Economic Transformation in India', *Economic and Political Weekly* 43(16): 53–62.
———. 2011. 'Against Corruption = Against Politics', *Kafila* [blog], 28 August.
Chikermane, G. with S. Banerjee. 2014. *The Disrupter: Arvind Kejriwal and the Audacious Rise of the Aam Aadmi*. New Delhi: Rupa Publications India.
Giri, S. 2014. 'India: Why the Aam Aadmi Party Needs a Small Lesson in Marxism', *Democracy and Class Struggle* [Blog], 5 April.

Jodkha, S. 2002. 'Nation and Village: Images of Rural India in Gandhi, Nehru and Ambedkar', *Economic and Political Weekly*, 10 August, 3343–353.
Hansen, T.B. 2014. 'The Sacrificial Self – Recasting Renunciation in South Asia'. Public lecture delivered at University of Copenhagen, 21 March.
Illaiah, K. 2014. 'Missing the Aurat in AAP', *New Age Islam*, 15 January.
Jaffrelot, C. 2003. *India's Silent Revolution: The Rise of the Lower Castes in North India*. New York: Columbia University Press.
Jenkins, M. 2014. 'Anna Hazare, Liberalisation and the Careers of Corruption in Modern India: 1974–2011', *Economic and Political Weekly* 49(33): 41–49.
Kejriwal, A. 2012. *Swaraj*. New Delhi: Harper Collins.
Khandekar, A. and D. Reddy. 2015. 'An Indian Summer: Corruption, Class and the Lokpal Protests', *Journal of Consumer Culture* 15(2): 221–47. Published online 13 August 2013.
Megwanshi, B. 2011. 'This is Why Team Anna Makes me Nervous', *Tehelka*. Retrieved 6 December 2017 from http://archive.tehelka.com/story_main50.asp?filename=Ws010911This_why.asp.
Menon, N. and A. Nigam. 2011. 'If Only There Were No People, Democracy Would be Fine …', *Kafila* [blog], 22 August.
Mosse, D. 2011. 'Uncertain Networks: NGOs, Dalit Rights and the Development Agenda in South India'. Background paper to ESRC 'Caste out of Development' project (RES-062-23-2227). https://casteout.files.wordpress.com/2013/07/david_uncertainnetworks.pdf.
Naqvi, S. 2015. *Capital Conquest: How the AAP's Incredible Victory Has Redefined Indian Elections*. Gurgaon: Hachette Book Publishing India.
Nigam, A. 2014. 'AAP and the Ideology Warriors', *Kafila* [blog], 11 January.
Palshikar, S. 2016. 'Who is Delhi's Common Man?', *New Left Review* 98: 113–28.
Patkar, M. 2004. 'Q & A Medha Patkar: "Politics is Also a Kind of Movement"', *The Hindu*, 28 March.
Patnaik, P. 2014. 'A Disturbing Phenomenon', *Frontline*, 24 January.
Pattenden, J. 2016. *Labour, State and Society in Rural India: A Class-Relational Approach*. Manchester: Manchester University Press.
Pinney, C. 2014. 'Gandhi, Camera, Action! India's "August spring"', in P. Werbner, M. Webb, and K. Spellman-Poots (eds), *The Political Aesthetics of Global Protest: The Arab Spring and Beyond*. Edinburgh: Edinburgh University Press, pp. 177–92.
Ramani, S. 2013. 'The Aam Aadmi Party's Win in Delhi: Dissecting it through Geographical Information Systems', *Economic and Political Weekly* 48(52).
Roy, S. 2014. 'Being the Change: The Aam Aadmi Party and the Politics of the Extraordinary in Indian Democracy', *Economic and Political Weekly* 49(15): 45–54.
Sharma, A. 2012. 'Finding Women among "Common Men"', *Kafila* [blog], 12 December.
Singh, P. 2014. 'History and Idealism in the Aam Aadmi Party's 2014 Victories in Punjab', *Kafila* [blog], 29 May.
Sonpimple, R. 2014. 'Aam Aadmi and Dalits', *Countercurrents*, 8 February.
Visvanathan, S. 2014. 'The Future and AAP', *The Hindu*, 16 April.
Webb, M. 2015. 'Contemporary Indian Anti-Corruption Movements and Political Aesthetics'. *FocaalBlog*, 23 April. Retrieved 6 December 2017 from http://www.focaalblog.com/2015/04/23/martin-webb-contemporary-indian-anti-corruption-movements-and-political-aesthetics/.
Zabiliute, E. 2014a. 'Delhi Assembly Elections, Daru and Politisation of Violence against Women', *Feminist Review* 107: 90–97.
———. 2014b. 'Going to a Mall, Disguising the Slum: Experiences of the "World Class City" among Urban Poor Young Males'. *European Conference on South Asia Studies, 23–26 July*. Switzerland: University of Zurich.

– Chapter 9 –

RE-ENVISIONING SOCIAL MOVEMENTS IN THE GLOBAL CITY
From Fordism to the Neoliberal Era
Ida Susser

This chapter is an effort to understand social movements in the United States with respect to regimes of accumulation. Following somewhat in the footsteps of social theorists such as Gavin Smith (2011) and Jane Collins (2012), I review recent approaches to theorizing social movements of the neoliberal era and then attempt to understand the emergence of various movements over time in New York City. As Don Kalb (2014: 174) has called for, this is part of an ongoing project 'to rediscover … the interconnected populist histories, contestations and emergent "class compasses"' generated in the urban capitalist context.

Following E.P. Thompson (1963), we can understand the new class formations or fault lines of society through the emerging social movements of the era. Thus, in the 1990s, the World Social Forum revealed a growing understanding of common global assaults through neoliberalism and the less than obvious connections between the privatization of water and the price of pharmaceuticals. In 2011, Occupy Wall Street (OWS), which focused on inequalities within the nation/state, told us something about a growing conception of the middle and working class finding themselves in the same structural position. The movement generated internal critiques and struggles over the representation of the poorest Americans, Native Americans, homeless people and racialized minorities, as well as the voices of women. Nevertheless, it was only after the OWS demonstrations that President Barack Obama introduced discussions of poverty into his 2012 re-election campaign. Since then, the 2016 victory of the far-right presidential candidate Donald Trump in the US elections has forced a re-examination of the ideas of populism, fascism and civil society intertwined with questions of class.

This chapter suggests that the emergence of OWS and the major nationwide demonstrations following the 2017 inauguration of the extreme right-wing president Donald Trump represent a crucial confrontation over ideas of class. Trump's support has been partly attributed to the disaffection of the old established working class combined with a backlash of racism. However, it also represents decades of organizing and corporate funding by the Republican Party at the state and federal level to limit access to voting; undermine the rights of women, immigrants and minority populations; and increase the power of money in elections, among much else. Thus, the reformulation of a commons with respect to the 99 per cent, which includes attention to gender and discrimination against minorities, is becoming an ever more critical counterpoint to the current regime.

This argument relies on a view of the working class, defined broadly by its lack of the ownership of production, becoming aware of common interests in opposition to the assault of concerted corporate interests. However, in line with a postwar hegemonic project in the US, since the 1950s, many working people have come to see themselves as middle class and, in fact, have denied common interests with the working poor, often defined by race (Kalb 2014). As in the discussion of Occupy above, here I use the term middle class as both an emic and a sociological category and then consider the ways in which such groups, increasingly in debt and with static or declining incomes, have recently begun to see themselves in more inclusive terms as the '99 per cent'. As the new economy has led to the bifurcation of the middle class, with the majority losing ground and a smaller upper group enjoying massive increases in wealth (Milanović 2016), the distinctions between the working class and the lower echelons of the middle class have been less evident. The importance of OWS and the idea of the 99 per cent lies precisely in the ways in which different groups have been able to come together in public space, forming a commons while maintaining multiple separate alliances around specific goals and identities with respect to gender, race and sexuality.

Overall, I will submit that we learn about class formation and the possibilities of transformation from the emergence of contingent movements (Thompson 1963). In other words, we need to analyse movements from the grassroots in the effort to develop an understanding of the politics of resistance to accumulation by dispossession (see also Kasmir and Carbonella 2008). Although we can recognize shifts in regimes of accumulation, the historical importance of the particular movements that seem inevitably to spring up in resistance to new modes of exploitation are not always readily understood when they first emerge, but frequently come to signal new class formations as they crystallize and evolve over time.

Although theorists of social movements have long looked past the shop floor (Harvey 1976; Susser 2012 [1982]; Kalb 2014; Lem 2014), the ways in which the social reproduction of the neighbourhood, the urban street and labour movements interact under particular regimes becomes ever more significant as we enter the neoliberal regime with the dispersed workforce facilitated by informational technology, in all spaces from taxi driving to home rentals (such as Airbnb). With less contractual benefits and ever fewer factories while business is being done from home by computer or smartphone, social media becomes more crucial for social movements as the shop floor and even shops disappear. However, social media does not negate the need for expression on the urban street or social movements in public spaces, and it is the relationship between these forms of social protest that we need to theorize.

In a theoretical discussion of social movements, Gavin Smith (2011) notes that, since the 1980s, crises of accumulation have precipitated shifts in ruling class policies that have led to the dismantling of government services and the narrow targeting of assistance, which he terms 'selective hegemony'. He uses the term 'selective hegemony' to specify that neoliberalism involves exclusions that foster narrow identity politics rather than universal policies. One of Smith's important contributions to ongoing discussions of the current neoliberal era is his exploration of different hegemonic processes associated with recent political economic transformations.

This schematic outline moves us major steps towards understanding the formation of distinctive groups under neoliberal global policies. However, class, as a conflicting or counter-hegemonic force is not a central theme of Smith's argument. Since the analysis starts from an effort to restate arguments of governmentality, with the ever-present aim of linking a Foucauldian analysis with a Marxist framework, such a top-down analysis of hegemony does not explain how the emergence of social movements may break through and redefine the class boundaries of previous regimes of accumulation.

To take a completely different approach to social movements, I refer back to Castells (1983), *The City and the Grassroots*. Like

Christopher Hill (1972), Eric Hobsbawm (1955), Herbert Gutman (1976) and other social historians, Castells (1983) sought to understand culturally available paths and ideals that opened the possibilities for democracy, whether or not the visionaries succeeded at any particular historical moment – and this is an essential aspect in the understanding of social movements. Political mobilization or the act of collective resistance in itself generates and legitimizes alternative visions, such as the ideas of the urban commons so widespread today. Thus, even as they fail, movements of land invasion, emerging from historically and spatially rooted social process, lead people to publicly question the priority of private property under capitalism. As I have argued elsewhere (Susser 2006, 2016), alternative visions and their practical reality expressed in settlements for the poor are themselves significant in the generation of future possibilities. As the Trump era takes hold, this perspective is crucial in recognizing the impact of mobilizations such as Occupy Wall Street in 2011 and the possibility for later mobilizations to affect US politics.

Recent work by the Human Economy school (Keith Hart, John Sharpe and others at http://thehumaneconomy.blogspot.com/) has begun to take this approach seriously in the post-recession era and show the ways in which communal efforts in Greece (Rakopoulos 2013) and elsewhere may be creating practices that hold the possibility to shift the dominant discourse and contribute to imagining alternatives. Such an approach also recalls the arguments from a feminist perspective, which decentres industrial work and analyses informal work, households and varying patterns of redistribution as important spaces where people may work cooperatively, and through such practice generates transformative visions of society (Federici 2004; Gibson-Graham 2006).

Clearly global movements today manifest themselves across traditional class lines. As many have suggested, they are better described in terms of a theory of the commons (Nonini 2007; Harvey 2012; Susser and Tonnelat 2013; Susser 2016). The idea of the commons connects with calls for human rights and environmental justice, as well as shared rights to health, land, air and water, rather than to a narrow interpretation of working-class politics. Don Nonini (2007) has argued that the battle over the commons responds to the capitalist degradation of the environment combined with the crisis of accumulation. Such powerful and multiple emerging movements are also responding to the newly emerging forms of stratification in the global economy, manifested or precipitated by the increasing privatization and reductions in the public weal. People are recognizing and struggling against a continuing process of capital accumulation by dispossession (Harvey 2003a; Kasmir and Carbonella 2008), but since this dispossession is affecting a much broader group of people than industrial workers, or, in fact, the Fordist definition of the working class, the emerging movements involve a much broader swathe of the population.

Building on the anthropological tradition of Marxist/feminist theorists, whose influence in theorizing social reproduction Winnie Lem (2014) reminded us of in a recent blog, Jane Collins (2012) expands our ideas of labour, unemployment and social reproduction, as she argues that in the context of the growing inequality and privatization of neoliberal regimes of accumulation, powerful movements have emerged among service providers and the families they serve, many of whom might think of themselves as middle class. This perspective was developed by Frances Fox Piven and Richard Cloward (1971) in their analysis of the Welfare Rights Movement of the 1960s. However, at that time, I would argue, the divisions of race and income between the two groups along with the contrasting opportunities available to the service workers, and the context of this struggle in a moment when industrial labour was still relatively well off and well established, prevented a wider social movement and the expression of joint class interests coming to the fore. Once the civil rights and feminist movements had won affirmative action legislation, and after the 1975 fiscal crisis and the departure of manufacturing from much of the north-eastern US, such cooperation between government service providers and those they served became evident and powerful, if in scattered situations. It is to explore these shifts in emphasis over time that I investigate the history of social movements in New York City in the next section.

The abrupt transformation from the expansive hegemony of the welfare state to selective hegemony (Smith 2011) is dramatically represented by the 1975 New York City fiscal crisis, which heralded the imposition of austerity and the beginning of the neoliberal era globally (Harvey 2003a; Susser 2012 [1982]). Between about 1965 and 1980, New York City changed from a primarily small manufacturing economy to a service economy for businesses focused on finance, insurance and real estate (Mollenkopf and Castells 1991 Castells 1989; Sassen 1991; Freeman 2000; Susser 2012 [1982]). The loss of unionized manufacturing jobs and the sudden stringent austerity policies imposed after 1975, along with the influx of immigrants recruited in an informal service economy, led to new forms of municipal governance and required new approaches to organization for working-class residents of the city.

Here, by concentrating geographically on social movements in one city, I examine how the changes in the regimes of accumulation lead to different forms of protest over time. I compare the combination of neighbourhood movements, movements around service access and labour movements as municipal priorities change from expansive to selective hegemony. The effort is to trace the dominant social movements through three moments, from the 1960s through the transition to neoliberalism of the 1970s and 1980s and then to the social movements during the massive gentrification, displacements and defaults of the 2000s.

In New York City, under the expansive hegemony of the welfare state (Smith 2011), we can trace effective and powerful labour movements from the 1950s to the 1970s (Freeman 2000). Through the 1960s, one of the main battles of the civil rights movement was not only against racial segregation of neighbourhoods but for entry into these well-unionized jobs. Feminists also fought, through unions and elsewhere, for equal pay, day care to allow women to work and entrance into male-defined fields. Freeman notes that after 1965, the labour unions, men in construction, the Brooklyn Navy Yard and the many small factories such as those concentrated in Red Hook and Greenpoint-Williamsburg, Brooklyn, declined in power. By the 1970s the jobs in well-organized garment manufacturing, predominantly women workers, had also shifted to the Pacific Rim and elsewhere and the garment workers' union was under assault.

In line with Smith's concept of expansive hegemony, the early 1960s in New York City was a time of continuing expansion, with the unifying of the borough colleges and the creation of the City University of New York, the continuing construction of municipal hospitals, affordable housing for the poor and the middle class, and municipal investment in the building of major cultural centres, such as the Lincoln Center for the Performing Arts. The massive investment in central cities in the 1960s, part of President Lyndon Johnson's War on Poverty and known as urban renewal, was seen by some as 'urban removal' (Piven and Cloward 1971) and early gentrification (Castells and Susser 2002). However, in spite of these tendencies, new social housing was constructed behind the Lincoln Center and in other parts of Manhattan. In contrast, from 1975, with the end of expansive hegemony, investments in social housing ended and almost no social housing has been constructed in Manhattan since then.

In 1966, as the Brooklyn Navy Yard, which employed 9,000 workers, closed, construction slowed and small manufacturing departed from the city. Industrial labour unions lost influence, while a new group of powerful unions emerged in New York City among hospital workers and service workers, including many minorities and women, teachers and even university faculty and staff. The police and firemen's unions strengthened, now subject to affirmative action laws that were implemented in the 1970s, although these were resisted for many years.

Near the end of the industrial era, in the early 1960s, the automation of cotton picking in the rural South led to a massive migration of African American workers to New York City (Piven and Cloward 1971) just as the jobs in New York City were being moved elsewhere, also facilitated by automation and information technology (Castells 1989; Sassen 1991).

An early manifestation of the fight against selective hegemony by people without work can be found in the Welfare Rights Movement of the late 1960s (Piven and Cloward 1971). We see the cooperation of the poor African American women, many just arrived from the South, with the social service workers, also predominantly women, who were employed as the gatekeepers of payments for public assistance. These groups together managed to redefine subsidies for poor families as a right and remove barriers such as home inspections and the specification of funds for particular purchases of clothes and furniture from the requirements. This transformation of welfare subsidies from a contingent charity to a right was greatly resented by conservative government officials. By the late 1990s, the neoliberal and conservative agenda had destroyed the programme and replaced it with time-limited subsidies tied to work requirements. However, the Welfare Rights Movement can be seen as one of the first protests by poor people, in the absence of industrial unions, to collaborate with members of the growing numbers of service providers against policies of selective hegemony.

Another significant social movement in NYC in the 1960s, also addressing issues of the new poor, was in opposition to the racialized control of public space and police violence. Although the incarceration rate was not nearly as high as it became later, the excessive use of force, a hallmark of the neoliberal era in the United States, was already an issue by the mid 1960s. A strong and ultimately successful movement, made up of middle- and working-class New Yorkers, was formed to create a civilian review board for the police department.

The anti-imperialist student movement was one of the major forces of the 1960s and certainly shaped the thinking of scholars of the era. In the context of social movements with respect to New York City, the student campus occupations of April 1968 had two main thrusts. The first was the fragile coalition between students, neighbourhood organizers and national black activists in the opposition to Columbia University's expansion into Morningside Park, which would privatize the public space accessible to Harlem residents. The second was the occupation of the campus over time as a commons, an early 'post-industrial' effort to redefine the uses of the new technology such as to allow a different future for all. In this category, we can include the hippie movement, the squatters, the first community garden occupations, the Up Against the Wall Motherfuckers (founded by Herbert Marcuse's two stepsons) and many other groups, whose positions were perhaps best expressed in Herbert Marcuse's *Eros and Civilization* (1966), a call for an alternative vision of work and leisure. These student movements of 1968 represented the historic takeover of the urban street, which led to the theorization of Henri Lefebvre (2003), Manuel Castells (Castells and Susser 2002) and the many who followed.

The 1975 Fiscal Crisis in New York City was the watershed moment in the transition from Fordism to flexible accumulation as industry left the city in the search for cheaper labour (Harvey 2003a; Susser 2012 [1982]). It also marks the change in Smith's terms from expansive to selective hegemony in municipal governance (Smith 2011). It precipitated an abrupt abandonment of major social service projects such as the closing of well-baby clinics, local hospitals and TB treatment centres, and public libraries, the firing of the new university faculty and the reduction or neglect of sanitation services, education, fire protection and many other kinds of city responsibilities, such as sealing up burned-out buildings. The newly entrenched service unions lent their pension funds to back up the city during the fiscal crisis, but many of their workers were still laid off in the following austerity.

During this period, working-class neighbourhood movements responded with rent strikes and sweat equity in the effort to preserve affordable housing. In several boroughs, residents took over firehouses in the effort to retain fire protection and worked with both the fire union and the police to defend their jobs and services (Susser 2012 [1982]). Like the Welfare Rights Movement, these events can be seen as early examples of the massive collaborations between service providers and residents that occurred in Wisconsin thirty years later (Collins 2012). However, we do not yet see movements in which the middle class was closely aligned with working-class interests.

In 1988, after thirteen years of the selective hegemony or neoliberal policies that followed the fiscal crisis, homeless people, anarchists and artists occupied Tomkins Square Park in an iconic event of resistance to escalating displacement through gentrification (Smith 1996; Marcus 2005). This cooperation between working-class youth, homeless people and politically informed anarchists and artists displaced from the Lower East Side was a harbinger of the kind of movements of the urban street that were to become prevalent in the next decades.

Gentrification and the displacement of the working poor continued through the 1990s. To combat the weakening of established unions and the hiring of informal workers, immigrant groups, in Chinatown and among Latino/a workers, began to organize worker centres as a way to include documented and undocumented workers. These centres frequently formed alliances or merged with neighbourhood organizations opposing displacement through gentrification. One such cooperation led to a neighbourhood boycott of an upscale delicatessen and fishmarket to protest the firing of legal workers who had tried to form a union and the expulsion of undocumented Mexican workers who also worked there (Nash 2001).

By 1998, antiglobal activists were organizing around the United States, but the first major demonstration in NYC was planned for September 2001, when the WTO was to meet in NYC. These protests were dramatically curtailed by the assault on the World Trade Centre and the reorganization of global perspectives that followed. Under the harsh police fortifications implemented by Mayor Giuliani, exacerbated by the horror and fear following the events of 9/11, comparatively few protestors turned up and the critique of the WTO was temporarily muted.

Selective hegemony reigned supreme after 9/11, as a major new onslaught of re-zoning and the displacement of populations for the construction of high income housing began in New York City under the Bloomberg mayoral administration (which came into power in 2002). The concept of wounded cities (Schneider and Susser 2003) highlights the ways in which the shock of the World Trade Center assault allowed corporate leaders to take control of the city and undermine democratic processes (Susser 2012 [1982]; Harvey 2003b). This vacuum led to a business/government plan to re-zone the city, causing the massive displacement of artists and middle-class professionals combined with the continuing harassment and displacement of working-class people. As a result, members of middle-class and working-class groups joined together in all boroughs to fight for affordable housing, public education and other services. The Great Recession of 2008 led to some slowing down in the displacement through gentrification but increased displacement through debt and house foreclosures (Susser 2012 [1982]). Neighbourhood organizing for housing and healthcare continued but with limited success.

Reacting to the austerity policies implemented in 2008, in September 2011, Occupy Wall Street protesters took over Zuccotti Park just a block from the centre of capital on Wall Street. They famously occupied that space for several months, unrelentingly through cold and wet. Led by youth as well as long-term anarchists and other activists, this occupation of public space reflected the total displacement of working-class people beyond the neighbourhood (Susser 2002) and forefronted the new economy of financialization and predatory debt (Williams 2004), particularly student debt. Implementing a variety of tactics honed over twenty years of antiglobal organizing, Occupy Wall Street served as a rallying ground for thousands of people. The occupied space became a rallying ground for alternative communal lifestyles, well-organized medical and food distribution, tents and blankets for the cold wet weather, a library of shared books, reconfigured forms of communication and sign language, a multimedia headquarters equipped with high-tech computers plugged in globally, in the open air, and a long series of world famous speakers combined with local NYC activists. This was followed by youth occupations across the nation and far beyond national boundaries.

Although fleeting, I suggest that OWS represented a new form of protest scaled to counteract the divisiveness of selective hegemony by emphasizing a commons. They included both the communal aspects stressed by feminists and human economy theorists (Gibson-Graham 2006; Federici 2004; Rakopoulos 2013; Susser 2016), and the occupation of public space and the urban street (Castells 1983; Lefebvre 2003; Harvey 2012). In this way, the protesters reconfigured the vision of New York City. Occupy Wall Street, followed by Occupy Sandy in 2012 and Black Lives Matter in 2013, led to changes in NYC politics and a concerted rethinking of the Bloomberg era.

By the elections of 2013 in NYC, I argue partly as a consequence of Occupy Wall Street and the ensuing organizing, we see the emergence of a different class consciousness. We see the effectiveness of a movement based on the outlined history of grassroots housing groups, anti-racist organizing, healthcare activists and others that cuts across identity politics and includes the different sectors that might be labelled the precariat: immigrants, working poor and underemployed millennial youth (Standing 2011).

As a result of this movement, an outlier in New York City politics, Bill de Blasio was elected as the first democratic mayor since the African American David Dinkins in 1990. He was primarily elected on the basis of a campaign against police harassment, this time the racial targeting implied in the 'stop and frisk' programme. De Blasio's campaign slogan was a recognition of 'the 99 per cent' intervention of Occupy Wall Street: 'A tale of two cities'. His campaign promises invoked a priority for affordable housing as well as universal kindergarten. His wife, Chirlane McCray, an African American poet, activist and political writer, who had once publicly identified as a lesbian, could have been portrayed as a vulnerability but, in fact, became a major asset in the campaign. In other words, in opposition to over three decades of selective hegemonic governance, middle- and working-class New Yorkers were voting for a candidate who directly confronted the unprecedented inequality in the city, the ongoing racial targeting and repression by the police and the shortage of housing for middle-class and working-class people.

This election represented an alternate vision of the city and set priorities for a new coalition of residents who, in fact, understood themselves as 'the 99 per cent' – perhaps a new class formation in this increasingly unequal world. Since his election, besides implementing citywide pre-kindergarten programmes and other policies, De Blasio called on the Democratic Party candidate in opposition to Trump, Hilary Clinton, to pay more attention to progressive issues during her election campaign. He also worked to implement universal Municipal Identification Cards to dispel discrimination against undocumented immigrants and homeless people and has led democratic opposition to Trump's efforts to identify undocumented immigrants through city records.

The election of De Blasio can be seen as indicative of a new recognition of growing inequality, reflected in the immense public acclaim at the publication of Thomas Piketty's (Piketty and Goldhammer 2014) volume on the accumulating wealth of the 0.1 per cent. E.P. Thompson (1963) takes the appearance of the term 'working class' in working men's newspapers of 1813 as indicative of the emergence of a class for itself. Perhaps the slogan 'the 99 per cent' can be seen in the same light. This broad coalition of interests among the displaced middle and working classes has become the baseline upon which to advocate for progressive policies in New York City, including, at the state level, the institutionalization of a higher minimum wage and the return to a tuition-free public university (Gonzalez 2017; Viteritti 2017). Certainly, the institutional establishment of a progressive mayor of the largest city in the United States serves as one bulwark against the opening assaults on public welfare and human rights of the Trump presidency.

The significance of these developments in New York City is only magnified by analysis of the presidential election returns of November 2016, with respect to Donald Trump and Hilary Clinton. The successful progressive alliance that brought De Blasio to power in 2013 can be contrasted with the losses suffered by protesters in Wisconsin and the implications of these losses for the victory of Donald Trump.

In the spring of 2011, major demonstrations took place in Wisconsin in opposition to an assault on the collective bargaining of civil service unions. Like Occupy, they represented an effort to combat selective hegemony and cutbacks in education, healthcare and other services. Reminiscent of the Welfare Rights Movement of the 1960s, and the firehouse demonstrations of 1975 in New York City, the protests involved professional providers in collaboration with those they served, including those who regarded themselves as middle class as well as working class. Over 300,000 demonstrators comprising civil service unions of police, firemen, nurses, teachers and others in cooperation with the families of their clients occupied the state capital buildings (Collins 2012). In the end, this movement lost the battle with the Republican governor and collective bargaining was outlawed in the state. The weakening of the unions combined with the Republican assault on voting rights led to Trump's surprise winning of Wisconsin, a long-time Democratic stronghold. This was an important component of his electoral college victory.

In contrast to the losses in Wisconsin, the interventions of Occupy Wall Street in New York City can be seen as relatively successful, as they became moderately institutionalized in the election of the progressive Mayor De Blasio. Trump lost the elections in his home state, New York. In addition, massive demonstrations began outside Trump's residence, Trump Tower, on Fifth Avenue immediately after the election, disrupting midtown traffic for weeks. The day after the inauguration, in support of the Women's March on Washington, more than 250,000 people assembled at Grand Central Station and marched down Park Avenue. The following Saturday, thousands of protesters poured into JFK airport to protest Donald Trump's Executive Order banning immigration from six Muslim countries and the next day many more gathered in protest in Battery Square Park. Reflecting the sense of the population, Mayor De Blasio adopted a strong stand in opposition to Trump's assault on immigrants, Muslims and others. Along with other major cities, New York City has taken a leading role as a sanctuary city and so far, in spite of new government demands, refused to provide information about immigrant status to the Trump regime. As this unpredictable presidency proceeds, the history of social movements in New York City and the legacy of Occupy may provide a platform from which to contest the challenges to come.

In conclusion, in the shift from regimes of 'Fordism' to flexible accumulation, the weakening of industrial unions in New York City and the increase in the service economy undermined the power and social conditions of the working class in New York City. This was accompanied by a shift in governance from an expansive to a selective hegemony. Social movements that emerged to address this shift have relied on the urban street and in some cases a coalition of service providers and their clients. Both of these kinds of movements have constructed alliances across identity and have rallied members who see themselves as 'middle class' to join with displaced urban residents, underemployed youth and immigrants in the fight for a more equitable distribution of income, including a minimum wage and an opposition to racism. In a city with a long progressive history, such movements have been effective in counteracting the divisiveness of selective hegemony, maintaining to some extent protections for the urban working class and the lower echelons of the bifurcated middle class. In the process they are making a new political bloc, or the emergence of a class, visible to itself.

Ida Susser is a Distinguished Professor of Anthropology at the Graduate Center, CUNY. Her recent book *The Yellow Vests and the Battle for Democracy: taking to the streets of Paris in the 21st Century* (2026) focuses on commoning movements and new visions. Previous books include *Norman Street* (2012) a study of working-class opposition to cutbacks during the New York City fiscal crisis, and *AIDS, Sex and Culture: Global Politics and Survival in Southern Africa* (2009).

Note

Some of this material appears in Susser, I. 2017. 'Commoning in New York City, Barcelona, and Paris: Notes and Queries from the Field', in Special Section: Exploring the Commons in *Focaal – Journal of Global and Historical Anthropology* 79: 6–22, and in Susser, I. 2016. 'Considering the Urban Commons: Anthropological Approaches to Social Movements', *Dialectical Anthropology* 40(3): 183–98.

References

Castells, M.1983. *The City and the Grassroots*. Berkeley: University of California Press.
──. 1989. *The Informational City*. Oxford: Blackwell.
Castells, M. and I. Susser. 2002. *The Castells Reader on Cities and Social Theory*. Oxford: Blackwell.
Collins, J. 2012. 'Theorizing Wisconsin's 2011 Protests: Community-Based Unionism Confronts Accumulation by Dispossession', *American Ethnologist* 39(1): 6–20.
Federici, S. 2004. *Caliban and the Witch*. Williamsburg, NY: Autonomedia.
Freeman, J. 2000. *Working Class New York*. New York: The New Press.
Gibson-Graham, J.K. 2006. *A Postcapitalist Politics*. Minneapolis, MN: University of Minnesota Press.
Gonzalez, J. 2017. *Reclaiming Gotham*. New York: The New Press.
Gutman, H. 1976. *Work, Culture and Society in Industrializing America*. New York: Vintage.
Harvey, D. 1976. 'Labor, Capital and Class Struggle around the Built Environment in Advanced Capitalist Societies', *Politics and Society* 6: 265–94.
──. 2003a. *The New Imperialism: Accumulation by Dispossession*. Oxford: Oxford University Press.
──. 2003b. 'The City as Body Politic', in J. Schneider and I. Susser (eds), *Wounded Cities*. Oxford: Berg, pp. 25–46.
Harvey, D. 2012. *Rebel Cities*. London: Verso.
Hill, C. 1972. *The World Turned Upside Down: Radical Ideas During the English Revolution*. London: Penguin.
Hobsbawm, E. 1955. *Primitive Rebels*. New York: Norton.
Kalb, D. 2014. 'Class: The Urban Commons and the "Empty Sign" of "the Middle Class" in the 21st Century', in D. Nonini (ed.), *A Companion to Urban Anthropology*. Oxford: Blackwell, pp. 157–76.
──. 2015. 'Introduction: Class and the New Anthropological Holism', in J. Carrier and D. Kalb (eds), *Anthropologies of Class: Power, Practice and Inequality*. Cambridge: Cambridge University Press, pp. 1–27.
Kasmir, S. and A. Carbonella. 2008. 'Dispossession and the Anthropology of Labor', *Critique of Anthropology* 28(1): 5–25.
Lefebvre, H. 2003. *The Urban Revolution*. Minneapolis, MN: Minnesota University Press.
Lem, W. 2014. 'Materialist Feminism, Migration and "Affective" Labor: Mediations in Capitalist Reproduction', *FocaalBlog*, 23 July. Retrieved from http://www.focaalblog.com/2014/07/23/materialist-feminism-migration-and-affective-labour-mediations-in-capitalist-reproduction-winnie-lem/#sthash.0ixmEIuU.dpuf.
Marcus, A. 2005. *Where Have all the Homeless Gone?* New York and Oxford: Berghahn Books.
Marcuse, H. 1966. *Eros and Civilization*. Boston, MA: Beacon.
Milanović, B. 2016. *Global Inequality: A New Approach for the Age of Globalization*. Cambridge, MA: Harvard University Press.

Mollenkopf, J. and M. Castells. 1991. *The Dual City*. New York: Russell Sage Foundation.
Nash, J. 2001. 'Labor Struggles: Gender, Ethnicity and the New Migration', in I. Susser and T. C. Patterson (eds), *Cultural Diversity in the United States*. Oxford: Blackwell, pp. 206–28.
Nonini, D. (ed.). 2007. *The Global Idea of 'The Commons'*. New York and Oxford: Berghahn Books.
Piketty, T. and A. Goldhammer. 2014. *Capital in the 21st Century*. Cambridge, MA: Harvard University Press.
Piven, F. and R. Cloward. 1971. *Regulating the Poor*. New York: Pantheon.
Rakopoulos, T. 2013. 'Responding to the Crisis: Food Co-operatives and the Solidarity Economy in Greece', *Anthropology Southern Africa* 36(3–4): 102–7. (Special Issue: The Human Economy Project: First Steps). Retrieved from http://thehumaneconomy.blogspot.com/2014/05/special-issue-human-economy-project.html.
Sassen, S. 1991. *The Global City*. Princeton, NJ: Princeton University Press.
Schneider, J. and I. Susser (eds). 2003. *Wounded Cities*. Oxford: Berg.
Smith, G. 2011. 'Selective Hegemony and Beyond-Populations with "No Productive Function": A Framework for Enquiry', *Identities* 18(1): 2–38.
Smith, N. 1996. *The New Urban Frontier*. New York: Routledge.
Standing, G. 2011. *The Precariat: The New Dangerous Class*. London: Bloomsbury Academic.
Susser, I. 2002. 'Losing Ground: Advancing Capitalism and the Relocation of Working Class Communities', in D. Nugent (ed.), *Locating Capitalism in Time in Space*. Stanford, CA: Stanford University Press, pp. 274–289.
_____. 2006. 'Global Visions and Grassroots Movements: An Anthropological Perspective', *International Journal of Urban and Regional Research* I 30(1): 212–18.
_____. 2012 [1982]. Updated, *Norman Street: Poverty and Politics in an Urban Neighborhood*. Oxford: Oxford University Press.
_____. 2016. 'Considering the Urban Commons: Anthropological Approaches to Social Movements', *Dialectical Anthropology* 40(3): 183–98.
Susser, I. and S. Tonnelat. 2013. 'Transformative Cities', *Focaal* 66: 105–21.
Thompson, E.P. 1963. *The Making of the English Working Class*. London: Victor Gollancz.
Viteritti, J. 2017. *The Pragmatist: Bill de Blasio's Quest to Save the Soul of New York*. Oxford: Oxford University Press.
Williams, B. 2004. *Debt for Sale*. Philadelphia, PA: University of Pennsylvania Press.

—Afterword—

NOTES FOR A CONTEMPORARY URBAN CLASS ANALYSIS

Massimiliano Mollona and Don Kalb

The remarkable contributions in this volume show that we are witnessing an exceptional period of worldwide global mobilizations with its epicentre in 'global cities'; uneven geographies made up of financial districts, sprawling slums, luxury developments and semi-rural neighbourhoods, enmeshed in post-industrial, financial, informal, indentured and subterranean economies. Some political analysts see the current urban mobilizations as part of the long wave of worldwide democratic uprisings that took off at the beginning of the twenty-first century in countries that do not have a long-standing democratic tradition and that are now championing new forms of anti-capitalism. Others feel more ambivalent about these protests, especially as they were followed by a global right-wing political turn,[1] including the end of the Pink Tide in Latin America, the election of Trump as US President and Brexit in the UK. In fact, the current global political shift marks the end of the inclusive and egalitarian populism of the left in the South – mostly Latin America but also Europe's South – and the sudden rise of 'authoritarian populism' among the conservative and far-right parties in the North. The right-wing authoritarian populism of Le Pen in France and Orban in Hungary built an 'unlikely' alliance with the white working class around an undefined centre, fuelled by nationalism, xenophobia and economic dispossession. Its emotional register is one of moral indignation, condemnation and outrage articulated through middle-class values and an identitarian and exclusionary narrative of class.

Laclau's *On Populist Reason* (2005) and Mouffe's (2005) notion of post-politics are possibly the most adopted theoretical frameworks to understand the contemporary political situation. For Laclau, populism is a political *form* (as opposed to content) that embraces and gathers diverse and contradictory ideological positions and political demands. Working through chains of equivalences, populism reconciles conflicting frameworks; for instance, xenophobia and autochthonous working-class solidarity, and brings together left-wing and right-wing demands within a unified social subjectivity antagonistic to the status quo and coalescing around 'empty signifiers' – 'the people' or 'the politicians' or 'capitalism'. Laclau also distinguishes between democratic demands (for instance, for increasing social welfare or against inequality) and popular demands (for instance, the undifferentiated rage against the government) and argues that globalized capitalism generates incremental leakages between the two. Bringing together psychoanalysis and political theory, Laclau shows the important affective and unconscious dimension of politics and the power of 'the people' *across* the Western political imaginary – from Rousseau to Le Bon, Lenin and Peron. The Freudian and Lacanian components of Laclau's theory help us to understand the 'strange' popular appeal of politicians such as Trump or Grillo, who rely on the fact that they are located in between the vertical position of the leader and the horizontal one of the common people. Laclau's discursive approach to politics is also central in Mouffe's notion of the post-political, another recurring frame in contemporary political analyses. For Mouffe the post-political is the ideal of the consensual administration that has characterized Western liberalism since the 1990s – from Habermas' deliberative democracy, to Blair's third-way and Fukuyama's 'end of history'. Consensus-based politics fails to acknowledge that pluralist politics is inherently divisive, conflictive and agonistic, and replaces adversaries with enemies.

Indeed, contemporary political analyses, including some in this volume, tend to stress the affective and discursive power of 'the people', their moral condemnation, outrage and indignation, their lack of positive identification and their identitarian and exclusionary frameworks that replaced class identification ('without colours'). In other terms, they endorse Laclau and Mouffe's ideas of the 'post-political' and populism. It is true, 'the people' gathered in the streets in Argentina, Brazil, Turkey, Spain, Portugal, Egypt and Greece in the early 2000s as well as more recently, when they were supported by right-wing and authoritarian populist leaders. But were they the same kind of people? Raymond William famously argued that 'there are no masses; there are only ways of seeing people as masses' (Williams 1973: 289). Indeed, our imaginary of crowds is historically contingent on broader trajectories of political economy. In Brazil, the demonstrations of June 2013 and those of 2015 were expressions of different class articulations. The demonstrations of 2013 were led by casualized workers and the subproletariat. They showed the deep crisis of the Brazilian Workers' Party – a working-class party generating labour precariousness – but also a remarkable rearticulation of the Brazilian left, including 'right to the city' organizations, student movements and new trade union articulations. The demonstrations of 2015 and the impeachment of Dilma showed the end of the populist consensus and the re-emergence of the old right-wing elites, who had been dormant during the democratic opening.

We must be weary of culturalist and discursive readings of contemporary politics that consider 'left' and 'right' as shifting signifiers operating within the same ideological realm. Rather, as the introduction argues, we should focus on the multilayered interplay of global structural conjunctures, regional trajectories and local contingent struggles. First let us consider regional specificity, starting from Latin America. The analysis of the end of the Pink Tide is beyond the scope of this piece. But it is clear that the main impulse for the end of Chavismo, Kirchnerismo and Lulismo was the collapse of the commodity cycle and the steep decline of oil prices, which constituted the backbone of these neo-extractivist regimes based on the combination of finance, logistic, commodities and land extraction (Mezzadra and Rossiter 2015; Mollona, this volume). Indeed, the hybrid model of 'neoliberalism-cum-neo-developmentalism' (Saad-Filho 2016) in Argentina, Brazil and Ecuador patched together contradictory measures such as formal wage increases, foreign exchange and price controls, universal programmes of poverty reduction, labour deregulation, tight fiscal policy and public debt reduction beyond credibility. This economic heterodoxy, often critical of Western economic orthodoxy, made possible the populist consensus between the middle class, the working classes and old power elites. By populist consensus I mean the economic emancipation of the working class and rural classes without their political emancipation. So the coming together of the middle classes and working classes in Latin America reflected the combination of specific forms of capitalist growth and social redistribution made possible by extractivism. The crisis of extractivism in the region marked the end of this left populism.

For Andre Singer (2012), 'Lulismo' was the specific phenomenon of incorporation of the subproletarian masses of the north-east inside the imagined national community, a passive revolution based on the combination of income redistribution and financialization. The election of Macri in Argentina, Pedro Pablo Kuczynski (a 77-year-old ex-banker) over Keiko Fujimori in Peru and the staffing of Temer's cabinet with (white and male) economists makes it clear that Latin American politics is shifting towards neoliberal economic orthodoxy. Commenting on the latest Latinobarometro poll, *The Economist* (3 September 2016) recently argued: 'Latin pragmatism looks like a welcome contrast to the rise in support for fringe candidates and causes in Europe and the United States'. Latin Americans, the article claims, are no more content with the status quo than are Brexiters or Trump supporters in the United States. In fact, 73 per cent of them think the elites govern in their own interests. But unlike in Europe or the United States they are not protectionists (77 per cent of them favour greater integration with other nations) nor are they identitarian and xenophobic. Their main worry is the economy, especially unemployment, inflation and poverty. But unlike the inclusive populism of the left, the economy championed by Macri or Temer is hierarchical and exclusionary – cuts in pensions and poverty programmes and other state spending, as well as limits to economic redistribution and lifting of protections against vulture funds. The crisis of the left in Latin America, and more broadly, is connected to the way left-wing parties in power have depoliticized the economy and subscribed to the dogma of capitalism. For Zizek (1999: 298), the depoliticization of the economy by the left marks the end of its inclusionary and universalizing political project. It is this surrendering to the neoliberal project by the PT that, according to Perry Anderson (2016), moved the working class against Dilma in 2015.

Reintroducing class analysis in the contemporary political context is not an easy task. The financialization of the economy, the fragmentation of industrial production along global commodity chains and the deregulation of labour, including the proliferation of zero-hour contracts, has exploded 'the factory walls' and expanded the reach of capital to the entire life cycle. Penetrating every human activity – from household reproduction to care, communication and sociability – capital now colonizes and subjugates the working class everywhere, from the heavy mortgages afflicting respectable workers to the extortionate microfinance loans imposed on slum dwellers. This diffuse omnipresence of capital makes class relations, to use Cornelius Castoriadis' (1994) term, 'magmatic', as they articulate around myriads of individual, contradictory and atomized dimensions. Together with Carbonella and Kasmir (2014) and Carrier and Kalb (2015) this volume argues that new experiments of class rearticulation are taking place in the context of major economic shifts, in which capital has left the shop floor and is colonizing the entire life. The acts of 'commoning' (Susser and Tonnelat 2013), and the cross-sectional politics in some of the urban mobilizations described in this volume, show that as well as 'parasitically multiplying labour' (Mezzadra and Rossiter 2015), the movement of capital creates possibilities of labour resocialization; for instance, by bringing together old and new traditions of labour activism, trade unions and social movements. This, according to Leo Panitch (2017), is the only viable strategy for labour.

Examples of these contradictory class articulations are the AAP party in India supported by both low-caste slum dwellers and upper-caste activists, as described by Steur in this volume, and the co-presence of favelados and IT workers in the same street protests in Rio, in Mollona's chapter. But class fragmentation does not imply the emergence of undifferentiated 'centres' or the resurgence of a revolutionary middle class as for Fukuyama or Standing. Favelados and IT workers, slum dwellers and upper-caste activists, Kirchnerists and supporters of Macri are not part of the same 'people'. The unemployed youth that took to the streets of Rio and Bulgaria in 2013 (70 per cent of which were below 30 years of age) was not expressing any exclusionary middle-class morality. It was demonstrating against those ex-communist parties that once in government subscribed to the TINA dogma. We argue that 'left' and 'right' are lost in different realms of the post-political. For the left, succumbing to the post-political means to have lost its universalizing and inclusive mission. For the right, the post-political is the familiar reproduction of exclusion and inequality through a moralizing economic discourse that naturalizes racialized, feminized, and spatially uneven trajectories of capital accumulation.

Indeed, we have seen authoritarian populism before. In an article in *Marxism Today* in 1980, Stuart Hall used Laclau's notion of authoritarian populism to make sense of the political ascent of Margaret Thatcher. In a context of deep economic crisis, Thatcher was tapping into the popular discontent with the bureaucratic and controlling statism and collectivism of the Labour Party and *discursively* associating that discontent with the left and socialism more broadly. Thatcher framed her opposition to the Labour Party as a struggle of the people against a bureaucratic and centralist state.

More importantly she understood that monetarism would become a central *political* force – in breaking the trade unions, privatizing the state, financializing the economy – and she supported it discursively, framing it as a progressive and 'moral' alternative to the corporatism of the Labour Party, and incorporating different and contradictory positions and components of Toryism (family, authority, patriarchy) with those of neoliberalism (individualism, mobility, success and anti-statism). Hall notes that in parallel to the authoritarian shift of the Labour Party, the working class was developing a 'moral panic about social anarchy and race' and endorsing a 'petty bourgeois morality'. He adds: 'In the light of Thatcher's critique of statism, democracy is at the very heart of the struggle … The definition of a new conception of socialism is the only practical way in which the crisis can be overcome and turned into a positive direction'. Central to the redefinition of the left, Hall argued, is the recomposition of the working class beyond identitarian lines. More than thirty years later Theresa May is capitalizing on similar racist discourses among the white working class. Besides, after the failure of the populist project of Blair's New Left (very similar to Lula's), on which new ground can the recomposition of the working class succeed? The contributions in this volume show that the articulation of social activism and class activism will play a central role in the renewal of the left today, in the same way in which, for instance, social service workers and the poor black working class came together in the welfare rights movement in NYC in the 1960s, highlighted by Susser in this volume. In the mobilizations in Turkey and Bosnia described in this book, the 'traditional working-class' organizations played a leading role. In the mobilizations in Brazil, Argentina, Turkey, Bosnia and Egypt, also discussed in this volume, trade unions and mainstream left parties joined the demonstrations only half way through and faced scepticism and resistance by the grassroots movements that had initiated them. But solidarities and collaborations between the new social movements and the old labour movement did develop, as in Brazil, leading to a new class articulation of the left. In other terms, new social movements may 'signal new class formations as they crystallize' (Susser in this volume) rather than being an alternative to traditional working-class action. Besides, practical alliances between the working classes and middle classes may develop around common livelihood projects, but without overidentification or mutual opposition.

The second important characteristic of contemporary mobilizations is their entanglement with the city and with the broader process of urban democratization initiated in the 1970s by 'right to the city' movements (Lefebvre 1991; Harvey 2013). The political geography of contemporary cities is uneven and multi-scalar. Cities are nested within different scales of political economy – regional, local, national and global – each of them with different dynamics and temporalities. In cities the spatial and temporal dynamics of capital and labour associated with factory work are replaced by the temporal and spatial dis-junctures, and critical junctures,[2] between 'life-spaces'[3] (the space of community and places) and the forces operating in the abstract economy (international investors, media and financial networks, global developers, multifunctional logistics, hoteliers and extractive companies). Such cognitive and experiential disconnect between 'economy' and 'life' in the urban context, coupled with the incessant privatization of public spaces, makes it difficult to develop sustained class solidarities and common political projects. But the connectivity, effervescence and intensity of cities may trigger unexpected counterinsurgencies, alliances and gatherings. Besides, the modern urban milieu complicates the traditional dichotomy between 'the country' and 'the city', famously highlighted by Williams (1973), which still underpins much of the contemporary political imaginary. Megacities blur rural peripheries and ultramodern centres, thus bringing together, for example, 'postmodern' rentierism (Harvey 2013 or Piketty 2014) and 'pre-capitalist' land grabbing (Sassen 2014) so that casual labourers, landless peasants, street vendors, cyber-proletarians, care workers and dispossessed slum dwellers become a unified marginal class within the urban centres (see also Therborn 2014). Indeed, in Brazil, the decline of the Landless Movement (MST) was accompanied by the rise of the movement of the homeless (MTST) and by the activism of slum dwellers. In other instances, anti-land grabbing movements are co-opted by high-caste demands and moralities, as in Steur's chapter; or by the rhetoric of land redistribution of the Maoist party, as described by Hoffmann. Moreover, cities complicate the dichotomies between production and circulation, industry and finance, which dominate much of the present political imaginary. Entangled with the abstract and invisible circulation of finance and urban rents are the material infrastructures of labour and the grassroots economies – informal trade, small and illegal production and street markets – that feed the immaterial circuits of capital. For every immaterial transaction that ends up in the dark pools of finance is in the end extracted from the labour of builders, electricians, welders, engineers and unskilled workers who make up the living urban infrastructure of capital. In addition, the peripheries of Buenos Aires, Istanbul, Delhi, Rio de Janeiro and Athens pullulate with small industrial shop floors, family-run firms and sweatshops that form a living economy both parasitical and counter-hegemonic to the main circuits of capital. Worker-run factories, neighbourhood-based labour councils, solidarity and women's cooperatives in Bolivia, Argentina, Athens, India and Brazil are experiments in direct and democratic production and livelihood[4] premised on diverse and yet pervasive forms of class solidarity. In other terms, the uneven political cartography of cities is complemented by their diverse economies and forms of livelihood.

In the fluid and disorganized context of late capitalism, contemporary anthropology faces the challenge of capturing specific critical junctions (including dis-junctions) within broader networks and instances of structural power. For Kalb (2011: 13), critical junctions are 'multi-level relational mechanisms that link the global levels of structural power with the respective institutional fields of tactical power on the scale of the nation-state and with the spaces of agential power of common people situated in everyday circumstances'. Methodologically, this multi-scalar and global analysis challenges us to combine traditional ethnography with the 'macroscopic' historical and political economy frameworks of Eric Wolf (2010) and Bill Roseberry (1988). Indeed, if Zizek (1999) is right to suggest that the left must rediscover the political dimension of the economy, one should note that this is what Marxist anthropology has always stood for.

With this volume we argue that anthropological analyses of contemporary urban activism, even when localized, must adopt a deeper comparative framework around a class analysis that should be framed within a broader global and historical anthropology of uneven and combined development. For instance, Therborn (2014: 8) recently argued that Latin America, because of its combined forces of anti-colonialism and anti-capitalism, developed its own tradition of socialism, based on 'ideological bricolage' rather than on neat class distinctions and on heterogeneous social formations including the middle classes, informal labourers, unemployed, migrants and indigenous people.

In her chapter, Lazar points to the notion of 'popular classes' so often used in Latin America. Identitarianism, horizontalism and personalistic support structures were integral to anti-capitalist struggles in Argentina (Sitrin 2006), Bolivia (Zibechi 2010) and Brazil (Singer 2012) long before the postmodern turn in politics (Jameson 1991).

And yet other traditions of identitarianism and ethnonationalism are the result of the capitalist advance in post-communist Eastern Europe. Besides, horizontalism, starfish organizations, decentralized networks, consensus and leaderlessness are also the modus operandi of mafia organizations, al-Qaida franchises, tea parties and the 'new spirit of capitalism' (Boltanski and Chiappello 2007). When looked at comparatively, practices of inclusiveness and commoning have been part of working-class struggles throughout history and so have been capitalist idioms of hierarchy, exclusion and separation.

Lastly, as scholars involved in the movements of the political and engaged in the revitalization of the Marxian project, we face the challenge to balance ethnographic immersion and analytical distance – the practical unfolding of immediate struggles and their crystallization in processes of knowledge production. As activists we take part in the immediate, contingent and direct actions with the intention of instituting contingent political projects in the present. As scholars, we look back at these moments and produce concepts and knowledge that may orient contingent struggles in the future. Through the lenses of geography and world history, we then reinscribe these contingent presents and futures in the broader trajectories of capitalism. A long view on capitalism and class struggle tells us that after a long period of what Gramsci (1971: 276) called an interregnum we are now facing a new era of direct action and the resurgence of the political from all sides, the meaning of which can only be fully grasped ex-post, not because its form is open-ended and empty but because its underlying class dynamics are as complex, opaque and contradictory as the forces of capital accumulation that underpin it.

Massimiliano Mollona is an anthropologist and filmmaker. He has conducted extensive fieldwork in Brazil and England around themes of class, work, racism and post-capitalism. He currently teaches at the Department of the Arts (DAR) at the University of Bologna. His most recent book is *Brazilian Steel Town: Machines, Land, Money and Commoning in the Making of the Working Class* (2020).

Don Kalb is professor of social anthropology at the University of Bergen, Norway. Recent books include *Financialization: Relational Approaches* (Edited with Chris Hann, 2020); *Insidious Capital: Frontlines of Value at the End of a Global Cycle* (Editor, 2024, winner of the Society for the Anthropology of Work prize); *Value and Worthlessness: The Rise of the Populist Right and Other Disruptions in the Anthropology of*

Capitalism (2025); and *Backlash: The Global Rise of the Radical Right* (Edited with Walden Bello, 2026). Don is Founding Editor of *Focaal – Journal of Global and Historical Anthropology*.

Notes

1. For Latin America, see Massimiliano Mollona (2016) on *FocaalBlog*.
2. Following Don Kalb (2011) we define critical junctions as 'spatio-temporal relations that have critical consequences on the ground'.
3. The term is used by David Harvey and Teresa Hayter (1994).
4. For a review of these, see Boaventura de Sousa Santos (2006).

References

Anderson, P. 2016. 'Crisis in Brazil'. *London Review of Books*, 21 April.
Boltanski, L. and E. Chiappello. 2007. *The New Spirit of Capitalism*. London: Verso.
Carbonella, A. and S. Kasmir. 2014. *Blood and Fire: Towards a Global Anthropology of Labour*. New York and Oxford: Berghahn Books.
Carrier, J. and D. Kalb (eds). 2015. *Anthropologies of Class: Power, Practice, and Inequality*. Cambridge: Cambridge University Press.
Castoriadis, C. 1994. 'The Logic of the Magma and the Question of Autonomy', *Philosophy and Social Criticism* 20(1/2): 123–54.
De Sousa Santos, B. 2006. *Another Production is Possible: Beyond the Capitalist Canon*. London: Verso.
Gramsci, A. 1971. *Selections from the Prison Notebooks* (ed. and trans. Q. Hoare and G. Nowell-Smith). London: Lawrence & Wishart.
Hall, S. 1980. 'Thatcherism: A New Stage?' *Marxism Today*, February.
Harvey, D. 2013. *Rebel Cities: From the Right to the City to the Urban Revolution*. London: Verso.
Harvey, D. and T. Hayter. 1994. *The Factory and the City: The History of the Cowley Automotive Workers in Oxford*. Cengage Learning EMEA.
Jameson, F. 1991. *Postmodernism or the Cultural Logic of Late Capitalism*. Durham, NC: Duke University Press.
Kalb, D. 2011. 'Introduction: Headlines of Nation, Subtext of Class: Working-class Populism and the Return of the Repressed in Neoliberal Europe', in D. Kalb and G. Halmai (eds), *Headlines of Nation, Subtexts of Class*. New York and Oxford: Berghahn Books, pp. 1–36.
――――. 2014. 'Class: The Urban Commons and the 'Empty Sign' of 'the Middle Class' in the 21st Century', in Donald Nonini (ed.), *A Companion to Urban Anthropology*. Oxford: Blackwell, pp. 157–76.
Laclau, E. 2005. *On Populist Reason*. London: Verso.
Lefebvre, H. 1991. *The Politics of Space*. Oxford: Wiley-Blackwell.
Mezzadra, S. and N. Rossiter. 2015. 'Extraction, Logistic and Finance,' *South Atlantic Quarterly* 114(1): 2–25.
Mollona, M. 2016. 'The End of the Latin American Pink Tide? An Introduction', *FocaalBlog*. http://www.focaalblog.com/2016/03/15/massimiliano-mollona-the-end-of-the-latin-american-pink-tide/.
Mouffe, C. 2005. *On the Political*. London: Verso.

Panitch, L. 2017. 'On Revolutionary Optimism of the Intellect', in G. Albo and L. Panitch (eds), *Rethinking Revolution* (Socialist Register). London: Merlin Press, pp. 356–63.
Piketty, T. 2014. *Capital in the Twenty-First Century*. Cambridge, MA: Harvard University Press.
Roseberry, W. 1988. 'Political Economy', *Annual Review of Anthropology* 17: 161–85.
Saad-Filho, A. 2016. 'Overthrowing Rousseff: It's Class War and their Class is Winning', *FocaalBlog*. http://www.focaalblog.com/2016/03/22/alfredo-saad-filho-overthrowing-rousseff-its-class-war-and-their-class-is-winning/.
Sassen, S. 2014. *Expulsions: Brutality and Complexity in the Global Economy*. Cambridge, MA: Harvard University Press.
Singer, A. 2012. *Os Sentidos do Lulismo: Reforma Gradual e Pacto Conservador*. São Paulo: Companhia Das Letras.
Sitrin, M. 2006. *Horizontalism: Voices of Popular Power in Argentina*. Oakland, CA: AK Press.
Susser, I. and S. Tonnelat. 'Transformative Cities: Three Urban Commons', *Focaal – Journal of Historical and Global Anthropology* 66: 105–121.
Therborn, G. 2014. 'New Masses? Social Bases of Resistance', *New Left Review* 85: 7–16.
Williams, R. 1973. *The Country and The City*. Oxford: Oxford University Press.
Wolf, E. 2010. *Europe and the People without History*. Berkeley, CA: University of California Press.
Zibechi, R. 2010. *Dispersing Powers: Social Movements as Anti-State Forces*. Oakland, CA: AK Press.
Zizek, S. 1999. *The Ticklish Subject*. Norwich: Heathwood Press.

INDEX

A

Aam Aadmi Party. *See* Common Man Party
AAP. *See* Common Man Party
Abbasağa Park Forum of Beşiktaş/Istanbul, 47
Action Aid, 146
affirmative ethnography, 55
agonistic politics, 20, 93, 111, 224
agribusiness, 108
AKP. *See* Justice and Development Party
alter-globalist movement, 1, 4
alt-right, 4
anarchism, 54, 55, 175
Anick, 199–202
antagonistic politics, 20
anthropology, 26n1
    class and, 18
    Marxist, 230
    schools of, 6–8
Anti-capitalist Muslims, 34, 37
anti-colonialist struggle, 180, 230
anti-imperialist student movement, 215
anti-materialist philosophy, 20, 119
anti-rationalism, 20, 119
Arab Spring, 2, 37
Argentina, 92, 102, 112
    neoliberalism and, 93
    political culture of, 111
    violent crime in, 104–5
Argentine Workers Centre (CTA), 97, 98, 107
Association of State Workers (ATE), 96, 107
austerity, 2, 74, 122
    'winter protests' against, 73, 76, 78

B

Backward Society Education (BASE), 143
becoming, politics of, 55
Bharatiya Janata Party (BJP), 193, 194, 195, 200, 201, 204, 205
Bharat Jan Andolan, 191
Bharti, Somnath, 192–93
BJP. *See* Bharatiya Janata Party
Black Lives Matter, 217
Bloomberg, Michael, 216
Blumberg, Axel, 105
Blumberg, Juan Carlos, 105
Bolsa Familia, 178
bonded labourers, 23, 143, 148. *See also* Kamaiya (ex-bonded labourers)
Bouazizi, Mohammed, 2, 11
Braga, Ruy, 172
brain-drain, 77, 80
Brazil, 163–64, 168, 173, 177–80, 225
    June Revolution, 21
Brazilian Workers' Party, 225
Brexit, 4, 13
Brigate Rosse (Red Brigades), 125
BSP. *See* Bulgarian Socialist Party
Buenos Aires, 95, 96, 99
    anti-insecurity demonstration in, 105
    key mass mobilizations in, 97
Bulgaria, 22–23, 73, 75, 88
    industrial decline in, 79
    informal networks, 87
    middle classes and, 77
    term 'communists' in, 76–77
Bulgarian Socialist Party (BSP), 73, 76

C

Cabral, Sergio, 171

– 235 –

Cacciolla, Biagio, 125
cacerolazos, 98, 99, 100, 104
capital, 226
   accumulation, 212
   capital flight, 96
   deterritorialization of, 181
   foreign capital, 42, 44, 168
   international capital markets, 114n2
Capital in the Twenty-First Century (Piketty), 6
capitalism, 14, 19, 41, 69, 77, 231. *See also* neoliberal capitalism
   contradictions of, 160
   economic downward trends of, 81
   financialized, 3
   globalized, 23, 38, 224
   homogenizing capacities of capitalist state, 10
   increasingly authoritarian, 38
   India and, 205
   Islam in discord with, 34
   non-capitalist moralities, 8
   'really existing capitalism', 9
   systemic global capitalist crisis, 42
Caradonna, Giulio, 126
Casaleggio, Gianroberto, 118
caste, 157, 189, 190, 193–96, 198, 199, 202, 204
Castells, Manuel, 210
Castro, Raul, 165
Central Bank of the Republic of Turkey, 42
Centre for Housing Rights and Evictions (COHRE), 183n10
CGIL. *See* Confederazione Generale Italiana del Lavoro
Chartist mobilizations, 16
Chaudhary, Tulsi, 151
Chavismo, 225
China, 3, 165
   slowdown in economy of, 109
The City and the Grassroots (Castells), 210
civil rights movement, 213
CLA. *See* Costruiamo l'Azione
class, 17, 209–10. *See also* middle classes; working classes

adversarial conception of politics organized around class lines, 136
anthropology and, 18
class analysis, 226
class conflict, 122
class consciousness, 218
class formation, 8, 15
class-related powerlessness, 75
conundrum of, 11–12, 15
Gezi Park and, 31
Marxian idea of, 14
neoliberal capitalism as class project, 45
clientelism, 123
   party clientelism, 59, 67
Clinton, Hillary, 12, 219
CNV. *See* National Commission of Truth
COHRE. *See* Centre for Housing Rights and Evictions
collective subjectivity-in-revolt, 58
colour revolutions, 1
commodified market relations, 46
commoning, 12, 46, 182, 227
   fledgling politics of, 66
   practices of, 13
   in Taksim Square, 47
Common Man Party (Aam Aadmi Party) (AAP), 25, 187–92, 197, 198, 200, 203–5, 227
commons, 66, 209, 211
Communist Party (PCI), 21
Communist Party of India (CPI), 203
Communist Party of India (Marxist) (CPI(M)), 203
Confederation Cup, 168
Confederation of Public Workers Unions (KESK), 36
Confederation of Revolutionary Trade Unions (DISK), 36
Confederazione Generale Italiana del Lavoro (CGIL), 124
Constitutional Amendment Proposal (PEC) 37, 166, 177
corruption, 2, 66, 77, 113, 193, 197
   accusations of, 87
   anti-corruption, 24, 177, 187, 195

India and, 204
    labour unions and, 86
    Macri and, 111
    outrage against, 108
    of police, 109
    political demands against, 73
Costruiamo l'Azione (CLA), 128, 131
counter-hegemonic projects, 56
CPI. *See* Communist Party of India
CPI(M). *See* Communist Party of India (Marxist)
critical junctions, 18
CTA. *See* Argentine Workers Centre
cultural difference, 18
currency controls, 112
cyber-proletariat, 17, 22, 229

D
Dayton BiH, 19, 52, 54, 56, 61, 67, 68
    antagonistic frontier in, 65
    average salary in 2014 in, 64
    conditions of existence of, 58
    'Dayton Meantime', 60
    dominant governmental rationality within, 66
    Federation of BiH, 62
    lack of reliable population statistics in, 57
    leftward swing of populism in, 69
    'normal lives' in, 63–64, 70n1
    protests in, 59
    social reproduction in, 69
    territorial-institutional set-up of, 59
Dayton Peace Agreement, 1995, 58
de Blasio, Bill, 25, 218, 220
debt, 78, 82, 88
deindustrialization, 180
de la Rúa, Fernando, 94
Delhi, 189, 198–201
    women in, 204
Democratic Unity Roundtable (MUD), 165
Demokratska fronta (DF), 68
Department of Information (DOI), 170
developmentalism, 127, 164, 168
DF. *See* Demokratska fronta
DFO. *See* District Forest Office
Dhangadhi, 148, 149, 154, 156

dictatorial politics, 106
direct democracy, 36
DISK. *See* Confederation of Revolutionary Trade Unions
dispossession, 79, 201, 210
    capital accumulation and, 212
District Forest Office (DFO), 157
District Land Reform Office (DLRO), 157
Dita, 67
DLRO. *See* District Land Reform Office
DOI. *See* Department of Information
Duhalde, Eduardo, 94

E
economic growth
    AKP and, 41–42
    inconsistent and fluctuating, 48
energy prices, 75, 82
Erdogan, Recep Tayyip, 35
Eros and Civilization (Marcuse), 215
ethnography, 60
ethnonationalism, 58, 59, 62–63, 65, 67, 231
European Recovery Plan, 122
everyday communism, 8
ex-bonded labourers. *See* Kamaiya
extractivism, 108

F
factory workers, 22, 52
Falklands War, 93
fascism, 119
    neo-fascist groups, 21, 129
Fédération Internationale de Football Association (FIFA), 169
financialization, 67, 226
'Financial Stability Report' (Central Bank of the Republic of Turkey), 42
Fioravanti, Valerio, 129
FKS. *See* Freed Kamaiya Movement
forced relocation, 169
Fordism, 13, 215, 220
foreign debt, 42, 43
Free Brazil (MBL), 164

Freed Bonded Labourers Society (Mukta Kamaiya Samaj), 143
Freed Kamaiya Movement (FKS), 143, 144–48, 156–57, 160
    four-point programme of, 154
    leaders of, 158
    members beaten by police, 153
Freed Kamaiya Society, 159
Free Fare Movement (MPL), 21, 166, 172–73
frictional heterogeneity, 34, 35–36, 45, 49
    formation of, 32
    middle classes and, 41
Front Line (Prima Linea), 125
Fukuyama, Francis, 38–40

G
GDP. *See* gross domestic product
general strike, 36
gentrification, 32, 168, 175, 181, 216
Gezi Park, 18, 31
    middle classes and, 37, 39
    social media and, 33
    solidarity-based self-management in, 47
Giuliani, Rudi, 216
global accumulation, 18
globalization, 12, 14, 23, 38, 120, 187, 224
Global North, 1, 5
Graeber, David, 8, 54
Gramsci, Antonio, 10, 17, 100, 231
grassroots movements, 124, 126–28, 137, 143
Great Recession of 2008, 217
Grillo, Beppe, 118
gross domestic product (GDP), 48, 178
Grupo Clarín, 100, 101, 110
Guglielmi, Constanza, 106

H
Hazare, Anna, 187, 190–91, 194, 195
health problems, 81
hooliganism, 53
Housing Development Administration of Turkey (TOKI), 44–45
housing maintenance, 83

I
IAC. *See* India Against Corruption
identitarianism, 62, 69, 224, 230–31
    fear-mongering, 59
ideological dispute, 127, 131
Illaiah, Kancha, 204
imaginations, 13, 14, 121, 187
    ethical and esthetical, 8
    liberation of, 15
    moral, 9
IMF. *See* International Monetary Fund
imperialism, 2, 215
impoverization, 74, 81, 85
India, 3, 5, 194, 196
    capitalism and, 205
    corruption and, 204
    neoliberal capitalism and, 24
India Against Corruption (IAC), 189, 193, 197
indignation, 101, 102, 123
    grassroots feelings of, 121
    sociality of indignation, 108
industrialization, 181
industrial modernization, 79
inflation, 107, 177
informal garment industry, 107
informal networks, 87
insecurity, 104–5, 106
intellectual workers, 175
internal solidarity, 127
international capital markets, 114n2
International Monetary Fund (IMF), 41, 71n12
Islam
    anti-capitalist Islamists, 19
    capitalism in discord with, 34
Israel, 3
Istanbul, 11, 33, 41, 45, 230
    police violence in, 31
    regimes of accumulation and, 20
    social movements in, 32
Italian Communist Party (PCI), 120, 124, 133, 136, 139n14
Italy, 118, 128, 131, 137
    labour force in, 122
    New Right in, 125

'Opposti Estremismi' in, 131
political reproduction of Italian
  left, 125
turmoil in, 123–24
working classes in, 132

J
Janatantrik Tarai Mukti Morcha
  (JTMM), 161n7
Al-Jazeera, 2
Jobbik, 14
Join the Street, 164
JTMM. *See* Janatantrik Tarai Mukti
  Morcha
June Revolution, 21, 22, 163, 166, 171
Justice and Development Party (AKP),
  33, 37, 45, 49
  conservative and Islamist politics
    of, 34
  economic growth and, 41–42
  GDP under, 48
  privatization and, 44
  worker rights and, 40

K
Kamaiya (ex-bonded labourers), 142,
  151, 157. *See also* Freed Kamaiya
    Movement
  rehabilitation of, 148, 154, 156,
    161n3
Kamaiya Abolition Act of 2001, 156
Kamaiya Movement, 143, 145
Karachi, 108
Kejriwal, Arvind, 188–90, 191, 193,
  197, 199–200
KESK. *See* Confederation of Public
  Workers Unions
Keyder, Caglar, 41
Khirki Extension incident, 192
Kirchner, Néstor, 95, 96, 98, 102
de Kirchner, Cristina Fernández, 92,
  95, 102–4, 112
Kuczynski, Pablo, 165
Kurdish movement, 37

L
labour, 11–12, 122, 227
  bonded labourers, 23, 143, 148
  Brazilian experience of labour
    struggle, 180
  flexibilization of, 40
  as political category, 13
  traditional labour movement, 176
Labour Party, 227–28
labour unions, 11, 36, 83
  perceptions of corruption among,
    86
  privatization and, 84
Laclau, Ernesto, 57–58, 63, 179, 224
'Lama episode', 124–26
Lanata, Jorge, 101, 102
Landless Movement (MST), 174, 176,
  229
Latin America, 5, 182, 223, 225–26
  Pink Tide in, 22, 163, 165, 223, 225
  socialism in, 163
'Law of the Father' (Keyder), 41
Lazar, Sian, 11, 12
Lefebvre, Henri, 37, 46
Le Pen, Marine, 13, 223
LGBTQ groups, 32, 33, 35
liberalism, 1, 16, 224
living expenses, 76, 82
London Stock Exchange, 3
Lula da Silva, 164, 165, 172, 178
Lulismo, 225, 226

M
Macri, Mauricio, 96, 108, 109, 111, 165
Mahila Kamaiya Samaj (Women
  Kamaiya Society), 145
'mano dura', 105, 106
Maoism, 23, 143
  necessity of liberation of poor
    people and, 158
  U-CPN Maoist Party, 145, 153, 155
Maoist Constitutional Assembly
  Members, 152
Maoist Party, 148, 152
Maracanã Stadium, 169, 170
Marcuse, Herbert, 215
Marlena, Atishi, 197
Marx, Karl, 10, 14, 16
Marxism, 6, 120, 160
  class conceived under, 14
  classical, 180

Marxist anthropology, 230
revitalization of Marxian project, 231
Maskovsky, Jeff, 14
Mauss, Marcel, 8
May, Theresa, 228
MBL. *See* Free Brazil
media conspiracy, 101
medical sector, neoliberalization of, 40
Member of the Legislative Assembly (MLA), 191
memes, 102
meso-level relational mechanisms, 8
middle-aged people, 84
middle classes, 16, 17, 88, 107, 110, 189, 208–9
   anti-left middle class, 167
   Bulgaria and, 77
   'class C', 177–79
   discourse of freedom-seeking, 31–32
   emersion and consolidation of, 122
   frictional heterogeneity and, 41
   Gezi Park and, 37, 39
   global middle class revolution, 43
   Goldman Sachs report on, 38–39
   morality of, 20
   post-industrial, 121, 135
   social unrest and, 38
   unproductive, 123
   youth in, 194
migration, 80
militancy, 138n5, 150, 161n7
MLA. *See* Member of the Legislative Assembly
modernity, 85
Modi, Narendra, 200–201, 204–5
Morales, Evo, 165
morality, 20, 76
   moral imaginations, 9
   non-capitalist moralities, 8
   of outrage, 92, 107, 111
   protests, moral politics of, 113
Mouffe, Chantal, 111, 121, 130, 136, 224
Movement of Homeless Workers (MTST), 174–75, 229

Movimento 5 Stelle, 118
Movimento Sociale Italiano (MSI), 126, 138n6
MPL. *See* Free Fare Movement
MSI. *See* Movimento Sociale Italiano
MST. *See* Landless Movement
MTST. *See* Movement of Homeless Workers
MUD. *See* Democratic Unity Roundtable
Muir, Sarah, 94, 107
Mukta Kamaiya Samaj (Freed Bonded Labourers Society), 143

N
La Nación, 100
NAP. *See* Nuclei Armati Proletari
NAPM. *See* National Alliance of People's Movements
NAR. *See* Nuclei Armati Rivoluzionari
de Narvaez, Francisco, 106
National Alliance of People's Movements (NAPM), 189, 195
National Campaign for People's Right to Information, 196
National Commission of Truth (CNV), 170
National Day of Struggle, 167
nationalism, 5, 37, 223
   ethnonationalism, 58, 59, 62–63, 65, 67, 231
   Roma people, nationalist discourses against, 88
National Rural Employment Guarantee Act (NREGA), 196
NC. *See* Nepali Congress
negative self-positioning, 61
neoliberal capitalism, 1, 198
   activist self-organization to reveal alternatives to, 54
   antineoliberal uprisings, 69
   as class project, 45
   crises and contradictions of, 7
   India and, 24
   intellectual omnipresence of, 6
   medical sector and, 40
   neoliberal orthodoxy, 42

obvious pitfalls of, 5
neoliberalism, 210, 212, 228
   Argentina and, 93
   neoliberal ideologies, 86
   neoliberalizing measures, 66
   structural adjustment, 94
Nepal, 23, 161n3
Nepali Congress (NC), 159
New Right (Italy), 125
New York City, 213–14, 215, 219
9/11, 216
non-capitalist moralities, 8
NREGA. *See* National Rural Employment Guarantee Act
Nuclei Armati Proletari (NAP), 125
Nuclei Armati Rivoluzionari (NAR), 128, 129

O
OAB. *See* Order of Lawyers of Brazil
Obama, Barack, 165, 208
Occupy movements in Slovenia, 55
Occupy Wall Street (OWS), 1, 3, 25, 208–9, 211, 217
Odebrecht, Norberto, 171
OECD. *See* Organisation for Economic Co-operation and Development
oil crisis of 1973, 121
Olympic Games, 166, 168
Ombudsman bill, 191, 195
On Populist Reason (Laclau), 57, 224
operação Lava Jato, 164
'Opposti Estremismi', 131
Order of Lawyers of Brazil (OAB), 173
Organisation for Economic Co-operation and Development (OECD), 48
Our Commons, 46
outrage
   against corruption, 108
   grassroots feelings of, 121
   morality of, 92, 107, 111
OWS. *See* Occupy Wall Street

P
Paci, Massimo, 132
Pakistan, 112

Panama Papers, 111
Pan American Games, 173
participatory democracies, 75
PCI. *See* Communist Party; Italian Communist Party
PCP. *See* Petty Commodity Production
PEC. *See* Constitutional Amendment Proposal
People's Political Front (PPF), 196
Pernik, 74
   industrial decline in, 79
   out migration and, 80
   steelworkers' district in, 83
   working classes in, 78–79
Perón, Juan, 93
   populist Peronist rhetoric, 99
personhood, alternative forms of, 8
Petrobras, 164
Petty Commodity Production (PCP), 182
Piketty, Thomas, 6, 218
Pink Tide, 22, 163, 165, 223, 225
Plaza de Mayo, 106, 107
police corruption, 109
Police Pacification Units (UPP), 169
police violence, 32, 35, 152–53
   police killings, 105
political engagement
   disappointment with, 85, 89
   lack of, 79
   rhetoric against, 78
   scepticism towards, 60
political establishment, 120
political oppression, 79
political representation, 121, 130
Popular Committee on the World Cup, 173
populism, 209, 225
   authoritarian, 223, 227
   leftward swing of Dayton BiH populism, 69
   populist articulatory practice, 58
   populist Peronist rhetoric, 99
   populist reason, 58, 68
   right-wing, 5
post-2011 urban mobilizations, 38, 39
post-ideological turn, 120

post-materialism, 178–79
postsocialist state formation, 64
PPF. *See* People's Political Front
Prachanda. *See* Pushba Kamal Dahal
precariatization, 17, 172, 176, 178
Prima Linea (Front Line), 125
primitive accumulation, 195
private property, 65
privatization, 31, 38, 44, 52, 68, 229
   debt-infused, 45
   labour unions and, 84
   in Sofia, 74
protests, 1–3, 108–10, 112, 118, 148, 149, 155, 159, 194, 213, 216–17, 223
   abstention from, 74–75, 87–88
   in Bulgaria, 75
   Dayton BiH and, 59
   in Delhi, 189
   against FIFA, 169
   by FKS, 143, 144, 147, 152, 156–57, 160
   Hazare and, 195
   by IAC, 193
   June Revolution and, 163, 166
   'lawless Friday', 170
   leaderless, 104
   moral politics of, 113
   by organized social forces, 92
   against police violence, 153
   political arithmetic of, 13
   in Rio de Janeiro, 168
   self-convened, spontaneous, 92, 98, 99–100, 113
   against Trump, 219–20
   types of, 20, 210
   violent state repression of, 110
   Welfare Rights Movement and, 214
   'winter protests' against austerity, 73, 76, 78
PSOL. *See* Socialist Party
PSTU. *See* Unified Socialist Workers' Party
PT. *See* Workers Party
public media, 15
public sector workers, 110
public wealth, 44

Pushba Kamal Dahal (Prachanda), 148
Pushkar, Pankaj, 191–92

R

racial discrimination, 175, 193, 208–9, 214
Radončić, Fahrudin, 53
Rakes Movement, 119, 135
Ramlila Maidan, 187
Razsa, Maple, 55–56
Red Brigades (Brigate Rosse), 125
regimes of accumulation, 20, 208, 213
rent strikes, 215
Resident Welfare Associations (RWAs), 193
Right to Information Act (RTI), 196
Right to the City Movements, 182, 229
Rio de Janeiro, 168–69, 170, 171, 180–81
Road to Europe, 57, 67
Roma people, 80–81
   nationalist discourses against, 88
Rome, 118–19, 129
Rousseff, Dilma, 108, 163, 164, 167, 171, 176
Roy, Srirupa, 198–99
RTI. *See* Right to Information Act
RWAs. *See* Resident Welfare Associations

S

Sapkota, Tika Ram, 149
Sarajevo, 54
   ethnographic study in, 60
   plena in, 57
   solidarity demonstrations in, 53
Sassen, Saskia, 14, 181
Savez za bolju budućnost (SBB), 53, 68
Scioli, Daniel, 109
SDA. *See* Stranka demokratske akcije
SDP. *See* Socijaldemokratska partija
self-immolation, 2, 76
self-organization, 54, 55
service workers, 175, 176, 214
Sitrín, Marina, 94
slavery, 180, 181
Slovenia, Occupy movement in, 55

Smith, Neil, 6
socialism, 182
   Europe collapse of, 85
   images of socialist past, 86
   in Latin America, 163
socialist feminists, 34
Socialist Party (PSOL), 174
social justice, 13, 54, 59, 62, 127
   counter-hegemonic projects focused on, 56
   with universalist aspirations, 63
social media, 15, 47, 100, 104, 210
   Gezi Park and, 33
social mobilization, 41
social property, 65
social reproduction, 65, 67, 69, 212
Socijaldemokratska partija (SDP), 53, 60, 68
Sofia, privatization in, 74
solidarity-based social and economic action, 95
solidarity demonstrations, 53
South Africa, 4
sovereignty, 58
Spontaneista groups, 20, 118, 135
   Fioravanti military leader of, 129
   main groups of, 128
   violence produced by, 134
steel production, 79, 82
stop and frisk, 218
Stranka demokratske akcije (SDA), 53, 68
Strathern, Marilyn, 8
swaraj, 189, 190, 192
Syntagma Square, Athens, 100, 101
Syrian refugees, 80

T

Taksim Solidarity Platform, 46
Taksim Square, 34, 46
   commoning in, 47
tertiarization, 122, 178, 180
Terza Posizione (TP), 128
Thatcher, Margaret, 227
Third Position, 128
Third Way politics, 93, 121
Tikapur Intellectual Society, 147

Tikapur Town Development Committee, 151
Tilly, Charles, 8
TOKI. *See* Housing Development Administration of Turkey
torture, 106
TP. *See* Terza Posizione
transitional justice interventions, 70n5
Trump, Donald, 4–5, 13, 209, 219–20
Tunisia, 11
Turkey, 48
   economy of, 42, 43
   IMF and, 41
   Turkish nationalists, 33
   youth unemployment rate in, 39
Turkish Medical Association, 40
Tuzla, 52, 57, 63
   participative-democratic citizens assembly in, 53

U

U-CPN Maoist Party, 145, 153, 155
Ukrainian Maidan rebellion, 11
umbrella revolution, 4
unemployment, 13, 64, 90n3
   youth unemployment rate in Turkey, 39
UNESCO World Heritage, 169
Unified Socialist Workers' Party (PSTU), 174
Union of National Civil Servants (UPCN), 98, 101
United Kingdom, 11
United States, 208
Universal Child Benefit, 95
Up Against the Wall Motherfuckers, 215
UPCN. *See* Union of National Civil Servants
UPP. *See* Police Pacification Units
urban insurrections, 15
urbanism
   aggressive, 19
   authoritarian, 31, 45, 49
   neoliberal, 44

V
violence against women, 97
violent crime, 104–5
voting, 89
voting rights, 219

W
wagelessness, 13
Washington Consensus, 94
Welfare Rights Movement, 214, 215, 219
'winter protests', 73, 76, 78
Wolf, Eric, 12
women, 97
    African American, 214
    campaigns against unequal treatment of, 175
    in Delhi, 204
    Valmiki, 199
    Women Kamaiya Society, 145
    Women Kamaiya Society (Mahila Kamaiya Samaj), 145
Women's March on Washington, 219
worker rights, 40
Workers Party (PT), 22, 164, 172, 176, 177, 179
working classes, 15, 133–34, 179, 208–9, 224
    displacement of, 31
    in Italy, 132
    pauperization of, 172
    in Pernik, 78–79
    Perón support from, 93
    as political category, 16
    struggles of, 12
    Western industrial working class, 164
    workers' resistance, 45
working conditions, 81–82
World Cup, 166, 168, 174
World Social Forum (WSF), 4, 163

X
xenophobia, 223, 224, 226

Y
Youth for Equality, 194
Yugoslavia, socialist, 65

Z
zero-hour workforces, 175
Zuccotti Park, 3, 9, 37, 217

DISLOCATIONS

General Editors: August Carbonella, *Memorial University of Newfoundland*; Don Kalb, *University of Bergen & Utrecht University*; Linda Green, *University of Arizona*

The immense dislocations and suffering caused by neoliberal globalization, the retreat of the welfare state in the last decades of the twentieth century, and the heightened military imperialism at the turn of the twenty-first century have raised urgent questions about the temporal and spatial dimensions of power. Through stimulating critical perspectives and new and cross-disciplinary frameworks that reflect recent innovations in the social and human sciences, this series provides a forum for politically engaged and theoretically imaginative responses to these important issues of late modernity.

Volume 1
Where Have All the Homeless Gone? The Making and Unmaking of a Crisis
Anthony Marcus

Volume 2
Blood and Oranges: Immigrant Labor and European Markets in Rural Greece
Christopher M. Lawrence

Volume 3
Struggles for Home: Violence, Hope and the Movement of People
Edited by Stef Jansen and Staffan Löfving

Volume 4
Slipping Away: Banana Politics and Fair Trade in the Eastern Caribbean
Mark Moberg

Volume 5
Made in Sheffield: An Ethnography of Industrial Work and Politics
Massimiliano Mollona

Volume 6
Biopolitics, Militarism, and Development: Eritrea in the Twenty-First Century
Edited by David O'Kane and Tricia Redeker Hepner

Volume 7
When Women Held the Dragon's Tongue and Other Essays in Historical Anthropology
Hermann Rebel

Volume 8
Class, Contention, and a World in Motion
Edited by Winnie Lem and Pauline Gardiner Barber

Volume 9
Crude Domination: An Anthropology of Oil
Edited by Andrea Behrends, Stephen P. Reyna, and Günther Schlee

Volume 10
Communities of Complicity: Everyday Ethics in Rural China
Hans Steinmüller

Volume 11
Elusive Promises: Planning in the Contemporary World
Edited by Simone Abram and Gisa Weszkalnys

Volume 12
Intellectuals and (Counter-) Politics: Essays in Historical Realism
Gavin Smith

Volume 13
Blood and Fire: Toward a Global Anthropology of Labor
Edited by Sharryn Kasmir and August Carbonella

Volume 14
The Neoliberal Landscape and the Rise of Islamist Capital in Turkey
Edited by Neşecan Balkan, Erol Balkan and Ahmet Öncü

Volume 15
Yearnings in the Meantime: 'Normal Lives' and the State in a Sarajevo Apartment Complex
Stef Jansen

Volume 16
Where Are All Our Sheep? Kyrgyzstan, a Global Political Arena
Boris Petric, translated by Cynthia Schoch

Volume 17
Enduring Uncertainty: Deportation, Punishment and Everyday Life
Ines Hasselberg

Volume 18
The Anthropology of Corporate Social Responsibility
Edited by Catherine Dolan and Dinah Rajak

Volume 19
Breaking Rocks: Music, Ideology and Economic Collapse, from Paris to Kinshasa
Joe Trapido

Volume 20
Indigenist Mobilization: Confronting Electoral Communism and Precarious Livelihoods in Post-Reform Kerala
Luisa Steur

Volume 21
The Partial Revolution: Labour, Social Movements and the Invisible Hand of Mao in Western Nepal
Michael Hoffmann

Volume 22
Frontiers of Civil Society: Government and Hegemony in Serbia
Marek Mikuš

Volume 23
The Revolt of the Provinces: Anti-Gypsyism and Right-Wing Politics in Hungary
Kristóf Szombati

Volume 24
Worldwide Mobilizations: Class Struggles and Urban Commoning
Edited by Don Kalb and Massimiliano Mollona

Innovative Approaches to Anthropology!

FOCAAL
JOURNAL OF GLOBAL AND HISTORICAL ANTHROPOLOGY

Editorial Board:
Don Kalb, *University of Bergen and Utrecht University*
Sharryn Kasmir, *Hofstra University, New York*
Mao Mollona, *Goldsmiths College, London*
Mathijs Pelkmans, *London School of Economics*
Oscar Salemink, *University of Copenhagen*
Alpa Shah, *London School of Economics*
Gavin Smith, *University of Toronto*

Managing & Lead Editor: **Luisa Steur**, *University of Amsterdam*

Focaal is a peer-reviewed journal advocating an approach that rests in the simultaneity of ethnography, processual analysis, local insights, and global vision. It is at the heart of debates on the ongoing conjunction of anthropology and history as well as the incorporation of local research settings in the wider spatial networks of coercion, imagination, and exchange that are often glossed as "globalization" or "empire."

Seeking contributions on all world regions, *Focaal* is unique among anthropology journals for consistently rejecting the old separations between "at home" and "abroad", "center" and "periphery." The journal therefore strives for the resurrection of an "anthropology at large," that can accomodate issues of postsocialism, mobility, capitalist power and popular resistance into integrated perspectives.

RECENT ARTICLES

Emptiness and its futures: Staying and leaving as tactics of life in Latvia
DACE DZENOVSKA

The desire for disinheritance in austerity Greece
DANIEL M. KNIGHT

Conjuring "the people": The 2013 Babylution protests & desire for political transformation in postwar Bosnia-Herzegovina
LARISA KURTOVIC

Finding a place in the world: Political subjectivities and the imagination of Iceland after the economic crash
KRISTIN LOFTSDOTTIR

Between Afropolitans and new Sankaras: Class mobility and the reproduction of academics in Burkina Faso
MICHELLE ENGELER

"Forging New Malay networks": Imagining global halal markets
JOHAN FISCHER

Shelling from the ivory tower: Project Camelot and the post–World War II operationalization of social science
PHILIP Y. KAO

The racial fix: White currency in the gentrification of black and Latino Chicago
JESSE MUMM

berghahnjournals.com/focaal

ISSN 0920-1297 (Print) • ISSN 1558-5263 (Online)
Issues 80, 81, & 82/2018, 3 issues p.a.

www.ingramcontent.com/pod-product-compliance
Lightning Source LLC
Chambersburg PA
CBHW051535020426
42333CB00016B/1936